Microsoft® ASP.NET and AJAX: Architecting Web Applications

Dino Esposito

PUBLISHED BY
Microsoft Press
A Division of Microsoft Corporation
One Microsoft Way
Redmond, Washington 98052-6399

Copyright © 2009 by Dino Esposito

Library of Congress Control Number: 2008940527

Printed and bound in the United States of America.

1 2 3 4 5 6 7 8 9 QWT 4 3 2 1 0 9

Distributed in Canada by H.B. Fenn and Company Ltd.

A CIP catalogue record for this book is available from the British Library.

Microsoft Press books are available through booksellers and distributors worldwide. For further information about international editions, contact your local Microsoft Corporation office or contact Microsoft Press International directly at fax (425) 936-7329. Visit our Web site at www.microsoft.com/mspress. Send comments to msinput@microsoft.com.

Acquisitions Editor: Ben Ryan
Developmental Editor: Lynn Finnel
Project Editor: Tracy Ball
Editorial Production: S4Carlisle Publishing Services
Technical Reviewer: Kenn Scribner; Technical Review services provided by Content Master, a member of CM Group, Ltd.
Cover: Tom Draper Design

Body Part No. X15-28134

To the people who help me to smile and often smile, play and laugh with me.

—Dino

Contents at a Glance

Table of Contents

What do you think of this book? We want to hear from you!

Microsoft is interested in hearing your feedback so we can continually improve our books and learning resources for you. To participate in a brief online survey, please visit:

www.microsoft.com/learning/booksurvey/

What do you think of this book? We want to hear from you!

Acknowledgments

A team of people helped me to assemble this book.

Ben Ryan was sneakily convinced to support the project on a colorful Las Vegas night, during an ethnic dinner during which we watched waiters coming up from and going down to the wine cellar in transparent elevators.

Lynn Finnel just didn't want to let Dino walk alone in this key project after brilliantly coordinating at least five book projects in the past.

Kenn Scribner is now Dino's official book alter ego. Kenn started working with Dino on books back in 1998 in the age of COM and the Active Template Library. How is it possible that a book with Dino's name on the cover isn't reviewed and inspired (and fixed) by Kenn's unique and broad perspective on the world of software? The extent to which Kenn can be helpful is just beyond human imagination.

Roger LeBlanc joined the team to make sure that all these geeks sitting together at the same virtual desktop could still communicate using true English syntax and semantics.

I owe you all the (non-rhetorically) monumental "Thank you" for being so kind, patient, and accurate.

—*Dino*

Introduction

This book is the Web counterpart to another recently released book I co-authored with Andrea Saltarello: *Microsoft .NET: Architecting Applications for the Enterprise* (Microsoft Press, 2008). I wrote it, in part, in response to the many architectural questions—both small questions and big ones—that I was asked repeatedly while teaching ASP.NET, AJAX, and Silverlight classes.

Everybody in the industry is committed to AJAX. Everybody understands the impact of it. Everybody recognizes the enormous power that can be derived from its employment in real-world solutions.

Very few, though, know exactly how to make it happen. There are so many variations to AJAX and so many implementations that even after you have found one that suits your needs, you are left wondering whether that is the best possible option.

The fact is that AJAX triggered a chain reaction in the world of the Web. AJAX represents a change of paradigm for Web applications. And, as the history of science proves, a paradigm shift has always had a deep impact, especially in scenarios that were previously stable and consolidated.

I estimate that it will take about five years to absorb the word *AJAX* (and all of its background) into the new definition of the Web. And the clock started ticking about four years ago. The time at which we say "the Web" without feeling the need to specify whether it contains AJAX or not…well, that time is getting closer and closer. But it is not that time yet.

Tools and programming paradigms for AJAX, which were very blurry just a few years ago, are getting sharper every day. Whether we are talking about JavaScript libraries or suites of server controls, I feel that pragmatic architectures can be identified. You find them thoroughly discussed in Chapter 3, "AJAX Architectures."

Architecting a Web application today is mostly about deciding whether to prefer the *richness* of the solution over the *reach* of the solution. Silverlight and ASP.NET AJAX are the two platforms to choose from as long as you remain in the Microsoft ecosystem. But the rich vs. reach dilemma is a general one and transcends platforms and vendors. A neat answer to that dilemma puts you on the right track to developing your next-generation Web solution.

Who This Book Is For

I believe that this book is ideal reading for any professionals involved with the ASP.NET platform and who are willing or needing to find a solution that delivers a modern and rich user experience.

Companion Content

Examples of techniques and patterns discussed in the book can be found at the following site: *http://www.microsoft.com/learning/en/us/books/12926.aspx.*

Hardware and Software Requirements

You'll need the following hardware and software to work with the companion content included with this book:

■ Nearly any version of Microsoft Windows, including Vista (Home Premium Edition, Business Edition, or Ultimate Edition), Windows Server 2003 and 2008, and Windows XP Pro.

■ Microsoft Visual Studio 2008 Standard Edition, Visual Studio 2008 Enterprise Edition, or Microsoft Visual C# 2008 Express Edition, and Microsoft Visual Web Developer 2008 Express Edition.

■ Microsoft SQL Server 2005 Express Edition, Service Pack 2 or Microsoft SQL Server 2005, Service Pack 3, or Microsoft SQL Server 2008.

■ The Northwind database of Microsoft SQL Server 2000 is used to demonstrate data-access techniques. You can obtain the Northwind database from the Microsoft Download Center (*http://www.microsoft.com/downloads/details.aspx?FamilyID=06616212-0356-46A0-8DA2-EEBC53A68034&displaylang=en*).

■ 1.6 GHz Pentium III+ processor, or faster.

■ 1 GB of available, physical RAM.

■ Video (800 by 600 or higher resolution) monitor with at least 256 colors.

■ CD-ROM or DVD-ROM drive.

■ Microsoft mouse or compatible pointing device.

Find Additional Content Online

As new or updated material becomes available that complements this book, it will be posted online on the Microsoft Press Online Developer Tools Web site. The type of material you might find includes updates to book content, articles, links to companion content, errata, sample chapters, and more. This Web site is available at *http://www.microsoft.com/learning/books/online/developer* and is updated periodically.

Support for This Book

Every effort has been made to ensure the accuracy of this book and the companion content. As corrections or changes are collected, they will be added to a Microsoft Knowledge Base article.

Microsoft Press provides support for books and companion content at the following Web site:

http://www.microsoft.com/learning/support/books

Questions and Comments

If you have comments, questions, or ideas regarding the book or the companion content, or questions that are not answered by visiting the sites above, please send them to Microsoft Press via e-mail to

mspinput@microsoft.com

Or via postal mail to

Microsoft Press
Attn: *Microsoft ASP.NET and AJAX: Architecting Web Applications* Editor
One Microsoft Way
Redmond, WA 98052-6399

Please note that Microsoft software product support is not offered through the above addresses.

Part I
The (Much Needed) Facelift for the Old Web

Chapter 1
Under the Umbrella of AJAX

Forget what we think we know about the limitations of the Web, and begin to imagine a wider, richer range of possibilities.

—*Jesse James Garrett*

In 2007, more or less at the same time I was proudly showcasing my hot new book on ASP.NET AJAX, an old friend of mine started investigating the features of AJAX and the still largely unknown Silverlight platform. He had just been given the task of planning and coordinating a huge migration project within his company.

He spent about ten years building, maintaining, and progressively enhancing a vertical application that had won an industry award and was aimed at some special categories of professionals, such as lawyers and public accountants. At some point, his company had been acquired by a larger group and the old application had to be integrated into an existing Web platform.

With the whole company about to abruptly switch from a desktop mindset to a Web paradigm, my friend was trying to be reasonably thoughtful. He was looking for the best available tools of the current Web paradigm to minimize the pain and costs of migration while delivering an effective, desktop-like experience to the existing users. With all the buzz and hype around AJAX (and that fancy new thing known as Silverlight), his efforts seemed to be a matter of prudence and the fruit of an innate "try before you buy" attitude.

I met my friend at TechEd 2007, where I was giving a couple of presentations on the subject of ASP.NET AJAX. To my greatest surprise, at the end of my last session he came by and whispered apologetically, "Sorry Dino, but is that all of it?" He was aware that his question might sound insolent or silly and that it undermined the beautiful story I had just told the audience.

My presentation had been about how a new age of prosperity and success was about to begin for all Web developers and architects. It included the success story of how one of the building blocks of Web 2.0 came along. I told the fantastic story of how the Web was, all of a sudden, about to offer the same set of functionality as the desktop.

Unfortunately, the Web is not the desktop.

And it will never be like that, no matter which moderating suffix you attach to the word *desktop*. You can label the Web as *desktop over HTTP* or *browser-hosted desktop* or even *desktop in the cloud*. It is, and will always be, a pure marketing gimmick.

What Web Do We Want?

My friend got it right quite quickly. The Web is the Web, with its pros and cons. Using AJAX (or even Silverlight) as a shortcut or, worse yet, as a magic wand to simplify development—from developing new commercial Web sites to performing complex enterprise migration projects—is just incorrect. And it's potentially a deadly decision with regard to the assets of a company.

My friend, who looked at AJAX with a totally unbiased mind, had the farsightedness to clearly and quickly see that AJAX was something important for Web-related development but that it was not the easy fix that many people were enthusiastically depicting it to be. (And to some extent, it's still being depicted that way today, two years later.)

In light of this, the following equation is not realistic:

```
desktop = Web + AJAX
```

It doesn't work outside the dreams of some IT managers.

Although my friend had perceived the key facts about AJAX, his insight didn't solve his primary concern. By figuring out AJAX quickly, though, he was able to focus his brainstorming in the right direction and center his thoughts around the right questions.

So what are the right questions to ask about AJAX?

It's All About User Experience

As I see things, there's just one key question, and a number of more technical and in-depth questions spread out from this question later. The fundamental question is, "What Web do we want?"

Admittedly, the question implies we are not entirely happy with today's Web and are looking for a different type of Web. At the end of the day, what we all want from the Web is a much better *user experience*, in the broadest possible meaning of both the term *user* and the term *experience*.

So what does *user experience* mean to various people?

User Experience for Dummies

Jesse James Garrett has made it into the history books as the man who coined the now ubiquitous and universal acronym *AJAX*, back in 2005. (To read the full story, pay a visit to *http://www.adaptivepath.com/ideas/essays/archives/000385.php*.)

For readers who might have spent the last three years in a remote rainforest with no connectivity at all, I'll spell out the acronym here—Asynchronous JavaScript And XML. (Later in the chapter, I'll comment on the role and importance of each part of the acronym.)

Jesse James Garrett, however, is neither a software architect nor a Web developer. He calls himself an experience designer, and he's also the author of a widely referenced book on Web design titled *The Elements of User Experience* (New Riders Press, 2002). In short, Jesse James Garrett is probably one of the most qualified people in the world to give us a concise and comprehensible definition of *user experience (UE)*.

Understanding the whys and wherefores of UE is the first step to understanding what Web we want and how to go forward and look for valid technologies to employ in its implementation.

The concept of UE is made of many disparate parts. Creating a positive user experience for a Web site involves enabling end users to use the site for their own purposes, which might include business, work, personal activities and interests, and entertainment. UE is about how a Web site (or, generally, any system) is perceived, learned about, and finally used; and how a user feels about that.

A brilliant team of developers, architects, and designers might be able to serve up a set of Web functions that meet the original strategic intent. But they might fail to provide a consistent and pleasant user experience. Using Garrett's wording, the concept of a good user experience sounds like this:

> *A site that really works fulfills your strategic objectives while meeting the needs of your users. Even the best content and the most sophisticated technology won't help you balance those goals without a cohesive, consistent user experience to support it.*

A superior UE springs from a powerful mix of usability, data and work flows (often referred to as *information architecture*), appealing graphics, and interaction model. As you can see, there's no code or software architecture involved at this level. Software comes later or is developed in parallel to figuring out how to implement these characteristics. For sure, it takes the overall Web development thing to another dimension.

User Experience for the Poor Web User

Let's set aside these concepts from the field of *experience design* as applied to the Web and focus on the software side of the *new* Web. For the purposes of this book, we'll happily assume that someone on the development team has valuable ideas they want to instill in the otherwise foggy minds of the team's members.

For the end user, the next WWW (short for the *Web We Want*) is centered on providing the user with a high-quality, first-class experience when passing through your site. Whatever that means. Figuring out what that means is the job of developers, designers, and UE people.

Note This is a sort of psychological note. For about ten years, the poor Web user navigated to a site to get some sort of information related to personal or business interests—documents, reports, charts, prices, best prices, timetables, account balances, various types of news, live scores, itineraries, guides, essays, and so on.

For part of this decade, the poor Web user felt lucky and happy to draw something of value from the bottomless well of the Internet. At some point, though, while the well remained largely bottomless, other critical resources began to be scarce—bandwidth and, more importantly, patience.

The poor Web user could accept slow responses when he had enthusiasm for this new thing. But when the exciting new thing turned to a commodity, the enthusiasm vanished and the poor Web user began to wonder if there could be a better way to accomplish the same tasks. Now if there's no better way, he feels unhappy and starts looking around for smarter and more cutting-edge competitors.

User Experience for Developers

In raw developer terms, a *high-quality user experience* means essentially a more responsive application that can better deal with network latency. Web users today are more sophisticated than they were ten years ago and demand higher performance and responsiveness regardless of the latency and bandwidth hurdles you, as a developer, might have to overcome.

However, you can't change the laws of physics. It still takes electrons a certain amount of time to move from one place to another. Therefore, developers work to optimize the server-side code and logic to tweak every ounce of performance and scalability from that code. But often even this isn't enough. That's when developers look to other tricks, perhaps even very new tricks that require rethinking how Web applications interact with the user.

The tricks mostly involve asking the application to do more work on the browser's side—even in the background, when the browser is idle—by sending and requesting much less data over the wire and by repainting smaller areas of the page. In summary, we will accept more roundtrips, but each carrying only a small chunk of data and only if the communication is performed in the background and results in partial page refreshes instead of complete page browser reloads.

From a developer's perspective, this is not a small step at all. It's not merely a smart form of optimization. Instead, it's a huge jump that changes our understanding of the foundation of the Web as we know it today.

A more responsive application is also more interactive from the user's perspective. It shows animations, visual effects, and sharp graphics that change quickly and smoothly to reflect the state of the page. This aspect of the new Web is an enhancement aimed at improving the experience. However, it doesn't have much to do with hard-core, server-side development and the information architecture.

It is rather more about having enhanced graphics and layout, which are more the purview of the Web designer and artist than the implementing developer. In the end, though, some browser-side code trickery will still be necessary to give the user the impression that the page is more responsive and easier to interact with. Building a nice user experience is a team effort—design plus browser-side script.

How can developers implement more responsive and interactive Web pages? Again, let me answer this question with another question. What is a Web page made of? HTML and JavaScript. These are the pillars of Web pages as we know and write them today. Any tricks you come up with will necessarily be applied here.

User Experience for Managers

Written four years ago, Garrett's aforementioned excellent essay on AJAX is starting to look a bit—yes, let's say it—outdated. The paper discusses incontrovertible facts about the mechanics of the Web with and without AJAX. But it also contains an introduction and a conclusion that are a bit misleading when read today, four years later. (As a rule of thumb, I consider five years of software progress as the logical equivalent to a geological era. So four years are definitely a lot of time.)

Managers might sometimes read through moderately technical stuff like what you find in Garrett's work, but it's very hard for them to read between the lines and grasp the implications of a technical description. What remains in their mind is that the interactivity and responsiveness gap between desktop and Web applications is now closing thanks to AJAX.

AJAX is a big innovation and a revolutionary change for the Web. However, it's not free and often costs you quite a bit in terms of resources.

Managers see the user experience as mashups and cool features. Building a mashup, though, is not like querying a database table on a local or remote server. Using mashups makes well-designed information architecture more essential than ever. It makes software architecture slightly different and raises a whole bunch of new development issues.

Making Web sites appealing and easy to navigate is more possible with AJAX than without it. But AJAX is not magic; it will never give you a desktop platform over HTTP. And, finally, there's the matter of tradeoffs and making (ideally, correct) decisions.

Origins of the Web

The Web We Want is a Web that can deliver a much better user experience. As a Web developer or architect, your role is to increase the responsiveness of pages and the interactivity of most features. The former will likely require some architectural work on code and information; the latter just requires more script code to be put to work.

The final destination for this book is to take you to the recommended architectural changes needed to get the Web We Want.

AJAX is a revolution. Great, but why? What is wrong with the old Web?

Let's begin by looking at the limitations imposed by the origins of the Web and take our first step toward understanding why the recommended architectural changes are necessary to shift to the new, more responsive Web.

The First Cry

The Web as we know it today was prototyped in the early 1990s at CERN, the European Organization for Nuclear Research. (The acronym originates from the French name of the organization.)

Scientists at CERN worked on the concept of hypertext and arranged an ad hoc markup language for expressing interlinked text-based documents and a communication protocol for retrieving such documents. Needless to say, the markup language is HTML and the communication protocol is HTTP. HTTP in particular works on top of a Transmission Control Protocol (TCP) connection occurring over port 80 by default.

The first experiment of connecting two machines over HTTP took place in the summer of 1991. Less than two years later, the CERN waived any copyrights on it, thus officially starting the era of the World Wide Web.

A lot has happened since. We had, for instance, the browser wars. This refers to a period in the late 1990s when basically each new browser release was made to edge out competitors by developing custom extensions to the markup and building in-house technologies to improve the programmability of sites and, only as a side effect, the user experience. Standardization via the World Wide Web Consortium (W3C) committees helped to have an official specification for some Web features such as CSS and HTML Document Object Model (DOM). To be effective, though, a Web standard must be widely supported by actual browsers. It took years before all major browsers aligned to support a common set of features (often only in the realm of standard specifications) that was powerful enough to begin a new era for the Web—the AJAX era.

The Mechanics of the Web

The Web is based on a request/response model that involves a client browser and the Web server. This is shown in Figure 1-1.

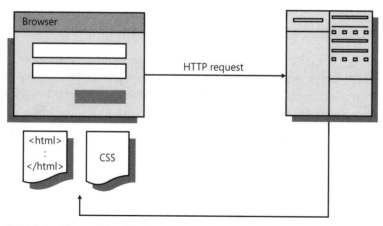

FIGURE 1-1 The traditional Web application model

According to this model, a continuous action originates a sort of stop-and-go pattern. The user interacts with the page and at some point sends a request back to the server. As the server processes the request, the user waits. Next, a new page is displayed to the user that requires some more work. The work produces a new request to the server, after which the user waits—over and over again.

In HTML, the user starts a request by hitting a submit button. Today, the standard implementation of the HTML Document Object Model also requires a script-based method, but that was not the case in the beginning. The browser interprets a submit click as the order of submitting the content of the host form to the specified action URL. Next, the browser freezes the user interface (UI) until a new HTML page is received.

In the classic Web model, the browser implements a request by sending out an HTML form and receiving a brand new HTML page.

The Original Purpose of HTML and HTTP

HTML and HTTP were created at CERN to serve a well-defined purpose: improving the flow of information across the network and sharing documents more easily using the hypertext model. A document created using HTML can contain links to other documents in the same network—for example, documents referenced in the bibliography of a scientific paper.

After they were released for public use in 1993, HTML and HTTP gained the incredible success we all know. An army of developers were able to use HTML and HTTP to build millions of pages in richer and richer Web sites. Since then, HTTP and HTML in particular have been squeezed to extract every single fragment of functionality.

Quite paradoxically, the Web was originally created to serve as an internal tool in a relatively small community of people—at least compared to today's communities. It turned out, instead, to be a monster that changed our personal lives and our businesses.

Paradox of the Web

The use of the adverb *paradoxically* is deliberate. So what is the paradox of the Web? In 15 years, developers and designers have been able to build the World Wide Web as we know it today using extremely simple tools that were not specifically designed for the job.

This process has given rise to two opposing forces. One is the force of progress, which wants the Web to become more powerful every day, with new features and applications. The other is the resistance from the limitations of the building blocks of the Web, which are not really designed to support the current workload.

The paradox lies in the fact that rebuilding the Web entirely is completely unrealistic. We need to improve it significantly, but without changing its (now inadequate) columns.

The Sturdy, Old Columns That Hold Up the Web

The Web wasn't designed for many of the purposes we use it for today. In particular, it wasn't designed to do any publishing. It wasn't specifically aimed at building the presentation layer for any distributed systems. Supporting multimedia content and rich graphics was certainly not a priority.

More importantly, it was not designed to secure its content. HTTP is an extremely simple and efficient protocol, but it's not *technologically* secure. What about HTTPS, then? HTTPS is essentially an extra layer of cryptography applied at the gate when the packet leaves or reaches the computer. HTTPS protects the message but doesn't help much with authentication and authorization. What about client certificates? Well, they certainly work. But like HTTPS, client certificates are a feature bolted onto the native (and unsecure) HTTP protocol.

Why was HTTP designed this way?

In 1991, the whole theme of Web security was unimaginable. Web security started to be a serious issue only after the bold success of the World Wide Web made it worthwhile for hackers to plan their attacks. Once we started sending money over the Web, with the associated personal information, then and only then did it make it worthwhile for malicious hackers. Before that, hacking was more a college prank than anything.

Born as a tool to manage HTTP connections and parse HTML pages, the browser became an increasingly powerful tool step by step with the rapid increase in the number of Web sites around the world.

One of the first enhancements that browsers made to the syntax of HTML was the support for a programming language—JavaScript. The first browser to deploy a JavaScript engine was Netscape Navigator 2.0 in December 1995. JavaScript was introduced to give authors of Web-deployed documents the ability to incorporate some logic and action in HTML pages.

Later on, other features were added, such as cookies, the Document Object Model (DOM) for publicly exposing in a programmable way the content being displayed, and cascading style sheets (CSS) to quickly style elements of the page. In the heat of the "war of the browsers," multiple browsers offered the same features with each using its own syntax and model. By the end of the last century, it was clear that serious Web programming couldn't be planned or actually done without common worldwide standards.

The W3C committees made it happen. As a result of their efforts, we have standard HTML and a standard JavaScript language. These are the pillars of today's Web. And for the purposes of today, they are tottering pillars.

Pillars Can't Be Changed

A pillar is not something you can replace without possibly causing the building to collapse. You can fix it or make it stronger, but you can't replace it. This is the situation we currently face with the pillars of the World Wide Web: HTML and JavaScript.

These twin supports for the Web are common and popular. Revolutionary changes to either of them would seriously affect activity on the Internet. Existing applications wouldn't be touched, but new browsers would be needed to run applications based on the modified pillars. The whole world of users would split in two—those who can change browsers and those who can't or don't want to change browsers. For the Web, which owes its popularity to being accessible to all, this is a nightmare scenario.

The Web grew too quickly to allow people to consider the adequacy or limitations of its pillars. Or, put another way, people found it easier to push the Web to the maximum instead of planning for an infrastructure with more capabilities. On the other hand, the Web is public and since 1993 it has not been the intellectual property of any company or organization. Changes to it are possible, but only if they're in compliance with accepted and recognized standards.

> **Note** Despite the *Java* prefix in its name, the JavaScript language has very little to do with the popular Java language. JavaScript was designed to look like a simpler Java for nonexpert page authors—hence, the name. JavaScript is an interpreted, dynamic-binding, and weakly typed language with first-class functions. It has some light flavors of object orientation, it's not compiled and, maybe more importantly, it's subject to the browser's implementation.
>
> Created to add action to Web pages, and kept simple on purpose, the JavaScript language perfectly met initial expectations for it, but it failed to exceed those expectations. That's why JavaScript is currently a pain in the neck for Web developers. But we can't replace it without breaking widely agreed upon and stable standards. This is a big part of the Web paradox.

The Biggest Benefit of AJAX

What users want is a better experience, and not all Web applications and sites offer that. For this reason, the world of the Web is moving toward AJAX.

AJAX is definitely a plus for the Web.

AJAX capabilities address the user's experience in the broadest sense—by providing a continuous feel, flicker-free updates, interface facilities, mashups, live data, and so on. AJAX is the way that's available to us to reinforce the tottering pillars safely and making them more stable.

AJAX is the only significant plus we can afford. This limitation is not merely a matter of money or economics. We simply can't get a new Web redesigned from the foundation up and implemented without disrupting or just slowing down service. The Web is now a fundamental commodity. We all need it. No serious disruptions are allowed.

What's AJAX, Exactly?

AJAX is not a technology. AJAX is not something you can install and run. AJAX doesn't require any plug-in modules and is not browser specific. Quite the opposite: the key to the success of AJAX is that virtually any browsers released in the past five years are great hosts for AJAX-based applications. So what's AJAX?

AJAX is a blanket term. As disappointing as it may sound, the term *AJAX* was coined primarily as a concise and cool way to sell a set of technologies and a new approach to Web development.

What initially was simply a clever approach to building pages, scaled to the size of an entire real-world Web front end, turned out to be the incarnation of a new paradigm for writing Web applications. The AJAX approach is probably destined to last for many years or until conditions exist for rebuilding the Web from scratch (whichever comes first).

A New Way to Do Web Programming

AJAX refers to using a set of specific browser technologies to build pages. It's amazing to note that all these technologies are nothing really new. We're talking about browser technologies that have been around for ten years now—*XMLHttpRequest*, DOM, and JavaScript.

It's simple to use these technologies to implement a given set of features in an individual page. It's much more complex to build an entire application according to the AJAX paradigm. Why?

Especially with the advent of ASP.NET, the world of Web programming has been simplified. Frameworks offer a thick layer of abstraction over basic HTML and HTTP interaction, and the ASP.NET development environment makes it easy with automated code generation and remote debugging. And all of it works on the assumption that the browser sends an HTML form to get back an HTML page, one of the foundational pillars of the Web.

It's relatively easy to change the paradigm for a single feature in a single page. It can be quite difficult, however, to extend the new paradigm to the whole application. Why? Because the world of AJAX programming has not been similarly simplified—most AJAX implementations (at least efficient and properly designed implementations) are still built by hand. But this will change.

The *XMLHttpRequest* Object

As I mentioned, AJAX stands for *Asynchronous JavaScript and XML*. Five years after its introduction, and from a more technological point of view, we can say that the first part of the acronym is acceptable but the second part is arguable.

The AJAX development model revolves around one common software element—the *XMLHttpRequest* object. The availability of this object in most browsers' object model is the key to the current ubiquity and success of AJAX applications.

Originally introduced with Internet Explorer 5.0, the *XMLHttpRequest* object is an internal object that the browser publishes to its scripting engine. In this way, the script code found in any client page—typically, JavaScript code—can invoke the object and take advantage of its functionality.

The *XMLHttpRequest* object allows script code to send HTTP requests and handle their responses. Functionally speaking, and despite the XML in the name, the *XMLHttpRequest* object is nothing more than a tiny object model to place HTTP calls via script in a non-browser-led way. The object is scripted from client JavaScript code and, with regard to the browser, it operates asynchronously. (With respect to your code, on the other hand, the call can be either synchronous or asynchronous.)

When a connection to a Web server is led by the browser, the current page displayed to the user is lost. The page becomes inactive and frozen as soon as the user clicks to submit the content to some remote server.

With *XMLHttpRequest*, conversely, developers directly control the placement and outcome of the request. The actual mechanics of the request/response don't make any difference to the user. However, the possibility of using *XMLHttpRequest* enables Web developers to build features that ultimately deliver a much better user experience.

The Document Object Model

In addition to *XMLHttpRequest*, a second technology contributes to making AJAX so effective and attractive—the availability of an object model that exposes the current content of the page in an updatable manner.

Microsoft pioneered updatable Web pages in the late 1990s. With Internet Explorer 4.0 (released back in 1997), Microsoft introduced Dynamic HTML (DHTML), which is a powerful combination of HTML, style sheets, and scripts that allows programmatic changes to any displayed page. Several companies since then have worked out their own DHTML object model—often referred to as the Browser Object Model (BOM). The W3C committee worked hard to get vendors to agree on an interoperable and language-neutral solution for exposing Web pages through an updatable programming interface. The result is the Document Object Model (DOM) as opposed to a browser-specific BOM.

The DOM is a platform-independent and language-neutral representation of the contents of a Web page that scripts can access and use to modify the content, structure, and style of the document.

Note I'd even dare say that without an updatable DOM the whole AJAX approach wouldn't be possible at all. Using *XMLHttpRequest*, a developer can asynchronously connect to a URL and grab some fresh data. However, how could she integrate such fresh data into the current page without an updatable representation of the page? That's why the DOM is required and critical.

The Paradigm Shift

We're all witnessing (and as users, we're also contributing) to an interesting and fairly unique phenomenon—the Web is undergoing an epochal change right before our eyes as a result of our actions.

Only ten years ago, the majority of developers considered an application far too serious a thing to reduce it to an unordered mix of script and markup code. In the late 1990s, the cost of an application was sweat, blood, tears, and endless debugging sessions. There was neither honor nor fame for the "real" programmer in writing Web applications.

As drastic as it might sound, the Web revolutionized the concept of an application. Now AJAX is revolutionizing the concept of a Web application.

The Web will always remain separate from the desktop, but Web applications are going to enter a new age.

The Pages-for-Forms Model

Today, communication between the browser and the Web server occurs through *forms*. A form is a collection of values stored in a group of HTML input fields.

From a user's perspective, the transition occurs through *pages*. A page is a piece of HTML markup returned by the Web server. Each user action that originates a new request for the server results in a new page (or a revamped version of the current page) being downloaded and displayed.

The browser-to-server communication employs the classic HTTP protocol. As is widely known, the HTTP protocol is stateless, which means that each request is not related to the next and no state is automatically maintained, neither on the client nor on the server.

The state objects developers know and use in, say, ASP.NET are nothing more than an abstraction provided by the server programming environment. The state objects developers know and use on the client (for example, cookies) are nothing more than an abstraction provided by the client browser.

The Pages-for-Forms model was just fine in the beginning of the Web age when pages contained little more than formatted text, hyperlinks, and maybe some images. The success of the Web has prompted users to ask for increasingly more powerful features, and it has led developers and designers to create more sophisticated services and graphics. As a result, today's pages are heavy and cumbersome.

Given the current architecture of Web applications, each user action requires a complete redraw of the page. Subsequently, heavier pages render out slowly and produce a good deal of flickering. Projected to the whole set of pages in a large, portal-like application, this mechanism is perfect for causing great frustration to the poor end user.

Because nobody is willing to come back to the scanty, "Times New Roman" pages of the mid-1990s, a new Web model is possible only via a smarter form of interaction between the client and the Web server.

The Data-for-Data Model

For too many years, the old Web model survived because of compatibility and reach. To accommodate businesses, Web sites had to be as easy as possible to reach for any potential customer. From a technology perspective, the AJAX revolution was ready to start back in 1999 when *XMLHttpRequest* and an updatable DOM were designed and implemented.

It took a few more years instead.

This happened because for quite some time only high-end browsers (also known as rich, up-level browsers) provided support for both *XMLHttpRequest* and an updatable DOM. For a long time, only companies that could exercise strict control over the capabilities of the client browsers were able to choose the AJAX model for their sites. In short, for too long a *rich* browser also has meant a browser with too limited *reach*. For too long, using such a browser definitely has been a bad choice for most businesses.

Around 2004, many people realized at the same time that, perhaps because of a rare astral convergence, 90 percent of the browsers available in the marketplace were supporting the same set of features—in particular, both *XMLHttpRequest* and an updatable DOM.

This made it possible for Web architects and developers to set up the Data-for-Data interaction model. According to this model, a Web page puts plain data in the body of a HTTP packet instead of inserting the content of an HTML form. And the Web server just returns plain data—not a whole new HTML page—as its response. Figure 1-2 offers a graphical view of the model.

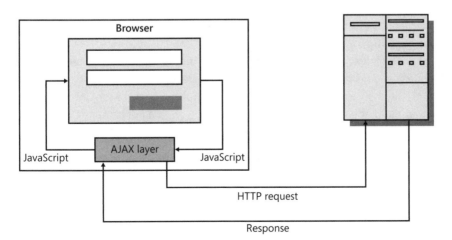

FIGURE 1-2 The AJAX Web application model

Some JavaScript code embedded in the client page triggers an HTTP request to the Web server using *XMLHttpRequest*. When the response comes back, another piece of client code parses it to some JavaScript object and, using DOM, integrates the new content in the current page.

From the user's perspective, the operation takes place asynchronously, and the user can keep on reading and scrolling the page without interruption.

Important Is the Data-for-Data interaction model—the essence of AJAX—really a faster model? Certainly, the Data-for-Data model moves around much less information than the classic HTTP page response. However, the big issue is network latency, which is more significant a factor than the transmitted quantity of data. And network latency affects the Data-for-Data interaction model because requested data is delayed. Moreover, the more roundtrips you make, the more network latency affects your application (that is, the effects are additive). So what's the point?

Performance, though, is not only made of raw numbers. Where a user and a user interface are concerned, the concept of performance morphs into the concept of *perceived* performance. A user who can keep on working with a page will feel much better than one who cannot. Therefore, data requests are made in the background and performed asynchronously. The user never knows the data was requested, and the user interface never "freezes" while waiting for new data. Most commonly, smaller portions of the page are independently updated, further providing the feeling of (increasing) perceived performance.

Is that all? As my old friend understood quite quickly, unfortunately *XMLHttpRequest* and an updatable DOM are only the starting point of a much longer revolution that necessarily will need to touch on the architecture of pages and applications.

Refactoring to AJAX: Features, Pages, and Applications

Gaining the ability to place asynchronous calls to the Web server while bypassing the browser's standard procedure is only the first, and largely preliminary, step to building an AJAX site.

When the benefits of the AJAX model are being discussed, often the following example is given. Suppose you want to know the balance of your bank account or any other simple and small piece of information. With the standard Web model, you submit a request to a server URL and wait for a new page to be (downloaded and) served. Intertwined with advertising, banners, graphics, menus, and disclaimers is the number you were looking for. With AJAX, on the other hand, the page remains up and running (with all of its banners, menus, and disclaimers) and only the number is downloaded.

Unfortunately, the example addresses only the *feature* level. It says nothing about the rest of the *page* and the rest of the *application*.

AJAX is a paradigm shift. And a paradigm shift always has a dramatic impact because it requires that people change their habits and embrace new and largely unknown practices.

Refactoring is a key word in AJAX.

What should you refactor in your application? The whole application? Or only a bunch of individual pages? Or should you simply consider optimizing just one critical feature or two?

AJAX and New Web Projects

After a decade of increasingly powerful tools and technologies designed for effective and quick development of Web sites and applications (such as ASP, Microsoft Visual InterDev, Dreamweaver, Java Server Pages, ASP.NET, and Microsoft Visual Studio), we've been pushed into the AJAX age where no such tools exist.

The world of AJAX development is not yet embraced by the tools you use. Everything you need can be manually created; however, very few tools exist. This is the issue that project leads (such as my old friend) and IT managers face when they get past the initial enthusiasm.

As I see things, there are three ways to approach AJAX. One is to just add AJAX capabilities to an existing solution or to a new solution designed in the traditional, non-AJAX way. Another is sticking to the Web paradigm (HTML and HTTP) but rethinking the architecture of the application and its implementation. This means learning new patterns, facing new issues, solving new problems, and using new tools. The third approach is to take the route of a Rich Internet Application (RIA)—a desktop-like application hosted in the Web browser via a plug-in.

I'm going to give a quick strategic overview of these three approaches in the rest of the chapter. The remainder of this book goes into more detail about a particular approach. Part I, "The (Much Needed) Facelift for the Old Web," covers the first approach in more technical depth. The second approach and RIAs are covered in Part II, "Power to the Client."

Adding AJAX Capabilities

Most Web sites today might be significantly improved in terms of usability and user experience with a touch of AJAX. As mentioned, the core of the AJAX model is an internal browser object and the DOM. The interface of both is defined according to standards—still a *de facto* standard for *XMLHttpRequest* and an official W3C standard for the DOM.

This means that adding AJAX capabilities requires only a bit of script code. You can add AJAX capabilities to any page regardless of the underlying programming platform—be it classic ASP, ASP.NET, Java Server Pages, PHP, or plain HTML.

Selective Updates

Adding AJAX capabilities entails working at the page level, when not directly at the feature level. The scaffolding of the application doesn't change, and so it is for the inspiring principles and overall architecture.

With this approach, you apply selective updates to the parts of a page that need a facelift. You do so by employing smart tricks to work around the classic behavior of the page.

Vendors provide some tools to make this process quick and effective. Effectiveness here is a critical parameter. A solution that applies AJAX updates to a Web page can be based only on JavaScript and must work well in a cross-browser manner.

The perfect example of what "adding AJAX capabilities" means is ASP.NET partial rendering, which I'll cover in Chapter 2, "The Easy Way to AJAX." Other possibilities exist, too. For example, vendors of UI suites such as Telerik, Infragistics, ComponentArt, and Gaiaware offer their own products that, in the ASP.NET world, allow you to reuse your skills entirely while getting a fully AJAX-enabled presentation layer.

Costs and Benefits

By simply adding AJAX capabilities, you don't turn your architecture upside down and you save significant time and costs. It's by far the cheapest option, and it still gets you a Web site that is perceived to be much faster than the old one.

For developers, the impact is limited, as all they have to learn is how to use a small set of new controls and features. Adding AJAX capabilities is the most conservative choice; take what you have and make it better.

In my opinion, this approach is ideal for existing Web sites when it's ascertained they need some updating. If you have a complex site and are concerned about the architecture, this option is probably as good (or as bad) as others. Selecting a different option certainly gives rise to additional issues, such as possible shortage of skills, higher learning curves, and longer development times. Like everything else in AJAX, there's a tradeoff to be considered.

Note Currently, the world of the Web is evolving and it's hard to see which products and approaches will emerge from the process. For what it's worth, this strategy has no significant future.

It certainly can be used, and it still makes your site work for you; however, the underlying approach is a dead end. It's likely that in a few years new tools will be created to make building AJAX solutions a walk in the park in much the same way it is today with classic ASP.NET.

Architecture Is the Concern

If ASP.NET fully embraces the old model of the Web, which is centered around JavaScript and HTML, should we conclude that ASP.NET is dead? And if so, what does the future have in store for us?

The ASP.NET application model based on postbacks and view states is, technologically speaking, probably a thing of the past. However, this doesn't mean that thousands of pages will be wiped out tomorrow and that hundreds of applications must be rewritten. More simply, a superior model is coming out that is more powerful both technologically and architecturally.

To take full advantage of the AJAX model, a different architecture is necessary and new patterns must be taken into account.

Some Common Architectural Concerns

If adding AJAX capabilities to an existing site doesn't have a huge impact on any of the parts involved, why on earth should we ever consider a different approach?

In ASP.NET, the classic Web model is implemented through the Web Forms API. The Web Forms API is based on the concept of the postback. The current page contains just one HTML form and one or more submit buttons. When the user clicks, the content is uploaded and the new page is downloaded. The new page is created based on the content that page controls have stored in the view state and based on the outcomes of the postback event.

The Web Forms model was created to make Windows and Web development nearly the same in the .NET platform. ASP.NET also has the merit of bringing a new family of developers to the arena of building Web applications. For years, Web development has required a radically different set of skills (such as HTML, JavaScript, DOM, and CSS) than smart C++ developers possessed. With ASP.NET, building Web applications has become a matter of doing plain old programming with a first-class language such as C#.

The Web Forms model sacrificed, almost entirely, JavaScript and client-side interaction. With AJAX, instead, we are moving back to the original characteristics of the Web. And the Web Forms model is less adequate every day.

The Web Forms model can still work if you plan to add only a few new features. It stops working if you want to design a more interactive application from scratch.

Two Tiers and a Data Format

The original enthusiasm for AJAX tends to wane when project leads figure out what it takes to build a true AJAX application from the ground up. They can see the benefits (interactivity, responsiveness, user experience, performance, and scalability) of an AJAX application, but they find it difficult to plan for it. Why? Most often it's the lack of tools and a clear vision of the final architecture.

Don't be too surprised to see different people talk about AJAX with different, often opposite, feelings—one saying it is the next big cool thing, and the other replying that its rate of adoption is slowing down.

AJAX is a plus and a necessity. But it requires a new architecture, new patterns, and a new ad hoc platform from vendors, including Microsoft. This is coming, but slowly.

Architecturally speaking, an AJAX application is not really complex. It's based on two layers: a client tier and a server tier. The front end sends requests to the back tier, and the back tier sends responses back. (See Figure 1-3.)

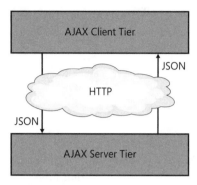

FIGURE 1-3 The classic AJAX architecture

The client tier contains JavaScript code and makes intensive use of the browser's native *XMLHttpRequest* object. The server tier represents a collection of public HTTP endpoints enabled to receive calls from the client browser. The server tier tops everything else the application back end needs to have—business logic, domain model, services, workflows, and data access layer.

JSON as the Fat-Free Alternative to XML

As mentioned, AJAX is all about the browser and Web server exchanging plain data over HTTP requests. The word *data*, though, is far too generic. What kind of data goes into the body of the packet? And how is it serialized?

A form of serialization/deserialization is required to exchange data over the wire. In the classic Web model, the content of the HTML form is serialized as shown here:

```
fieldname1=value1&fieldname2=value2& ... & fieldnameN=valueN
```

In a nutshell, it represents a collection of name/value pairs. The value, though, needs to be a string or, at least, a string representation of a given typed value or object.

All browsers know how to serialize the content of an HTML form to such a string and how to deserialize back. When you set up a mechanism that bypasses the browser, you are also charged with this additional serialization task.

For many years, XML has been touted as the *lingua franca* of the Web. XML can be used to express any value using proper schemas. And XML is also part of the acronym AJAX. But XML is not really suited for the task. A better option does exist—JavaScript Object Notation, or JSON for short.

Since the early days of AJAX, JSON has been the *de facto* standard for browsers and Web servers to exchange data. Just like XML, JSON is text based, but it's simpler and more human readable than full XML.

JSON doesn't compete with XML everywhere XML is used. However, as far as browser/Web server communication is concerned, it is a more lightweight and efficient alternative to XML. JSON is not as good as XML in terms of interoperability, but interoperability is not the point here. Conversely, JSON is much quicker to parse than XML and gets you JavaScript-typed objects rather than untyped DOM trees as the XML DOM. Finally, to use XML from JavaScript you need a client-side XML parser in addition to the JavaScript parser, and XML parser programmable interfaces aren't as standardized as those of JavaScript and the HTML DOM.

Writing your own XML parser in JavaScript is certainly not impossible, but it's not really practical. Standard XML is too big for the purpose because it includes a schema, validation, processing instructions, comments, and white spaces. If we reduce XML to something simpler that just includes attributes and nodes, all that we have is JSON that uses angle brackets instead of curly brackets. Here's a sample JSON serialization that represents an object with a property *id* holding a value of 5:

```
{id="5"}
```

And here's the same code segment in "simple" XML:

```
<id>5</id>
```

The key reason for choosing JSON is that a free JSON parser already exists in all browsers—JavaScript's *eval* function. In summary, when an AJAX request is made, the JavaScript code in the page prepares the JSON string and fills the body of the HTTP packet. On the way back, the JavaScript code in the page uses the *eval* function to evaluate the returned JSON response to some JavaScript object for further use.

To use JSON—and subsequently enable AJAX—you need ad hoc endpoints on the server side that understand and manage JSON strings. These endpoints can be anything the available technologies let you create—ASMX Web services, WCF services, REST services, ADO.NET services, as well as plain HTTP handlers, ISAPI, or CGI applications.

Costs and Benefits

An AJAX architecture doesn't seem much different from a classic multitier architecture. So why does it seem so problematic to embrace it? After all, it should be nothing new to many architects and developers. Really?

The success of ASP.NET and the power of visual tools and wizards in Visual Studio made it so convenient to skim over architectural considerations. Data source controls, autogenerated typed DataSets, and catch-all code-behind page classes are too often used arbitrarily just to make it work. The extreme flexibility of the ASP.NET platform makes it work in one way or another. However, when architectural changes are required, the costs increase significantly.

A well-architected ASP.NET application already has its own business layer neatly separated from the rest that incorporates the data model, application services, and workflows. A well-architected ASP.NET application has its own data access layer and model of data that the business layer works with. Finally, the "perfect" ASP.NET application includes a UI layer (typically, in the code-behind class) where application-specific, server-side operations are orchestrated.

If you already have all of this, how much will AJAX cost you? You probably need an extra layer of AJAX-specific services (which I'll discuss in Chapter 3, " AJAX Architectures,") and some enrichment on client pages (as discussed in Part II). It's not a picnic, but also it's not a tragedy.

If you don't have any of this already, well, you just need to rearchitect the application.

The Case for Rich Internet Applications

AJAX remains a Web feature, and Web solutions are characterized by *reach*. If your solution has to have wide reach and penetration, it has to work with the Web. And AJAX makes for a richer Web.

AJAX, though, will never be applied to building desktop applications for the Web. AJAX will remain limited to HTML for presentation and JavaScript for logic—more power to the client, but within the constraints of HTML and JavaScript.

An RIA, instead, gives you a flavor of a desktop application because it leverages the programming power of more powerful and tailor-made technologies for presentation and logic. An RIA comes out of a browser extension—a plug-in—that basically adds a virtual machine to produce the output. For years, Adobe Flash has taken this road to success and gained adoption mostly because it was the only RIA—even though it was not particularly easy to program.

In 2008, Microsoft released Silverlight. Silverlight is a cross-browser and cross-platform environment for building RIAs using C# as the programming language and a subset of Windows Presentation Foundation (WPF) as the delivery format for the presentation. Silverlight definitely provides the right tools for rich applications.

Reach vs. Rich

Should you opt for an AJAX solution or for Silverlight? What's the role of AJAX now that Silverlight is here? Will Silverlight be the killer of AJAX?

Let's face it. The Web is a whole step backward in terms of interactivity and responsiveness if you compare it to desktop solutions. But the Web compensates for this limitation with wide reach and ease of deployment.

If, in your vision, the factor *reach* is the predominant factor, go for a Web-based AJAX solution. If the winner is the factor *richness*, you should take the Silverlight route.

RIA Offers Better HTML

Today's Web pages use HTML to express their contents. But what's HTML, exactly? Is it a document format? Or is it an application delivery format? If you look at the origins of the Web, you should conclude that HTML is a document format designed to contain information, some images, and, more importantly, links to other documents.

This is not the way we use HTML today.

Today, we use HTML pages with tons of tables, CSS styles, and zillions of images sometimes used for the pictures they contain, but often also used to add compelling separators and rounded and shadowed borders to otherwise ugly and squared blocks of markup.

We actually use HTML for publishing and as a delivery format for our user interfaces. Admittedly, HTML is not the perfect fit for this job. To be a good application delivery format, HTML lacks at least a richer layout model, built-in graphics, and media capabilities.

An RIA platform such as Silverlight has a lot more to offer. In particular, Silverlight offers a large subset of WPF—the presentation platform introduced with the .NET Framework 3.0. It gives you layout tools, advanced input, rich controls, graphics, media, animation, data binding, and styles.

For a developer, building a Silverlight application is not much different than writing a desktop application. Forget about HTML and its unique features to be learned and digested before proceeding.

> **Note** Silverlight allows you to write WPF-style applications to run over the Web. In what way is this different from having the desktop over the Web? First, a Silverlight application requires a host HTML page and a browser plug-in. Second, a Silverlight application remains a partially trusted, sandboxed application. Third, a Silverlight application doesn't have full access to all of the available classes offered by the .NET Framework.

RIA Offers Better JavaScript

Rich Internet solutions are all about doing more work on the client. However, as long as the client environment remains the Web browser, the only tool we can leverage to do such work is JavaScript.

As mentioned, JavaScript is an interpreted language subject to the implementation that each distinct browser provides for it and limited by an object-based—not object-oriented—syntax and a weak type system.

Some libraries exist to give developers a better coding experience with JavaScript, but it'll never be like having the luxury of a compiled language in the browser. Silverlight gets you exactly this through its embedded core CLR, which supports C#, Visual Basic .NET, and even dynamic languages such as Ruby and Python.

> **Note** A fourth approach exists to design AJAX solutions in the real world. It's not based on ASP.NET or analogous Web frameworks. The approach consists of writing the Web front end in an intermediate language and then processing the classes through an ad hoc compiler that will produce HTML and JavaScript. This approach was first heralded by Google with the Google Web Toolkit (GWT). With GWT, you write your application front end using Java classes and the GWT compiler then parses the code and produces equivalent Web pages made of HTML and JavaScript.
>
> Backbase is another product in the same category. With Backbase, you write code in a custom language and the code is then translated to HTML and JavaScript before being executed. To express the expected behavior, Backbase offers a dual application programming interface (API): a declarative XML-based API and a procedural JavaScript API. The code is processed by a browser-hosted runtime, which renders it to the DOM. Widgets and JavaScript utilities are available to simplify and speed up coding.
>
> Microsoft Volta is a product currently under development that gets inspiration from this model and extends it to other non-Web platforms such as Silverlight and Windows Forms.

Summary

Most attentive developers in the community have been developing around interactive and highly responsive Web technologies since the late 1990s. So both AJAX and Silverlight are not brand new ideas. Indirect evidence of this statement is the fact that all real technologies behind AJAX, and even the plug-in technology behind Silverlight, are nothing new.

So what stopped such highly responsive technologies from gaining success and adoption for all this time? The primary factor that slowed down *XMLHttpRequest* and DOM was certainly the lack of cross-browser support for these techniques, which hindered them from reaching a critical mass of acceptance and use. For this reason, cutting-edge client technologies have been pushed to the corner for some years, where they've been forced to observe the success of ASP.NET and the triumph of the classic Web model.

A significant share of these applications today would need a bit of facelift to look better and run faster, and the addition of some AJAX capabilities is the perfect remedy. However, AJAX is a much more pervasive paradigm that might inspire a complete redesign of some other applications.

When it comes to this, though, many wonder whether AJAX is ready for prime time. As of today, the ASP.NET platform provides decent, but not excellent, support for AJAX development. AJAX support for ASP.NET excels in the task of building the server tier of an AJAX application, but it is insufficient as far as the presentation layer is concerned. The next version of ASP.NET is expected to fill the gap significantly.

Silverlight is another option to improve the Web. The challenge of Silverlight is to emulate the Microsoft Windows interface and build a desktop-like application with the same language and presentation technologies. Silverlight is an attractive option that in one way or another falls under the umbrella of AJAX and rich presentation for the Web.

In summary, the Web needs a facelift and AJAX is the new paradigm to evolve and regenerate the Web. You can revamp the Web in three ways. You can simply spice up existing solutions with new features. You can refactor the architecture to meet new requirements and employ new design patterns. Or you can build a truly rich Web application using Silverlight. The tradeoff is reach versus richness.

Chapter 2
The Easy Way to AJAX

If you know how to spend less than you get, you have the philosopher's stone.

—Benjamin Franklin

The core technology of the whole AJAX paradigm is the *XMLHttpRequest* object. Any AJAX frameworks you might happen to work with will use this object under the hood. If you end up using a different application programming interface (API), well, it's only an abstraction layer built to overcome browser differences and simplify programming.

By this definition, the programming model of AJAX applications seems to be clear and unquestionable. You write code that captures client-side events, conduct an operation on the server via *XMLHttpRequest*, get the results, and update the user interface. All the client-side programming is done through JavaScript. Sounds exciting? It is, but the devil is in the details.

The *XMLHttpRequest* object alone won't take you far. An approach to AJAX based on scripting an HTTP automation object is effective only when applied to individual features or bottlenecks in existing pages. It doesn't scale if you try to apply it to large applications—it's too expensive in terms of skills to acquire it and time to implement it. On the other hand, *XMLHttpRequest* is a small but critical object; it's a building block and it's essential.

AJAX applications require a change of paradigm and some imagination. When it comes to rewriting Web applications for AJAX, nearly all aspects of the application need to be redesigned, reconsidered, refactored, and often rewritten. Opting for AJAX all the way through might be too much for too many companies, and it's not a step you should take lightheartedly.

There has to be a simpler and easier way to apply AJAX patterns.

A simpler way to write AJAX applications involves maintaining, to a large extent, the same ASP.NET architecture based on view state and postbacks. A simpler way to work with AJAX involves using a new set of server controls that surround an area of the page and refresh that independently from the rest of the page.

A simpler way to AJAX passes through a component that, using *XMLHttpRequest*, could exchange HTML messages with the Web server having the same page URL as its server-side counterpart. In ASP.NET AJAX, this approach goes under the name of *partial rendering*.

The ASP.NET AJAX Infrastructure

ASP.NET partial rendering is centered around a new container control—the *UpdatePanel* control—that you use to surround portions of existing pages, or portions of new pages developed with the usual programming model of ASP.NET. A postback request that originates within any of these updatable regions is captured by the *UpdatePanel* control and resolved asynchronously using *XMLHttpRequest*. In this way, fresh HTML is downloaded for the selected region, bypassing the browser and reducing page flickering.

Partial rendering is offered natively in ASP.NET 3.5 and also works in ASP.NET 2.0 through a separate download—the ASP.NET AJAX Extensions. (For more information, see the following Web site: *http://www.asp.net/downloads*.)

Partial rendering is the tip of the iceberg, though. It is built on top of the Microsoft ASP.NET AJAX infrastructure that includes a few other server controls—primarily, the *ScriptManager* control—and a general-purpose JavaScript library.

Before delving deep into the mechanics and design goals of partial rendering, let's take a closer look at the underlying infrastructure.

The Page's Script Manager

I can never say this enough: If you want AJAX, be ready to write (or import) a lot of JavaScript code. AJAX involves doing more work on the client. For a Web application, the client is the browser, and the browser can be programmed only by using JavaScript (with the obvious exception of special plug-ins, such as Adobe Flash or Silverlight).

So JavaScript is important, but who writes all the (nontrivial) code you need? It might be you; more likely, it might be some third-party vendor, some organization behind an open-source project or, why not, just Microsoft.

For a variety of reasons (both cultural and historical), a large share of developers have a love/hate relationship with JavaScript. Some even feel sick solely at the appearance of the *<script>* tag. Others prefer to write an entire application of tens of thousands of lines of code in JavaScript.

To keep everybody happy and productive, the emerging form of compromise consists of hiding JavaScript from view when you use AJAX in a simple form. It sounds like a reasonable approach. In a simple form, like in partial rendering, AJAX is just an extension to the classic application model of ASP.NET. And JavaScript doesn't play a central role in classic ASP.NET. So although JavaScript is necessary for AJAX to work, minimizing the developer's exposure to JavaScript is definitely a gentle touch.

In ASP.NET, the *ScriptManager* control is a multifaceted new server control that silently manages most of the script code around an AJAX page.

The *ScriptManager* Control

ScriptManager is by far the most important control in the server infrastructure of ASP.NET AJAX because it performs a number of essential tasks. For example, the *ScriptManager* control manages and delivers common script resources, such as the files that form the Microsoft JavaScript client library. It also enables or disables general features such as partial rendering, page method calls, and history management. The *ScriptManager* is also the component that triggers the creation of JavaScript proxies for invoking Web services and Windows Communication Foundation (WCF) services from within a client page.

Regardless of its numerous capabilities, the *ScriptManager* control is primarily a helper control made available for the convenience of an army of ASP.NET developers. It represents a sort of declarative interface for a number of common tasks in an ASP.NET AJAX page. As we'll see in more detail in just a moment, you can certainly link script files to a page using the plain old HTML *<script>* tag. However, if you do it through the *ScriptManager* control, you have—free of charge—additional services, such as automatic support for localized and debugged versions of the same script. To link the Microsoft JavaScript client library to a page, you can certainly use the *<script>* tag again and make it point to all the files in the library that you need. However, by simply dropping a *ScriptManager* control in the page, you have it for free and without needing to have any intimate knowledge of the library details.

The following code shows the simplest and most common way to insert the script manager in an ASP.NET page:

```
<asp:ScriptManager runat="server" ID="ScriptManager1" />
```

The control produces no user interface, works exclusively on the server, and doesn't add any extra bytes to the page download.

The control should be considered as a sort of script console in the page; as such, you don't need (and don't want) to have multiple instances of it in the same page. If multiple script managers are defined in the same page, you are going to get an exception.

Let's learn more about the main services the *ScriptManager* control provides.

Important What about using the *ScriptManager* control in master pages? Should you define and configure the script manager in the master and let all content pages inherit it? And what if one content page out of, say, 300 pages needs a different configuration?

The suggested practice is to place *ScriptManager* in the master page using the most common configuration (that is, using the most commonly valid values for its properties). Next, when you need to write a content page that requires different settings, you get a proxy for the manager and enter changes through the proxy. The proxy is a control named *ScriptManagerProxy*. From a syntax standpoint, it's allowed to have *ScriptManager* in the master and *ScriptManagerProxy* in the content page. And the proxy can overwrite settings defined in the manager. Note, though, that the *ScriptManagerProxy* supports only a subset of the properties defined on the *ScriptManager* control. To override just one of the manager's properties that are not replicated through the proxy, you might want to write some code in the *Page_Load* event of the page and access the local script manager instance through the following code:

```
// Find a reference to the script manager defined for this page
ScriptManager proxy = ScriptManager.GetCurrent(this);
```

Once you hold the reference to the real manager, you can enter your changes safely. Note that the same *ScriptManagerProxy* control uses this technique internally.

Logistics for Partial Rendering

The *ScriptManager* control orchestrates partial rendering. It exposes a Boolean property—the *EnablePartialRendering* property—through which developers can enable and disable partial rendering on a given page. Partial rendering is enabled by default. As a result, the *ScriptManager* injects ad hoc pieces of script code in the HTML of the host page to initialize the partial rendering, client-side engine.

In addition, the *ScriptManager* control exposes a server-side interface for various tasks related to partial rendering. For example, it offers a property—the *AsyncPostBackSourceElementID* property—to check whether the current postback is because of a standard ASP.NET request or a partial rendering request. Likewise, it lets you set a timeout for the partial rendering operation and offers to capture any resulting exception.

The *ScriptManager* also lets you programmatically register triggers for updatable panels, and it supplies a mechanism to return server-generated data along with the updated markup. Last, but certainly not least, the script manager is also responsible for coordinating the process that generates the fragment of fresh HTML to send to the requesting browser.

Scripts, Just Served Better

By extensively relying on client capabilities, ASP.NET AJAX requires a lot of script code. The only HTML-supported way of linking script files to a page is the *<script>* tag and its *src* attribute. The *ScriptManager* control can be used to save yourself the direct manipulation of quite a few *<script>* tags and also obtain richer features, such as built-in management of localized and debug versions of scripts.

You use the *Scripts* collection to tell the *ScriptManager* about the scripts you want to add to the page. The collection can be accessed either declaratively or programmatically. The following example illustrates the script-loading model you can use to load optional and custom scripts:

```
<asp:ScriptManager runat="server" ID="ScriptManager1">
  <Scripts>
    <asp:ScriptReference
        Name="YourCompany.ScriptLibrary.Timer.js"
        Assembly="YourCompany.ScriptLib" />
```

```
      <asp:ScriptReference
          Path="~/Scripts/MyFavoriteLib.js" />
    </Scripts>
</asp:ScriptManager>
```

You can reference script files, including ASP.NET AJAX system scripts, either from an assembly or from a disk file.

One of the additional free services offered by *ScriptManager* that isn't offered by the classic *<script>* tag is the ability to automatically link debug or release script files, as appropriate. ASP.NET uses a special naming convention to distinguish between debug and release script files. Given a release script file named *script.js*, its debug version is expected to be filed as *script.debug.js*.

In general, the main difference between debug and release scripts is that the release scripts remove unnecessary blank characters, comments, trace statements, and assertions. Normally, the burden of switching the links to debug and release scripts when needed in a page falls upon the developer. The *ScriptManager* control takes on this burden and, based on run-time conditions, picks debug scripts when the *debug* attribute of the *<compilation>* section in the *web.config* file is *true* and picks release scripts otherwise.

Script files can have localizable elements such as text strings for messages and user-interface elements. When the *EnableScriptLocalization* property of the *ScriptManager* control is set to *true* and the page's UI culture is set, the script manager automatically retrieves script files for the current culture, if there are any, and if properly registered. Localization is driven by the *UICulture* attribute in the *@Page* directive and the *UICulture* property in the *Page* class:

```
<%@ Page Language="C#" UICulture="it-IT" ... %>
```

This information is not enough for the *ScriptManager* to pick up localized scripts. You also need to specify which UI cultures you intend to support for each referenced script. You indicate the supported cultures through the *ResourceUICultures* property on individual script references. The property is a comma-separated string of culture symbols. Here's an example:

```
<asp:ScriptManager ID="ScriptManager1" runat="server" EnableScriptLocalization="true">
    <Scripts>
        <asp:ScriptReference Path="Person.js" ResourceUICultures="it-IT, en-US" />
    </Scripts>
</asp:ScriptManager>
```

Note that *ResourceUICultures* is ignored if the *Path* attribute is not specified on the script reference tag. At this point, if the page requires a script named *person.js* and the UI culture is set to *it-IT*, the *ScriptManager* object attempts to retrieve a script file named *person.it-IT.js* from the indicated path.

> **Note** If you use the *ScriptManager* control, you don't have to worry about linking the Microsoft JavaScript client library. In addition to the user-requested scripts, the *ScriptManager* control automatically emits in the client page any ASP.NET AJAX required scripts.

Scripts, Just Made Global

Globalization is a programming feature that refers to the code's ability to support multiple cultures. A request processed on the server has a number of ways to get and set the current culture settings. For example, you can use the *Culture* attribute on the @*Page* directive, the *Culture* property on the *Page* class, or perhaps the *<globalization>* section in the *web.config* file. How can you access the same information on the client from JavaScript?

When the *EnableScriptGlobalization* property is *true*, the *ScriptManager* emits proper script code that sets up a client-side global *Sys.CultureInfo* object that JavaScript classes can consume to display their contents in a culture-based way. Only a few methods and a few JavaScript objects support globalization. In particular, it will work for the *localeFormat* method of *Date*, *String*, and *Number* types. Custom JavaScript classes, though, can be made global by simply calling into these methods or accepting a *Sys.CultureInfo* object in their signatures.

The following line of code shows how to get the culture-specific format for a short date representation:

```
var dateFormat = Sys.CultureInfo.CurrentCulture.dateTimeFormat.ShortDatePattern;
```

The *ScriptManager* control reads globalization data through server-side objects and then arranges and emits a JavaScript array that contains it all.

> **Note** The class *Page* has two properties with a similar name that are both necessary when you want to support multiple languages in a page. The properties are *Culture* and *UICulture*. Both properties are of type *String*, but they can only be assigned some predefined culture names and not just any strings. What's the purpose of having both?
>
> The two properties refer to distinct capabilities and affect different areas of the user interface. The *Culture* property affects the results of functions such as date, number, and currency formatting. The *UICulture* property, on the other hand, determines the localized resource file from which page resources are loaded.

Adding Service References to Pages

The *ScriptManager* control also plays a role in creating the conditions for some client-side JavaScript function to invoke a remote Web or WCF service. The *Services* section of the control hosts references to *.asmx* or *.svc* endpoints that refer to ASP.NET XML Web services and WCF services, respectively.

```
<asp:ScriptManager ID="ScriptManager1" runat="server">
    <Services>
        <asp:ServiceReference Path="~/LiveQuotes.svc" />
        <asp:ServiceReference Path="~/DataService.asmx" />
    </Services>
</asp:ScriptManager>
```

The *Services* section also has a programmatic counterpart in the *Services* collection exposed by the *ScriptManager* control.

Invoking a service is merely a matter of arranging an HTTP request to a public service endpoint using the proper content type, headers, and body format. As far as AJAX-enabled Web and WCF services are concerned, the body format is expressed as a JSON string. This means that you need code that prepares the request and serializes input data to JSON. On the way back, you also need some code that parses the JSON response into JavaScript objects.

A proxy class does just this. In JavaScript, as well as in classic server-side ASP.NET, to invoke a remote service you need a proxy. When processing a *ServiceReference* object, the *ScriptManager* control just emits a *<script>* tag and makes it point to a service URL that generates the much-needed JavaScript proxy, as shown here:

```
<script src="/LiveQuotes.svc/js" type="text/javascript"></script>
```

The service infrastructure (both for *.asmx* and *.svc* endpoints) understands the special syntax of adding */js* to the URL and generates and returns a JavaScript proxy for the service.

Defining History Points Within Pages

An AJAX application tends to replace classic URL-to-URL browser navigation with script-driven HTTP requests. The history feature of an AJAX application doesn't necessarily coincide with the list of visited URLs. More likely, the history of an AJAX application is a list of action points scattered through one or a few pages. In a nutshell, AJAX breaks the assumption that the previous state of a Web application coincides with the previously visited URL.

Clearly, this is a big change.

The net effect is that all the user interaction with an AJAX page produces a single entry in the browser's history. Hence, when you click the Back button you are redirected to the previously visited distinct URL, which might be an entirely new page—even a page in a different application.

There's no simple solution to this problem; there are only hacks to work around it. The most common hack that works is adding a hash string to the URL whenever the page moves to a state that you want to track. A hash is a string appended to the URL prefixed by a pound sign (#) symbol. Here's a sample AJAX-trackable URL:

```
http://www.contoso.com/default.aspx#s=1
```

When you change the URL to simply add or modify a hash, the browser doesn't navigate away from the current page. In addition, it also adds the new URL to its history list. As a result, the user now can navigate back and forward to the URL with the hash and can even bookmark it.

In the .NET Framework 3.5 Service Pack 1, the *ScriptManager* control provides an ad hoc API to add a hash to the URL when the flow reaches a particular point. Adding a hash to the current URL at a given point is a practice referred to as "adding a *history point.*"

A history point refers to a state of the page that is significant for the page and the application. This state is so significant that you want to bookmark it for a future reference. For example, if you offer a pageable control such as a *DetailsView*, any page change is a possible history point. Here's the corresponding code:

```
protected void DetailsView1_PageIndexChanged(object sender, EventArgs e)
{
    // Get significant information to create the hash (that is, the page index)
    string state = (sender as DetailsView).PageIndex.ToString();

    // Add the history point(s) (Name/Value)
    ScriptManager.GetCurrent(this).AddHistoryPoint("s", state);
    :
}
```

A history point is a set of name/value pairs, where the name is an arbitrary but unique string and the value is a string-based representation of any information that will let you restore the bookmarked state.

Whenever the browser navigates to a URL with an attached hash, the *ScriptManager* control detects it and fires a *Navigate* event. By handling this event, you read the hash, figure out the page state to restore, and restore it.

```
protected void ScriptManager1_Navigate(object sender, HistoryEventArgs e){
    string key = e.State.AllKeys[0];  // First key
    string state = String.Empty;

    if (String.Equals(key, "s"))
    {
        // Get the hash and convert to an integer (uses an extension method)
        state = e.State[key];
        int pageIndex = state.ToInt32();

        // Restore the state
        DetailsView1.PageIndex = pageIndex;
    }
}
```

In classic Back/Forward navigation, the browser retrieves and restores the page. In AJAX navigation, the browser can provide us only with the hash string we associated with a visited pseudo-URL. It's up to the page to re-create the desired state based on the information stored in the hash.

History management is disabled by default. To turn it on, you must set the property *EnableHistory* of the *ScriptManager* to *true*. Finally, note that in ASP.NET AJAX managing history also can be done from within JavaScript in the client side.

The Microsoft JavaScript Library

No AJAX capability would ever be possible without a client-side engine right in the page. With today's browsers, a similar engine can be written only in JavaScript. The page engine governs the execution of out-of-band calls, provides a first level of validation of input data, implements simple calculations, caches frequently used data, operates as a controller behind the user's view, and supplies developers more powerful tools (and more abstraction) to manipulate the page DOM and arrange needed operations.

To do any serious programming on the client side of a Web application, therefore, you need a rich, cross-browser extension to the core JavaScript language and the standard DOM. Enter the Microsoft JavaScript client library.

A Richer JavaScript Is Here

The JavaScript package you find in most browsers includes primitive types and a few smarter types to manage regular expressions and custom objects. Beyond that, a client page mostly uses JavaScript to program the page DOM. The DOM represents the programming gateway to the page constituent elements, but it's not designed to provide programming facilities such as those you can find in a general-purpose library.

The Microsoft JavaScript client library is a set of JavaScript files that, all together, power up the language with object-oriented features while hiding differences in the various browsers' implementation of JavaScript and in the DOM implementations. The library also offers a stub for the *XMLHttpRequest* object and facilities for handling events—a feature that often browsers implement in different ways.

You can get the Microsoft JavaScript client library from *http://www.asp.net/downloads*. The library is made of three files, as described in Table 2-1.

TABLE 2-1 Script Files Forming the Microsoft JavaScript Client Library

Script	Description
MicrosoftAjax.js	Core part of the library. It contains object-oriented extensions, the network stack, and a number of facilities, such as those for tracing and debugging.
MicrosoftAjaxWebForms.js	This file contains script functions to support ASP.NET partial rendering. In particular, it defines the client-side engine and programming interface for partial rendering.
MicrosoftAjaxTimer.js	This file contains the client-side programming interface of the Timer server control, a built-in control that comes with ASP.NET AJAX. The control creates a timer on the client and makes it post back upon timeout.

The library is self-contained in the sense that it has no dependencies other than on the JavaScript language and standard interfaces of the DOM. This means that after you have loaded the library in a page, you can start using it regardless of the type of browser you're using. (OK, the library, itself, takes care of the many little differences that exist between browsers' DOM implementation.) It also means that you can use the Microsoft JavaScript library regardless of the technology used to write the host page. It doesn't have to be ASP.NET with AJAX extensions. It can be the classic ASP.NET, ASP, plain HTML, or even PHP. Just link the files in the page and go.

> **Note** Why, instead of discussing script-based ways to enhance JavaScript, aren't we all planning a new and standard version of the language? JavaScript is currently versioned only as 1.2 and is probably still in its infancy.
>
> A 2.0 version of JavaScript is still in the works, but a general agreement on the features to implement is far from being reached. Since the beginning, JavaScript has been the language for quick-and-dirty-but-especially-quick things and tricks. It has always been good enough for everything that was attempted with it, which basically is the main reason for its limited growth. You only make the effort to change things when something dire forces you to.

Pros and Cons of the JavaScript Language

Introduced around 1995 to add more action to HTML pages, the JavaScript language was not expressly designed for developers. Rather, it was devised as a tool for Web designers to script page elements and styles.

JavaScript is not a classic object-oriented language, and its objects are different in nature than those you work with in languages such as C#. In C#, an object is the instance of a class, but in JavaScript there's no explicit idea of a class. In a true object-oriented language, a class is a template for object creation and defines the properties and methods an object will have. Once defined, these properties and methods are set in stone. You can't manipulate an object by adding or removing properties or methods at runtime. In JavaScript, conversely, an object is a sort of dictionary. It's a collection of *<string, object>* pairs that can be modified at any time through its prototype.

JavaScript also pays for the lack of great development tools and subtle differences between browsers in the implementation of the language engine and DOM representation.

For all these reasons, not many developers really like JavaScript and few can write high-quality JavaScript code. It seems easy and trivial to do, but it's much tougher than one might think at first.

On the other hand, JavaScript is a mature and consolidated language. Its dynamic-binding capability makes it extremely powerful in the right hands. Successful libraries such as Dojo, jQuery, Prototype, Script.aculo.us, and Yahoo UI are solid proof of its usefulness.

Adding Object-Orientation to JavaScript

The most important objective of the Microsoft JavaScript client library is adding a stronger sense of object orientation to JavaScript. This is accomplished by adding some type-system extensions and the notions of namespace, inheritance, and interface.

Inheritance, in particular, is obtained through the *prototype* property of JavaScript objects. Encapsulation, on the other hand, depends on the model used to create (pseudo) classes. If the class results from a single function (closure), encapsulation is total; if a prototype-based model is used, encapsulation is purely nominal.

As mentioned, JavaScript classes you get through the Microsoft JavaScript library are not real classes. They're simply JavaScript objects that group together other objects, including functions. They're, in a sense, pseudo-classes. We'll cover programming aspects of the Microsoft JavaScript library in Chapter 4, "A Better and Richer JavaScript."

> **Note** Where are we headed as far as Web programming is concerned? If you're a developer who feels sick when exposed to JavaScript for too long, the next couple of years might be hard for you.
>
> It seems that at least in the near future we'll be using more plain HTML, much more JavaScript, and fewer server controls. For years, server controls have been the primary and preferred tool for building Web pages with ASP.NET. Server controls, though, are barely configurable black boxes as far as their HTML output is concerned. If their HTML doesn't fully work for you (not accessible enough, not easy to style, not XHTML compliant, or whatever), it's hard to change. For this reason, we're predicting a return to using plain HTML and cascading style sheets (CSS) to style. Full control over HTML is what Web people want. We'll return to this topic in Chapter 5, "JavaScript Libraries," to discuss the possible evolution of server controls, from HTML producer to script code producer.

Partial Rendering

The problem with today's Web pages is that they are cumbersome. Or should I more elegantly say, *rich*? Such pages take a while to download and refresh. And having a significant set of interactive features, they tend to refresh quite often. The result is that their users spend a lot of time just waiting for the browser's window to redraw.

This waste of time would even be valuable if only the new content could justify it. Instead, for the most part, the *new* content is the *old* content with some very small exceptions. Fact is, in nearly all postbacks only a small fraction of the page is really updated, but the whole page is served.

After all, this is just the reason that led to the introduction of the AJAX paradigm. The AJAX paradigm, though, might be expensive to apply all the way through. In the real world, a postback-based control like the *UpdatePanel* control turns out to be really handy.

The *UpdatePanel* Control

Let's suppose you want to minimize page refreshes by using the *XMLHttpRequest* object. You write some JavaScript code that intercepts, say, a button click and then places a call to some URL exposed by the application—for example, a custom HTTP handler. When the response is received, the same JavaScript code parses it, extracts usable data, and updates the DOM. This is how it works in theory and in all public demos of the AJAX paradigm.

In the real world, you have no ready-made URL to invoke that can return just the data you want. You have to create it, and you have to put code behind it. This code must be factored out of the existing mainstream and moved from, say, a button click event handler to a separate function. In this way, you can invoke the code easily from the invoked HTTP handler. And what about input and output parameters? They must be marshaled from JavaScript to .NET and vice versa. Your code is also responsible for that.

As you can see, using *XMLHttpRequest* in the real world requires a nontrivial redesign of each page and likely of the whole application.

Motivation for Partial Rendering

Partial rendering is an interesting form of compromise between a pure AJAX approach and the existing ASP.NET codebase. The idea behind partial rendering is that you wrap any portions of the page that might be updated by some user in an ad hoc panel control. When a postback that refreshes that panel is requested, some *special code* executes that hooks up the postback process and returns only the delta of the page that has changed. That same *special code* then will take care of updating the current DOM tree with the fresh content just downloaded.

You don't need to change anything in your server-side code. A postback always occurs, and the page life cycle is entirely preserved. The only difference between a partial rendering postback (sometimes referred to as *async postback*) and a classic postback is the involvement of the browser. The browser does it all in a classic postback model; the browser is bypassed in an async postback and doesn't directly manage the request from start to finish.

The impact of partial rendering on existing code is close to zero. All that you need to learn is how to use a small set of new server controls—*UpdatePanel*, *ScriptManager*, and *UpdateProgress*. No new application architecture is required, and no code refactoring needs to be done. At the same time, by maintaining the classic ASP.NET application model, partial rendering doesn't deliver you the full power of AJAX. (See the upcoming section "Shades of Partial Rendering.")

The Syntax at a Glance

The *UpdatePanel* control is a container control defined in the *System.Web.Extensions* assembly. It belongs specifically to the *System.Web.UI* namespace. The control class is declared as follows:

```
public class UpdatePanel : Control
{
    :
    :
}
```

Although it's logically similar to the classic ASP.NET *Panel* control, the *UpdatePanel* control differs from the classic panel control in a number of respects. In particular, it doesn't derive from *Panel* and, subsequently, it doesn't feature the same set of capabilities as ASP.NET panels, such as scrolling, styling, wrapping, and content management. The *UpdatePanel* control derives directly from *Control*, meaning that it acts as a mere AJAX-aware container of child controls and provides no UI-related facilities.

To use partial rendering in an ASP.NET page, you place one or more *UpdatePanel* controls and use them to surround a group of contiguous controls that might be subject to updates during the page lifetime, as shown here:

```
<asp:UpdatePanel runat="server" ID="UpdatePanel1">
    <ContentTemplate>
        <%--
            This region of the page can be updated separately from the rest.
            You only have to configure how and when.
        --%>
    </ContentTemplate>
    <Triggers>
        <%--
            List here server-side events that will cause the content
            of this panel to update asynchronously.
        --%>
    </Triggers>
</asp:UpdatePanel>
```

In addition, you need to add a *ScriptManager* control to the page. That's the essence of partial rendering. And it just magically works. Well, not just magically, but it works.

Each *UpdatePanel* must be associated with a set of triggers that determine when the content of the panel will be refreshed. A trigger is essentially a server-side event handled through a postback. A typical trigger is the *Click* event of a *Button* control or the *SelectedIndexChanged* event of a *DropDownList* control with the autopostback feature enabled.

Note At this point, a common thought shows up in many developers' minds. Wouldn't it suffice to surround the whole body of the page with an *UpdatePanel* control?

If you do this, it certainly works. However, let's consider possible drawbacks. By having a single *UpdatePanel* control to wrap the whole page, you receive a partial rendering response that has nearly the same size as a classic ASP.NET postback. So it won't certainly be worse than in classic ASP.NET. In addition, partial rendering gives your users the pleasure of a continuous experience with the page—no wait, no full refresh, no flickering.

The point is that with limited extra effort, you can do much better and limit the response returned for each update to just a fraction of the page size, making better use of bandwidth.

Mechanics of Partial Rendering

A partial rendering operation is always triggered by a postback request, such as when the user clicks a submit button, clicks a hyperlink button, or changes the selection in an autopostback list control. This means that the browser kicks in and starts the procedure for a regular form submission.

The HTML 4.0 DOM standard states that a compliant browser must fire a *submit* event to its JavaScript scripting engine before opening the socket and letting the HTTP packet go. This is a key point.

When partial rendering is enabled on a page, the *ScriptManager* control emits ad hoc script code that just registers a built-in handler for the *submit* event on the (single) ASP.NET page form. The following script code actually triggers the magic of partial rendering. You can find it in the HTML produced by any ASP.NET page where partial rendering is enabled.

```
<script type="text/javascript">
//<![CDATA[
Sys.WebForms.PageRequestManager._initialize(
    'ctl00$ScriptManager1', document.getElementById('Form1'));
//]]>
</script>
```

Sys.WebForms.PageRequestManager is a JavaScript object defined in the Microsoft JavaScript client library. (The *ScriptManager* control therefore adds a reference to the library, too.) In the code snippet, the *_initialize* method registers a handler for the *submit* event of the *Form1* HTML form element. The built-in handler is defined in the Microsoft JavaScript client library.

First, the handler cancels the browser request, thus preventing the browser from killing the present UI and HTML page. Next, it rewrites the content of the captured HTML form to add some extra information and then conducts the request in person by placing a JavaScript call via *XMLHttpRequest*. Figure 2-1 provides a comparison of classic ASP.NET and A SP.NET partial rendering.

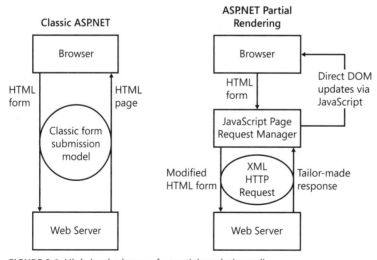

FIGURE 2-1 High-level schema of a partial rendering call

In a partial rendering scenario, the size of the HTTP packet that is uploaded to the server is slightly larger than in a classic postback scenario. This is because of the amount of extra information to be passed to handle the partial rendering. In particular, the form submitted in a partial rendering operation also includes the name of the instance of the *ScriptManager* control that will govern the process on the server. Most of the time, this is the only extra information being passed.

Server-Side Partial Rendering

The ASP.NET runtime doesn't treat an asynchronous postback request differently from a standard one. It finds a proper HTTP handler and sets it to work. The page life cycle continues as usual until rendering time approaches. This means that your code-behind class will receive regular *Init* and *Load* events, the view state is properly deserialized, and state on controls is restored and updated with posted data. The postback event is then executed, and controls are further updated according to the results. At this point, you need to render out some response for the caller.

Did you remember I mentioned that an extra parameter gets added to the HTML form in an asynchronous postback? Well, that extra parameter is just the ID of the *ScriptManager* that is active on the page. Here's an example of the extra parameter:

```
// The ID of the script manager is associated with the UpdatePanel to be refreshed
ScriptManager1=UpdatePanel1
```

During the page life cycle, the page HTTP handler, somewhere in between the *Init* and *Load* events, loops through the form's parameter and matches IDs to server control instances. If a valid match is found, the HTTP handler attempts to talk to the control through the members of the *IPostBackDataHandler* interface—a standard ASP.NET interface that has been around since the first version of ASP.NET.

The *ScriptManager*'s implementation of this interface saves in some internal state the list of panels to be updated. Finally, at rendering time—precisely from its *PreRender* event handler, the *ScriptManager* switches the rendering algorithm to a custom one that takes into account only panels.

The normal rendering algorithm for an ASP.NET page consists of a recursive visit of the tree of controls, starting from the root of the page. In a partial rendering scenario, the modified algorithm begins its recursive visit from the root of the *UpdatePanel* to refresh. Post-rendering steps (that is, serializing the new view state) are accomplished as usual and are in no way different from a standard postback.

The markup produced is serialized as text into a buffer using an internal record-based representation format. This string is the response written to the output stream and received by the calling instance of *XMLHttpRequest*.

> **Important** A partial rendering operation might involve multiple updatable panels. More often than not, the need to refresh a second or third panel manifests during the execution of server-side code. On purpose, the *UpdatePanel* control provides an *Update* method for programmatically ordering a refresh of the panel. The rendering algorithm simply looks at the list of panels to update in the *ScriptManager*'s state and loops over them.

Role of View State

As you can clearly see from Figure 2-1, partial rendering is just a smart trick to bypass the browser and optimize the rendering of ASP.NET pages. Any other aspect of the ASP.NET application model remains intact, including view state.

Too often belittled (mostly because of programmer misuse), the view state plays a key role in the Web Forms model of ASP.NET. It's the storage that allows you to write stateful code over a stateless protocol. The impact of view state on well-designed pages is significantly less today than in the past. More exactly, the bad reputation of the view state grew out of the first version of ASP.NET and poorly designed pages. Starting with ASP.NET 2.0, Microsoft largely improved the serialization algorithm, getting you an average 50 percent savings on the view state size for any page. For well-designed pages, therefore, the size of the view state these days is no longer a significant issue.

This said, with the view state on board, the size of a postback is much larger than with a specific, well-defined AJAX operation. Partial rendering is not immune from view state. If the page has the view state enabled, the view state will be serialized back to the page and added to the response along with the new markup.

The view state served within a partial rendering operation is always the view state of the whole page. In no case will the view state be limited to the subset of controls involved with the update.

Smooth Page Updates

After the generated response is served back to the page request manager in the browser's context (as shown in Figure 2-1), another piece of the Microsoft JavaScript library will take care of parsing it up. The response looks like an array of records where each record might refer to an *UpdatePanel* section, a hidden field, or perhaps a block of server-generated data to share with the JavaScript environment.

Any *UpdatePanel* record is resolved by extracting the markup and attaching that to the corresponding *<div>* or *<span>* tag in the DOM with a matching ID. The DOM update occurs through the *innerHTML* property, as shown here:

```
document.getElementById("UpdatePanel1").innerHTML = markup;
```

Similarly, hidden fields are resolved by loading the new content into the matching DOM elements. Finally, server-generated data (referred to as *data items*) that needs to be loaded into the JavaScript engine is copied into the state of the *PageRequestManager* object and made available to JavaScript functions and event handlers. Figure 2-2 shows a graphical representation of the content received by the browser after a partial rendering operation.

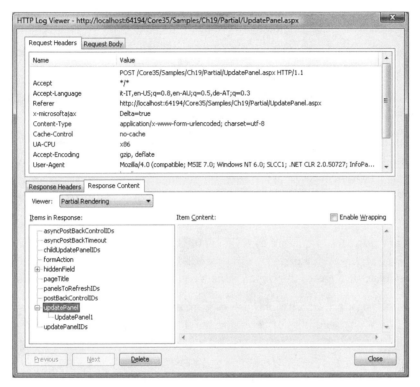

FIGURE 2-2 Anatomy of a partial rendering response

Note In Figure 2-2, you also see in the list of request headers an extra header that appears only in case of partial rendering postbacks. It is the *x-microsoftajax* header set to a value of *Delta=true*. If you're writing a run-time module (for example, the HTTP module) and need to distinguish regular and asynchronous postbacks, you can use that header as a discriminant. In a run-time module, in fact, you have access only to the request object and you have none of the *ScriptManager* facilities at hand. The header is your only help.

Programming Updatable Panels

The *UpdatePanel* control has a fairly rich programming interface that boils down to three main areas: conditional updates, programmatic updates, and dynamic templates.

Conditional Updates

If you use an *UpdatePanel* control as-is—that is, without setting any of its properties—you get the following behavior:

- Any postbacks originated by controls contained in the updatable panel will refresh the panel.

- Any other panel refresh originated in the page will refresh the page, too.

- The subtree contained in the *UpdatePanel* control is rendered as an HTML block, namely within a *<div>* tag.

In the real world, this behavior is rarely what you want. In particular, you might want to gain much tighter control over the conditions that, if met, take the panel to refresh.

Two properties are available to help. They are *ChildrenAsTriggers* and *UpdateMode*. The former is a Boolean property and indicates whether child controls of an *UpdatePanel* act as implicit triggers. By default, any child control is a potential trigger. As we'll see in a moment, any *UpdatePanel* can also have a separate list of explicit triggers. What happens if you set *ChildrenAsTriggers* to *false*?

In this case, any postback originated by child controls is processed as usual by the browser and determines whether a full page refresh is needed. What's the purpose? It gives you a chance to enable only a few of the *UpdatePanel*'s child controls as (explicit) triggers.

The *UpdateMode* property accepts only values from an enumerated type. Feasible values are *Always* and *Conditional*, with the former being the default value. When you set the property to *Conditional*, the panel stops refreshing with any partial rendering operation that goes on within the page. It refreshes only if any of its triggers (both implicit and explicit) fire. By properly using the *UpdateMode* property, you can reduce the payload of asynchronous postbacks as well as display up-to-date information without setting up a timer and polling the server.

As mentioned, you can associate an *UpdatePanel* control with a list of explicit triggers for the refresh. Triggers can be defined either declaratively or programmatically. You add an event trigger declaratively using the *<Triggers>* section of the *UpdatePanel* control:

```
<asp:UpdatePanel runat="server" ID="UpdatePanel1" UpdateMode="Conditional">
   <ContentTemplate>
      ⋮
   </ContentTemplate>
   <Triggers>
      <asp:AsyncPostBackTrigger
           ControlID="DropDownList1"
           EventName="SelectedIndexChanged" />
   </Triggers>
</asp:UpdatePanel>
```

You need to specify two pieces of information for each trigger—the ID of the control to monitor, and the name of the event to catch. It is essential to note that the *AsyncPostBackTrigger* component is a server-side component that can work only on server-side events. The real trigger of the action is on the client when the user clicks. This action originates a postback which, in turn, results in a server-side event fired against the controls in the ASP.NET page. These server-side events—not client events—can be caught in a partial rendering operation. In the previous code snippet, the panel is refreshed when the selection changes on a drop-down list control named *DropDownList1*.

Usually, the *AsyncPostBackTrigger* component points to controls placed outside the *UpdatePanel*. However, if the panel has the *ChildrenAsTriggers* property set to *false*, it could make sense for you to define a child control of the *UpdatePanel* as the asynchronous trigger.

> **Note** You can register controls (typically, buttons) to perform an asynchronous postback instead of a synchronous postback, which would update the entire page. This is what happens when you invoke the *RegisterAsyncPostBackControl* method, as shown here:
>
> ```
> protected void Page_Load(object sender, EventArgs e)
> {
>     // When Button1 is clicked, a partial rendering operation occurs.
>     ScriptManager1.RegisterAsyncPostBackControl(Button1);
> }
> ```
>
> Reasonably, the control you pass as an argument should be a control not included in any updatable panels and not listed as a trigger—otherwise, why bother calling this method? So which panel will be updated? If there's just one update panel, that panel will be updated. Otherwise, it's up to you to indicate in the postback event handler which panel to update by using the *Update* method on the *UpdatePanel* control.

Commanding Programmatic Updates

As mentioned, the content of an *UpdatePanel* control can be refreshed programmatically via the *Update* method. Here's the method's signature:

```
public void Update()
```

The method doesn't take any special action itself but is limited to informing the script manager in the page that another panel has to be refreshed. You resort to using the method if you have some server logic to determine whether an additional *UpdatePanel* control should be updated as the side effect of an asynchronous postback.

An invalid operation exception can be thrown from within the *Update* method in a couple of well-known situations. One situation is if you call the method when the *UpdateMode* property of the *UpdatePanel* is set to *Always*. The exception is thrown in this case because a method invocation prefigures a conditional update—you do it when you need it—which is just the opposite of what the *Always* value of the *UpdateMode* property indicates. The other situation in which the exception is thrown is when the *Update* method is called during or after the page's rendering stage.

Dynamic Templates

The content of an updatable panel is defined through a template property—the *ContentTemplate* property. Just like any other template property in ASP.NET controls, *ContentTemplate* can be set programmatically. Consider the following page fragment:

```
<asp:ScriptManager ID="ScriptManager1" runat="server" />
<asp:UpdatePanel ID="UpdatePanel1" runat="server">
    <%-- Left empty deliberately. Will be filled out programmatically --%>
</asp:UpdatePanel>
```

In the *PreInit* event of the code-behind page, you can set the *ContentTemplate* programmatically, as shown here:

```
protected void Page_PreInit(object sender, EventArgs e)
{
    // You could also read the URL of the user control from a configuration file
    string ascx = "SomeUserControl.ascx";
    UpdatePanel1.ContentTemplate = this.LoadTemplate(ascx);
}
```

You are not allowed to set the content template past the *PreInit* event. However, at any time before the rendering stage, you can add child controls programmatically. Note that you should use the following code:

```
LiteralControl lit = new LiteralControl("Test");
UpdatePanel1.ContentTemplateContainer.Controls.Add(lit);
```

If you try to add a child control programmatically to the *Controls* collection of an *UpdatePanel* directly—as you would probably try at first—all that you get is a run-time exception. You should use the *ContentTemplateContainer* property instead. The reason is that what you really want to do is add controls to or remove controls from the content template, not add them to or remove them from the *UpdatePanel* itself.

Additional Capabilities

You can use any number of *UpdatePanel* controls in your page. The only limitation might be the total number of controls you end up having in the page. Likewise, *UpdatePanel* controls can be freely nested.

Because a partial rendering page doesn't interfere much with the standard page life cycle, any security barrier you might have in your application remains functional. The timing of an asynchronous postback, in fact, is like that of a postback and occurs after all authentication and authorization steps have been taken.

Asynchronous pages are an ASP.NET feature designed to mitigate the impact of long-running tasks. By flagging as *asynchronous* a page that carries a potentially lengthy task, you instruct the ASP.NET runtime to split the page execution in two parts—before and after the lengthy task—picking twice an available thread from the pool. If you apply partial rendering to such a page, it will behave just fine and in the same way as with a classic postback model.

Note In this context, a lengthy task is a task started within a postback event handler that might take awhile to complete. However, the server is required to return the page containing the results produced by this task to the browser. The task is expected to return some content to the user regardless of the time it takes to produce those results. The problem with this operation is that an ASP.NET thread will wait until the task terminates, which might pose scalability issues. Asynchronous pages avoid this bottleneck and increase scalability.

By default, the *UpdatePanel* wraps the HTML generated by its child controls with a *<div>* tag named after the ID of the control. You switch to a *<span>* inline tag by setting the property *RenderMode* to *Inline*, whereas the default value is *Block*.

Minimizing Data Transfer

The *UpdatePanel* control works with the idea of limiting the refresh of the page to only the portions of it that are touched by the postback. A clear mapping between user actions and portions of the page that are updated consequently is key to successfully adopting the *UpdatePanel* control in an ASP.NET site.

Golden Rules for Placing *UpdatePanels*

The first practical step for successfully migrating page behavior to partial rendering entails that you, given the expected behavior of the page, identify the portions of the page subject to refresh. If you have, say, a complex table layout but only a small fragment of only one cell changes in the page lifetime, there's no reason to keep the whole table in an *UpdatePanel* control. Only the server-side control that displays the modifiable text should be wrapped by the panel.

The portions of the page that you should consider to be candidates to be wrapped by an *UpdatePanel* control should be as small as possible. They also should include the minimum amount of markup and the fewest number of ASP.NET controls. Note, though, that you can't wrap in an *UpdatePanel* an incomplete chunk of HTML. For example, you can't wrap a single table row; you either wrap the entire table or the content of individual cells.

The second step consists of associating each candidate region with a list of refresh conditions. You basically answer the question, "When does this region get updated?" After you have compiled a list of candidate regions, and for each you have a list of refresh events, you're pretty much done.

The final step is mapping this information to *UpdatePanel* controls and triggers. If all the regions you have identified are disjointed, you're fine. If not, you use properties and triggers on the *UpdatePanel* control to obtain the expected page behavior, thereby minimizing the impact of postbacks and page flickering.

If needed, updatable panels can be nested. There's no syntax limitation to the levels of nesting allowed. Just consider that any nested panel refreshes when its parent is refreshed, regardless of the settings.

Let's be honest. Identifying the perfect location for an *UpdatePanel* might not be a trivial task. Covering a disjoint set of regions with a collection of *UpdatePanels* is not always possible. Multiple smaller *UpdatePanels* are better than one big panel—if you can find a disjoint set of regions to update individually. However, given the number of properties supported by the *UpdatePanel* control, there's always room for a good compromise between user experience and performance.

Crunching the Numbers for Partial Rendering

The size of the partial rendering response is made of two components: the delta of the page and view state. With proper techniques like those just described, you can minimize the size of the delta. No partial rendering techniques help you to minimize the size of the view state.

To minimize the size of the view state, you resort to classic ASP.NET techniques that share nothing with partial rendering. You can, for instance, disable the view state for the entire page or for some of the constituent controls. Disabling the view state requires a different programming style because all controls will no longer retain their previous state. In many cases, disabling the view state for popular controls such as *Button* and *TextBox* doesn't even require developers to change anything in their code. The same can be said for controls, such as the *GridView*, with a lot of style properties.

Even though the overall size of the view state is much smaller than in the first version of ASP.NET, it's always a chunk of data that is not used on the client and that is uploaded and downloaded with each request.

Note Starting with ASP.NET 2.0, Microsoft introduces control state within the view state. *Control state* refers to some control properties that are saved to the view state whether the view state is disabled or not. Each control is responsible for defining its own control state and, as a page developer, you can't modify that. This means that even if you disable the view state altogether, an extra block of data is always attached to the response as the page view state.

Shades of Partial Rendering

Partial rendering is definitely the easiest way to add AJAX capabilities to an ASP.NET Web site. It has a relatively low impact on the structure of existing pages, doesn't require significant new skills, doesn't require exposure to JavaScript, and leaves the application model intact. Advocates of a pure AJAX approach might say that partial rendering completely misses the whole point of AJAX. And such a statement is not a false one.

Haven't we said that AJAX is key because it puts forth a new programming paradigm for building Web applications? And now we're back to giving kudos to partial rendering—an approach that admittedly maintains the old programming model of classic Web applications? What's the point?

Overall, partial rendering is only one possible way to approach AJAX. It preserves most of your current investments and is relatively cheap to implement. Partial rendering just makes your pages refresh in a smarter way, thus delivering the same pleasant effect of a canonical AJAX feature.

Partial rendering doesn't turn your existing application into a true AJAX application. There's no architectural new point in partial rendering. It's a great technique to quickly update legacy applications, and it's an excellent choice when you lack the time, skills, or budget to move on and redesign the application. But in a good number of cases, an improved user interface and optimized rendering are all that your users demand. So partial rendering would perfectly fit in.

On the other hand, building true AJAX applications where all the presentation logic lives on the client written in JavaScript is not trivial either, no matter how much help third-party libraries might offer.

In the end, you should be aware of the structural limitations that partial rendering has. You might want to start with partial rendering to improve your pages and then move on to other, more purely AJAX, solutions to fix particular bottlenecks that still remain. My advice is that a pure AJAX approach where a lot of JavaScript is involved is a solution that should be considered carefully; and that you should have good reasons for both adopting or refusing it.

JavaScript will never make you productive; a server-side application model will never give you the responsiveness and interactivity users loudly demand. Finding the right balance and making the correct tradeoffs is entirely up to you and your creativity. AJAX is cool, but AJAX is structurally a tough tradeoff to make.

Important Why is it so darned hard to write pure AJAX applications? AJAX applications are all about the client, and the client is JavaScript and HTML. Both have significant limitations in light of the complexity of applications these days.

JavaScript is an interpreted language, and it does not have a particularly modern syntax. Additionally, JavaScript is subject to the implementation that browsers provide. So a feature might be flaky in one browser and super-optimized in another. Originally born as a document format, HTML is used more as an application delivery format. But for this purpose, HTML is simply inadequate because it lacks strong, built-in graphics and layout capabilities. Silverlight 2.0 with its embedded Common Language Runtime (CLR), support for managed languages, and full support for Windows Presentation Foundation (WPF) tries to address both issues.

User Feedback

Partial rendering is a small and simple AJAX framework living within the boundaries of classic ASP.NET. It offers a great way to add basic AJAX capabilities to ASP.NET pages, but it also suffers from a number of limitations. I'll present three areas of functionality where partial rendering just can't do better than it does—and it can't be improved because of some structural limitations. Let's start with the visual feedback provided to the user during update operations.

In a classic Web scenario, each postback requires a full page refresh. Every time the user makes a request to the server, she's mentally prepared to wait. The browser freezes the current page, making it inaccessible to users. Operations then follow one another, but only one executes at a time.

There's often no need for showing an update progress panel. The browser's progress bar shown in the status bar is normally enough. Some sites—commonly travel Web sites—strive to offer a slightly better experience by using some nice tricks, such as using script to display an animated GIF (image) as the new page loads up. In any case, the user has clues of what's going on. In an AJAX scenario, this is different.

The mechanics of the asynchronous postback keeps the displayed page up and running. So the biggest improvement of AJAX—the continuous feel with the page—can become its major weakness if not handled properly. Having the computer engaged in a potentially long task might be problematic. Will the user resist the temptation of reclicking that button over and over again? Will the user patiently wait for the results to show up? Finally, will the user be frustrated and annoyed by waiting without any clue of what's going on?

The partial rendering API comes with a helper control—the *UpdateProgress* control—that has been specifically designed to provide user feedback while one or more *UpdatePanel* controls are being updated. The control just displays a panel with some information about what is going on. You use CSS to style and position the panel at your leisure—for example, you can center it within the page.

The user interface associated with an *UpdateProgress* control is displayed and hidden by the ASP.NET AJAX framework and doesn't require you to do any work on your own. Here's the structure of an *UpdateProgress* control:

```
<asp:UpdateProgress runat="server" ID="UpdateProgress1">
    <ProgressTemplate>
        :
    </ProgressTemplate>
</asp:UpdateProgress>
```

The ASP.NET AJAX framework displays the contents of the *ProgressTemplate* property while the user is waiting for a panel to update. You can specify the template either declaratively or programmatically. In the latter case, you assign the property any object that implements the *ITemplate* interface. For the former situation, you can easily specify the progress control's markup declaratively. You can place any combination of controls in the progress template. However, most of the time, you'll probably just put some text there and an animated GIF. (See Figure 2-3.)

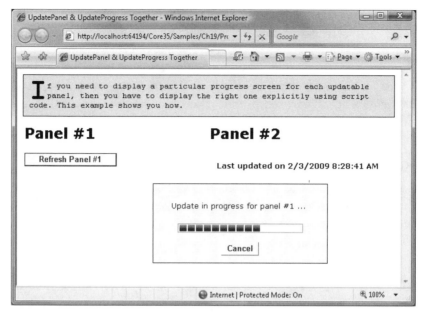

FIGURE 2-3 The *UpdateProgress* control in action

A nice feature to mention about the *UpdateProgress* control is its *DisplayAfter* property. Through this property, you can control how long the framework should wait before popping up the progress panel. By default, the property is set to 0.5 seconds—meaning that if a partial rendering operation hasn't terminated after 0.5 seconds, a progress panel will be displayed to notify the user about what the system is doing.

The *UpdateProgress* control is much less enticing than you might think at first. The control is great at showing some free progress messages, but it's not designed to be a gauge component. It's merely a container for the user-defined panel that the *ScriptManager* control shows before the panel refresh begins and that it hides immediately after completion. If you're looking for a real gauge bar to monitor the progress of a server-side task, partial rendering and the *UpdateProgress* control are not the right tools. As you'll see in a moment, polling is one of the main drawbacks of partial rendering and polling is unavoidable for monitoring server tasks from the client.

Likewise, the Cancel button you see in the figure is less powerful than expected. It's a client-side button with a piece of JavaScript code attached. Here's the typical code it contains:

```
function abortPostBack()
{
  var manager = Sys.WebForms.PageRequestManager.getInstance();
  if (manager.get_isInAsyncPostBack())
      manager.abortPostBack();
}
```

The *Sys.WebForms.PageRequestManager* object is a JavaScript class that governs the execution of any partial rendering calls. In the preceding code, this object checks whether an asynchronous postback is going on and then just kills it. As you can imagine, canceling the pending operation has no impact at all on what is happening on the server. All that it does is close the socket through which the browser will receive any response. In other words, if your postback triggered a transaction, canceling the client request won't stop, let alone roll back, that transaction.

Disabling Visual Elements During Updates

Any AJAX operation, including partial rendering operations, requires you to take care of the user interface to prevent users from clicking where they're not allowed to. This is an entirely new problem that Web developers face, but it's an important one.

In addition, with partial rendering, disabling input elements is almost a necessity. Any clicking, in fact, that fires a postback while another one is pending would abort the current call. No facilities in ASP.NET AJAX provide for a queue where postback requests are accumulated to be further serviced sequentially.

Issues with Concurrent Calls

Partial rendering doesn't support concurrent asynchronous postbacks. This means that you are not allowed to have two asynchronous postbacks going on at the same time. Partial rendering bypasses the standard browser mechanism that handles an HTTP request. It hooks up the *submit* event of the form, cuts the standard browser handler out, and finally places the HTTP request using *XMLHttpRequest*.

The request that reaches the Web server differs from a regular ASP.NET request only in that it has an extra HTTP header. The request sends in the contents of the posting form, including the view-state hidden field. The response is not pure HTML but represents a text record where each field describes the new status of a page element—update panels, hidden fields, and scripts to run on loading.

As you can see, the underlying model of partial rendering is still the model of classic ASP. NET pages. It's a sort of stop-and-go model where the users posts back, waits for a while, and then receives a new page. While waiting for the next page, there's not much the user can do. Only one server operation per session occurs at a time. Partial rendering is only a smarter way of implementing the old model.

From a technical standpoint, the major factor that prevents multiple asynchronous postbacks is the persistence of the view-state information. When two requests go, both send out the same copy of the view state, but each reasonably returns a different view state. Which one is good for the page, then?

Whenever a request for an asynchronous postback is raised, the partial rendering framework checks whether another operation is pending. If so, by default, it silently kills the ongoing request to make room for the new one—a *last-win* discipline.

This fact has a clear impact on developers. In fact, you should always modify the user interface to ensure that users can't start a second operation before the first is terminated. Otherwise, the first operation is aborted in favor of the second. This happens even when the two operations are logically unrelated.

> **Note** When concurrent calls are necessary, you should consider moving that page (if not the whole application) to a more AJAX-oriented design. Alternatively, you can consider implementing that feature within the page using some of the features covered in the next chapter, such as page methods or script services.

Issues with Polling

Among other things, AJAX pages are popular because they can deliver the client information in a timely manner. A page starts polling a remote URL, grabs fresh information, and returns it to the client for the actual display. Implemented via partial rendering, polling is subject to being interrupted when the user starts a new partial rendering operation that restarts automatically upon the response of the previous poll request.

Polling can't just happen effectively with partial rendering. If you need to poll a given server resource, do that via direct *XMLHttpRequest* calls.

AJAX and JavaScript Injections

For architects of Web solutions, finding the right way to AJAX today might not be trivial. The overall community of experts is still exploring the main street for getting to AJAX and attempting to find an approach that is clearly superior.

ASP.NET partial rendering is definitely an easy way to AJAX, although it has some drawbacks and architectural limitations. At the end of the day, AJAX is about having more action on the client. And more action on the client is only possible via more JavaScript in Web pages.

To embrace AJAX on a large scale, you probably need a framework—be it the ASP.NET partial rendering or a commercial framework such as those you can get from companies like Gaiaware, Telerik, Infragistics, ComponentArt, and so on. However, it's always possible, and in some cases even desirable, to have certain features in pages implemented (or re-implemented) using JavaScript and plain calls to *XMLHttpRequest*.

Spot injections of JavaScript code can improve the performance of your pages today without requiring you to invest (and, to some extent, also bet) on a framework. No perfect AJAX framework exists today—be aware of this.

Remote Methods

The whole AJAX movement started when people realized that a powerful combination of *XMLHttpRequest* and DOM manipulation could refresh portions of pages nicely and effectively. Keep in mind that this approach, although functional, is very simple and doesn't scale to large applications with hundreds of pages and complex transition workflows. On the other hand, this is just the class of applications for which classic ASP.NET rocks.

Simple and direct calls to remote HTTP endpoints, on the other hand, can bring to the client just the data you need in a particular situation without spinning up the whole page life cycle and rendering the full page. You can program HTTP direct calls in various ways. You can use the *XMLHttpRequest* object directly; you can use the simplified programming interface offered by popular JavaScript libraries such as Prototype or jQuery; or you can use page methods in ASP.NET AJAX.

Page Methods

Page methods are public and static methods exposed by the code-behind class of an ASP. NET page. These methods are decorated with the *WebMethod* attribute. These methods can be invoked directly via JavaScript and return their response to a JavaScript callback. Methods are static and, as such, they have no access to controls in the page and communicate without view state.

Using page methods saves you from the burden of creating and publishing a Web or a WCF service that is JSON enabled. At the same time, though, it binds you to having page-scoped methods that can't be called from within a page different from the one where they are defined. Here's a sample page method:

```
public class TestPage : System.Web.UI.Page
{
    [WebMethod]
    public static DateTime GetTime()
    {
        return DateTime.Now;
    }
}
```

You can use any data type in the signature of page methods, including .NET Framework types as well as user-defined types. All types will be transparently JSON-serialized during each call.

The page class where you define methods might be the direct code-behind class or, better yet, a parent class. In this way, in the parent class you can implement the contract of the public server API and keep it somewhat separated from the rest of event handlers and methods that are specific to the page life cycle and behavior. Because page methods are required to be static methods, you can't use the syntax of interfaces to define the contract. You have to resort to abstract base classes instead.

Alternatively, you can define Web methods as inline code in the *.aspx* source file as follows:

```
<script type="text/C#" runat="server">
    [WebMethod]
    public static DateTime GetTime()
    {
        return DateTime.Now;
    }
</script>
```

As mentioned, page methods are specific to a given ASP.NET page. Only the host page can call its methods. Cross-page method calls are not supported. If they are critical for your scenario, I suggest that you move to using Web or WCF services.

Invoking Page Methods

Page methods are not enabled by default. No client-side support for them is generated unless you set the *EnablePageMethods* property to *true* in the page's script manager:

```
<asp:ScriptManager runat="server" ID="ScriptManager1" EnablePageMethods="true" />
```

For the successful execution of a page method, the ASP.NET AJAX application must have the *ScriptModule* HTTP module enabled in the *web.config* file:

```
<httpModules>
  <add name="ScriptModule"
     type="System.Web.Handlers.ScriptModule, System.Web.Extensions" />
</httpModules>
```

Among other things, the module intercepts the application event that follows the loading of the session state, executes the method, and then serves the response to the caller. Acquiring session state is the step that precedes the start of the page life cycle. For page method calls, therefore, there's no page life cycle and child controls are not initialized and processed.

When the code-behind class of an ASP.NET AJAX page contains *WebMethod*-decorated static methods, the run-time engine emits a JavaScript proxy class nearly identical to the class that gets generated for a Web service. You use a global instance of this JavaScript class to call server methods. The name of the class is hard-coded to *PageMethods*.

The *PageMethods* proxy class has as many methods as there are Web methods in the code-behind class of the page. In the proxy class, each mapping method takes some additional parameters necessary to an asynchronous callback: completed callback, failed callback, and user context data. The completed callback is necessary to update the page with the results of the call. The other parameters are optional. The following code snippet shows a JavaScript function that calls a page method and leaves the *methodCompleted* callback the burden of updating the user interface as appropriate:

```
function fnButton1Clicked()
{
    PageMethods.GetTime(methodCompleted);
}
function methodCompleted(results, context, methodName)
{
    // Format the date-time object to a more readable string
    var displayString = results.format("ddd, dd MMMM yyyy");
    $get("Label1").innerHTML = displayString;
}
```

In the next chapter, we'll delve deeper into the mechanics of calling HTTP endpoints from JavaScript and discuss features such as timeout and error handling for page and Web and WCF service method calls.

Finally, from page methods you can access session state, the ASP.NET *Cache*, and *User* objects, as well as any other intrinsic objects. You can do that using the *Current* property on *HttpContext*. The HTTP context is not specific to the page life cycle and is, instead, a piece of information that accompanies the request from the start.

Page Methods vs. Services

Services are global to the application, whereas page methods are specific to a page. This said, from a programming standpoint no difference exists between service methods and page methods. Performance is nearly identical. A minor difference is the fact that page methods are always emitted as inline JavaScript, whereas this aspect is configurable for services.

Web and WCF services are publicly exposed over the Web and, as such, they're publicly callable by other clients. A method exposed through a Web or WCF service is visible from multiple pages; a page method, conversely, is scoped to the page that defines it. On the other hand, a set of page methods saves you from the additional work of developing a service.

In a real-world application, services you call from within a Web page are hardly the same services that populate your business layer. To isolate core services from front-end services and avoid possible Web attacks, I recommend that you create your own façade of ad hoc services that internally script the core services of the application and the business logic.

Widgets and Effects

AJAX is about placing out-of-band remote calls, but it's also about implementing a richer user experience. *Rich user experience* means implementing advanced UI features such as drag-and-drop, modality, resize, graphics, and visual effects. There's no way to add rich capabilities and functionalities to Web pages other than by crafting good and tricky JavaScript code.

Commercial frameworks provide rich controls that automatically deliver a better experience and make your UI look more appealing. Commercial frameworks, though, are rarely a lightweight choice in the sense that they have a significant impact on your presentation layer. A commercial framework gives you a lot, but it's a pervasive programming experience.

Are there simpler solutions? You can try Microsoft's control extenders, or you can go with ad hoc JavaScript libraries such as jQuery.

AJAX Control Toolkit

The AJAX Control Toolkit is a shared-source library of Web widgets specifically designed for ASP.NET. It's not included in the ASP.NET 3.5 platform and should be downloaded separately. You can get it from *http://www.codeplex.com/AjaxControlToolkit*.

Widgets in the toolkit are known as *extenders*. First and foremost, an extender is an ASP.NET server control. An extender represents a logical behavior that can be attached to one or more control types to extend their base capabilities. Extenders decouple controls from behaviors and make it possible to extend existing controls with new behaviors. In a certain way, extenders come to mean the same thing as aspects that add new capabilities to existing controls.

In the AJAX Control Toolkit, you find more than 30 extenders that you can use to enrich controls, especially input controls. Let's briefly consider a common example: adding a popup date-picker widget to a text box used to collect a date.

You start by linking the AJAX Control Toolkit assembly to the project and then place an extendee *TextBox* control in the page:

```
<%@ Register Assembly="AjaxControlToolkit" Namespace="AjaxControlToolkit" TagPrefix="act" %>
:
<asp:TextBox ID="Birthday" runat="server" />
```

Later in the ASPX source, you add a new control—the *CalendarExtender* control:

```
<act:CalendarExtender runat="server" ID="CalendarExtender1"
    TargetControlID="Birthday"
    Format="dd/MM/yyyy" />
```

The extender targets the page control with the specified ID and adds a new behavior to it. The behavior is further configured using a few public properties on the extender control, such as *Format* to indicate the desired date format.

The preceding code snippet is sufficient to display a popup calendar as the associated text box receives the focus. As an alternative, you can display the popup when the user clicks a page button. In this case, the ID of the button is set through the extender's *PopupButtonID* property. As mentioned, the *Format* property indicates the format of the date as it will be written to the text box when the user dismisses the calendar popup. (See Figure 2-4.)

FIGURE 2-4 The calendar extender and other extenders in action

The code necessary to create and display the date picker lives entirely on the client side and is contained in a JavaScript file. It therefore displays instantaneously, which increases the level of responsiveness of the page and improves the overall user experience.

The page displayed in Figure 2-4 also features a few other extenders from the AJAX Control Toolkit. In particular, you see the *TextBoxWatermark* extender that applies to text boxes and displays help text when the text box is empty. The *Slider* extender, on the other hand, uses JavaScript to hide the controlled text box element and show its own user interface as a replacement. The *NumericUpDown* extender adds some extra markup to the text box and attaches JavaScript code to properly edit the content of the text box as the user clicks the up and down buttons.

In all cases, an extender doesn't interfere with the programming interface of the underlying HTML elements. In other words, no matter how many (and which) extenders you attached to, say, a text box, the *value* property of the *<input>* element always returns the expected value. The companion JavaScript code guarantees that and overrides the process that retrieves and returns the content of the *value* property.

Finally, note that not all extenders can be applied to all server controls. The source code of the extender server control declares through an attribute the base class of extendee controls. Most of the time, an extender control is limited to injecting some JavaScript code in the body of the host page. More sophisticated extender controls, such as the one that supports modal panels, can also feature a server-side programming interface. For more information and samples, visit *http://www.asp.net/ajax/ajaxcontroltoolkit/samples*.

The jQuery Library

Written by John Resig, the jQuery library consists of a single *.js* file you can download from *http://docs.jquery.com/Downloading_jQuery*. The whole set of jQuery functionality can be divided into a few areas: DOM query and manipulation, effects and animation, AJAX, core functions to work with arrays, filter data, and "detect browser" capabilities. I'll cover jQuery and JavaScript programming in more detail in Chapters 4 and 5. For now, I just want to focus on jQuery widgets.

Widgets for the user interface belong to a special variation of the jQuery library—the jQuery UI library, which is available and described at *http://ui.jquery.com*. The UI library contains features such as drag-and-drop, sorting, and resizing, as well as free visual effects. The core functionalities are combined into a number of reusable widgets, including accordions, date pickers, dialog boxes, sliders, and tab containers.

The programming style of UI widgets is similar to the core jQuery library. For example, to add date-picking capabilities to a text box, here's what you need:

```
$("#birthday").datepicker();
```

In this case, the *birthday* ID refers to an *<input>* element in the page; the *datepicker()* function just registers a handler for the *onfocus* DOM event and pops up a calendar when the event is fired.

Similarly, given the following HTML you can build up a slider:

```
<div id="slider1">
    <div class="ui-slider-handle"></div>
</div>
```

To attach the slider widget to the HTML, you run a piece of JavaScript, as shown here:

```
$("#slider1").slider();
```

In jQuery, the *$* function is a shorthand notation to get a DOM reference to the ID prefixed with the # symbol. Figure 2-5 shows the final effect of the slider, with the default CSS style.

Slider Demo

FIGURE 2-5 A slider widget created with jQuery UI

Widgets are essential to making your Web pages more appealing and interactive. Widgets, though, require nontrivial JavaScript code. For this reason, libraries of widgets are very popular today, with Microsoft's AJAX Control Toolkit and jQuery being two of the most used. With jQuery, you write the JavaScript code yourself; with the AJAX Control Toolkit you rely on a server-side extender control. Widgets are just another aspect of AJAX—an aspect geared toward interactivity and user experience.

Summary

Cheap and effective, partial rendering is the easy way to AJAX, but it doesn't embody the demand for a change of paradigm for Web applications. Partial rendering is normally an excellent starting point in the journey to AJAX and doesn't prevent further optimization and even radical refactoring. Opting for partial rendering or a pure AJAX design is a matter of considering the tradeoffs. But in case it isn't clear enough already, the whole AJAX matter is a huge tradeoff.

Partial rendering provides an excellent compromise between the need to implement asynchronous and out-of-band functionality and the desire to use the same familiar ASP.NET application model. As you've seen in this chapter, any ASP.NET page can be easily transformed into an ASP.NET AJAX page. You divide the original page into regions and assign each markup region to a distinct *UpdatePanel* control. From that point on, each updatable region can be refreshed individually through independent and asynchronous calls that do not affect the rest of the page. The current page remains up and active while regions are updated.

The combination between partial rendering and widgets delivers a powerful solution that's not so revolutionary that it embraces full AJAX or requires new design and coding. Partial rendering is always worth a look. And, once again, because AJAX is a huge tradeoff you should feel free to build your solution piecemeal and as a puzzle of different techniques and technologies.

Chapter 3
AJAX Architectures

Freedom is not worth having if it does not include the freedom to make mistakes.

—Mahatma Gandhi

In the previous chapter, we examined strategies for getting AJAX easily and smoothly into our ASP.NET applications. Partial rendering is definitely worth a try because it doesn't require a steep and long learning curve and has a limited, often low, impact on the existing code.

Unfortunately, though, partial rendering doesn't really capture the heart of the AJAX paradigm. A very similar metaphor to describe partial rendering in the context of AJAX is the following. Partial rendering doesn't teach you how to fish; rather, it opens up a new fish market nearby where you can order nearly all types of fish and pay for it. In the fish market, though, deliveries are not possible every day and the fish is not always the catch of the day. All things considered, if you want your seafood shopping to be easy and are ready to make some compromises, this fish market is an excellent solution—just as partial rendering might be a good solution in the AJAX world.

What alternatives exist to partial rendering?

Pushing the focus to the server was ASP.NET's remarkable contribution to the success of the Web platform. Before ASP.NET, Web professionals and software professionals were two distinct categories of developers, with different skills. With ASP.NET, many C++ developers approached the Web without needing to learn JavaScript and HTML in depth. AJAX moves the focus back to the client, and the Web client platform is made of JavaScript and HTML. This means that at the other extreme of partial rendering you find a handcrafted combination of JavaScript and HTML.

Frankly, a similar solution can hardly be employed in a large enterprise solution with hundreds of pages because such an approach is too risky, fragile, and error prone. An alternative that can really speed up development while remaining reliable and effective is to use specialized server controls that offer AJAX functionalities out of the box. Many commercial frameworks do exactly this. Depending on the level of abstraction of the various frameworks, you might feel like you're using a brand new component-based language on top of ASP.NET or just an enhanced version of ASP.NET.

Regardless of the level of abstraction, the underlying architecture remains the same. You essentially design the user interface using server controls that emit both JavaScript and HTML. The output of each server control is bound to some JavaScript event handlers that fire HTTP calls to the Web server as the user interacts with input elements. The server-side recipients of HTTP calls might also take different shapes (for example, SOAP, JSON, or REST services), depending on the design principles and vision that inspired the framework you're using.

In this chapter, we'll review the two main AJAX application architectures that have emerged as the most popular and effective. No recognized names exist (that I'm aware of) to indicate these two architectural patterns. I'll (kind of arbitrarily) refer to them as *AJAX Service Layer* and *AJAX Server Pages*.

The AJAX Service Layer Pattern

At the highest level of abstraction, Web applications are client/server applications that require an Internet connection between the two layers. Before AJAX, this connection was incorporated in the special client application—the browser. The browser opens the connection, clears the user interface, and then updates the screen with the results of a server operation.

With AJAX, the client code has the ability to bypass the browser and can handle connections itself. This enables the client to enter user interface updates without fully refreshing the displayed page—a great step forward toward usability and rich user experiences.

To make the usability of Web applications grow as close as possible to that of desktop applications, the overall software platform must fulfill two key requirements. As mentioned, one is a client-side infrastructure that can manage the Internet connection with the server. The other requirement is the availability of a public and known programming interface on the server—the AJAX-specific service layer.

Architectural Overview

Any AJAX solution is made of two main layers that are neatly separated but communicating—the JavaScript and HTML presentation layer and a service layer that acts as a façade for HTTP endpoints. Figure 3-1 gives an overview of the architecture.

The presentation layer is hosted in the browser and communicates via HTTP with an ad hoc façade made of URLs. Behind the URLs, you have server code at work. The server code can be exposed in a number of ways determined by the programming API you choose—for example, Windows Communication Foundation (WCF) services.

The data being exchanged between the presentation layer and the HTTP façade depends on the client and server APIs and their capabilities. However, most of the time, albeit not always and not necessarily, JSON is the serialization format of choice.

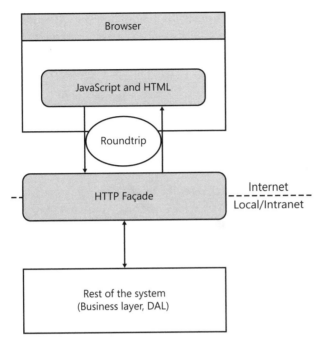

FIGURE 3-1 A typical AJAX architecture

The communication between the HTTP façade and the rest of the system happens either locally or over a protected network environment where only trusted callers are allowed.

HTTP Façade

As shown in Figure 3-1, the HTTP façade just reworks a more convenient API for the presentation layer to call. The API is built on top of application services and workflows. The HTTP façade just scripts these middle-tier components from the client.

The architectural relevance of the HTTP façade is that it decouples the middle tier from a very special presentation layer, such as an AJAX presentation layer. An AJAX presentation layer is special essentially because it's a partial trust Web client.

For security reasons, service technologies hosted on the Web server require special adjustments to enable JavaScript callers. In addition, it's likely that some of the application services you have in the middle tier run critical procedures. Any piece of code bound to a URL in the HTTP façade, instead, is publicly exposed over the Internet. Not an ideal situation for a business-critical service. So decoupling application services from the AJAX presentation layer is a measure of design but also a matter of security.

As an architect, you know that a business layer might sometimes include an outermost layer of code that is used to script the domain model and business components and services. The structure of this layer is inspired by the Service Layer pattern. In general, a service layer defines an interface for the presentation layer to trigger predefined system actions. As the name suggests, the service layer is a sort of boundary that marks where the presentation layer ends and the business logic begins. The service layer is designed to keep coupling between the presentation layer and business logic to a minimum, regardless of how the business logic is organized within the business logic layer.

How does the HTTP façade relate to a service layer?

HTTP Façade and the Service Layer Pattern

A service layer doesn't really perform any task directly. All that it does is orchestrate the set of business objects in the middle tier. The service layer has an intimate knowledge of the business logic (including components, workflows, and services), and likewise it knows the domain model, if any, very well. The service layer is, therefore, part of the business layer.

Ideally, the HTTP façade lives on top of the business layer and, subsequently, it lives on top of the service layer. Despite the word *service* in the name, a service layer is not necessarily made of services such as WCF or Web services. The service layer also can be a plain collection of classes. This is not uncommon in classic ASP.NET applications, where the code-behind class lives on the server and doesn't need a Web or WCF interface to call into the middle tier. A service-based service layer is more common when you have a smart client and need a physical connection to the server to operate. In this case, a WCF service is the best option.

In general, I suggest you opt for a WCF service only if you really need it. Note that having a WCF service only to connect presentation and business components might be overkill in some simple cases. On the other hand, when the client is an AJAX platform, you do need an HTTP endpoint to start server-side operations. In the .NET Framework 3.5, a simple WCF service is an excellent HTTP endpoint, but other options exist as well. The endpoint exposed to the client can be made of the services in the service layer (if you have services there), or it can be an additional layer of ad hoc AJAX services that just talk to the service layer or, more in general, to the business layer. (See Figure 3-2.)

The service layer (if you have one) is the layer invoked by the presentation layer. In the case of an AJAX presentation layer, either the service layer is publicly exposed to the Internet (becoming itself the HTTP façade) or it's shielded by a made-to-measure HTTP façade.

Let's expand on the technologies available to build an HTTP façade.

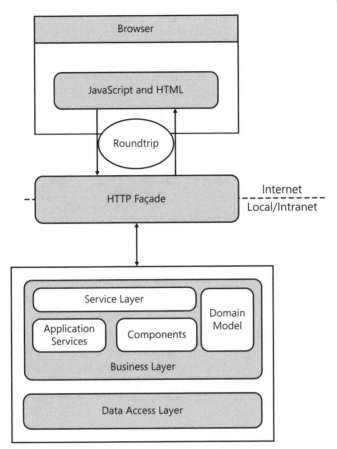

FIGURE 3-2 The HTTP façade and the middle tier

Technologies for the HTTP Façade

The HTTP façade is the list of public URLs known to and managed by the AJAX presentation layer. In an AJAX scenario, the presentation layer is made of only JavaScript code. All the logic you can't or don't want to code in JavaScript must be referenced on the server.

Public HTTP endpoints are the only point of contact between AJAX clients and server applications. In the .NET Framework 3.5, you can write endpoints callable by AJAX clients using a number of technologies.

To start off, an AJAX-callable endpoint can be an *.asmx* ASP.NET Web service. If this is your choice, you need to configure the host application so that its hosted Web services can accept JSON calls in addition to, or instead of, SOAP calls.

Note In the context of ASP.NET AJAX, Web-hosted services are instrumental to the definition of a public, contract-based API that JavaScript code can invoke. It doesn't mean that you can call just any public Web services from an AJAX client. More precisely, you can call only services that live in the same domain as the calling page in full respect of the Same Origin Policy (SOP) implemented by most browsers. This is a security measure, not a technical limitation. In the context of ASP.NET AJAX, you should think of Web services as a sort of application-specific façade to expose some server-side logic to a JavaScript (or Silverlight) client.

Starting with the .NET Framework 3.5, you can also use a WCF service to contain all the logic you want to expose to AJAX clients. As you'll see later in the chapter, though, you get only the Web WCF programming interface and, as such, only a subset of the typical WCF features. In particular, the area of security is thinned down.

Either through the WCF platform or via manual implementation, you can build custom services that operate according to the principles of Representational State Transfer (REST). Abstractly speaking, the ideal service for AJAX applications is centered around the idea of having data and resources to expose to Web clients. It's reachable over HTTP and requires that clients use URLs (and optionally HTTP headers) to access data and command operations. Clients interact with the service using HTTP verbs such as GET, POST, PUT, and DELETE. Put another way, the URL is a representation of a resource and the HTTP verb describes the action you want to take regarding the resource's representation. Data exchanged in those interactions is represented in simple formats such as JSON and plain XML, or even in syndication formats such as RSS and ATOM.

A service with these characteristics is a REST service. For more information about REST, have a look at the original paper that describes the vision behind it at: *http://www.ics.uci.edu/~fielding/ pubs/dissertation/top.htm*.

If you don't want to add WCF to your application but still need a service, you can then opt for a custom, handmade HTTP handler. An HTTP handler is just a public URL exposed by a Web application, so it can reliably serve any purpose the presentation needs to address. Compared to WCF services, plain HTTP handlers lack a lot of facilities, including the automatic JSON serialization of input and output data. (You can use the same tools that WCF uses, but you'll need to use them directly—they're not used on your behalf automatically.)

The long list of technologies through which you can implement your HTTP façade also includes ADO.NET services. Introduced with the .NET Framework 3.5 Service Pack 1, ADO.NET services wrap a domain model built with Entity Framework and expose it through a REST interface. For CRUDy user interfaces, when you hold a data model on the server, ADO.NET Data Services (formerly known as Astoria) might make some sense. Expect some good news with respect to consuming ADO.NET services from ASP.NET pages in the next version of the platform.

In the end, no matter how you physically implement HTTP endpoints, they point to code meant to be the back end of the application. Services in the HTTP façade are application-specific chunks of server-side code that implement some of the presentation logic. Services in the HTTP façade are not autonomous services in the SOA sense of the expression and are not expected to be available outside of the realm of the application.

Services in the HTTP façade are devised to be private services of the application, but they happen to be reachable through public HTTP endpoints. This impedance mismatch should be carefully addressed to prevent security holes in the overall system. (I'll return to this point later in the chapter.)

Data Transfer and Data Formats

In a rich Web application, at some point, you need to call some server-based code. In doing so, you likely need to pass some input data and wait to receive some other data back. Clearly, a serialization format is required to transform platform-specific data (for example, a .NET object) into an HTTP network packet. For years, this field has been the reign of XML. To a large extent, this is still the reign of XML, but not when a Web browser is used as the client.

Shorthand for JavaScript Object Notation, JSON is the emerging standard format for browsers and Web servers to exchange data over HTTP when a script-led request is made. The main reasons for preferring JSON over XML can be summarized by saying that overall JSON is simpler than full-blown XML and gets a free deserialization engine in virtually any browser that supports JavaScript. I'll return to this point in a moment. Meanwhile, you can learn more about the syntax and purposes of JSON at *http://www.json.org*.

JSON is a text-based format specifically designed to move the state of an object across tiers. It's natively supported by JavaScript in the sense that a JSON-compatible string can be evaluated to a JavaScript object through the JavaScript *eval* function. However, if the JSON string represents the state of a custom object, it's your responsibility to ensure that the definition of the corresponding class is available on the client.

The ASP.NET AJAX network stack (see Chapter 4, "A Better and Richer JavaScript," for details) takes care of creating JSON strings for each parameter to pass to a service in the HTTP façade. On the server, formatter classes receive the data and use .NET reflection to populate matching managed classes. On the way back, .NET managed objects are serialized to JSON strings and sent over. The script manager is called to guarantee that proper classes referenced in the JSON strings—the Web service proxy classes—exist on the client. The nicest thing is that all this machinery is transparent to programmers.

The JSON format describes the state of the object, an example of which is shown here:

```
{"ID"="ALFKI", "Company":"Alfred Futterkiste"}
```

The string indicates an object with two properties—*ID* and *Company*—and their respective, text-serialized values. If a property is assigned a nonprimitive value—say, a custom object—the value is recursively serialized to JSON, as in the code snippet shown here:

```
{"ID"="ALFKI",
  "Company":"Alfred Futterkiste",
  "Address":{"Street"="543 Oberstr", "City"="Berlin", "Country":"Germany"} }
```

Services in the HTTP façade preferably receive and return HTTP packets with JSON content. Commonly used technologies for implementing services didn't support JSON until recently. In the .NET platform, both the ASP.NET Web service and WCF platforms underwent some rework to enable JavaScript clients. The WCF platform, in particular, introduced in .NET 3.5 a new type of binding specifically aimed at JavaScript clients. In this way, the core service remains isolated from the binding details and the specific features of the AJAX caller.

Why JSON Is Preferable to XML

For years, XML has been touted as the lingua franca of the Web. Now that AJAX has become a key milestone for the entire Web, XML has been pushed to the side in favor of JSON as far as data representation over the Web is concerned.

Why is JSON preferable to XML in AJAX scenarios?

The main reason for dropping XML and SOAP in favor of JSON is that JSON is much easier to handle from within a JavaScript-powered client than any XML-based format. JSON is slightly simpler and more appropriate for the JavaScript language to process than XML. Although JSON might not be easier for humans to understand than XML—this is just my thought, by the way—it's certainly easier for a machine to process than XML. Nothing like an XML parser is required for JSON. Everything you need to parse the text is built into the JavaScript language. JSON is also less verbose than XML and less ambitious, too. JSON, in fact, is not as good as XML for interoperability purposes.

The JSON syntax is not perfect either. The industrial quantity of commas and quotes it requires makes it a rather quirky format. But can you honestly say that XML is more forgiving?

With JSON, you also gain a key architectural benefit at a relatively low cost. You always reason in terms of objects instead of dealing with untyped Document Object Model (DOM) trees. On the server, you define your entities and implement them as classes in your favorite managed language. When a service method needs to return an instance of any class, the state of the object is serialized to JSON and travels over the wire. On the client, the JSON string is received and processed, and its contents are loaded into an array, or a kind of mirror JavaScript object, with the same interface as the server class. The interface of the class is inferred from the JSON stream. In this way, both the service and the client page code use the same logical definition of an entity.

Obviously, from a purely technical standpoint, the preservation of the data contract doesn't strictly require JSON to be implemented. You could get to the same point using XML as well. In that case, though, you need to get yourself an XML parser that can be used from JavaScript.

Parsing some simple XML text in JavaScript might not be an issue, but getting a full-blown parser is another story completely. Performance and functionality issues will likely lead to a proliferation of similar components with little in common. And then you must decide whether such a JavaScript XML parser should support things such as namespaces, schemas, whitespaces, comments, and processing instructions.

As I see it, for the sake of compatibility you will end up with a subset of XML limited to nodes and attributes. At that point, it's merely a matter of choosing between the angle brackets of XML and the curly brackets of JSON. Additionally, JSON has a free parser already built into the JavaScript engine—the aforementioned function *eval*.

Also labeled as the fat-free alternative to XML, JSON has ultimately been a very convenient choice for architects of Web frameworks and is today the real currency exchanged by browsers and AJAX-enabled services. As JSON's popularity has grown, its use has become harder and harder to ignore.

HTML Presentation Layer

The presentation layer of an AJAX solution can't be anything significantly different than a powerful mix of HTML and JavaScript. The only issue that needs to be decided is who writes the JavaScript code for the page and how the HTML markup for the user interface is generated. Is that the responsibility of the development team? Is that something that can be safely delegated to a library of controls?

For a number of reasons, more and more Web applications need to gain control of every single pixel of their user interface. Accessibility, styling, and the need to work well on the largest possible number of browsers require that a Web application must have extremely flexible HTML presentation capabilities that the developer can fully control.

This seems to be a development that precludes the use of server controls—meaning you won't be able to use one of the hottest features of ASP.NET and probably the main reason behind ASP.NET's success. Server controls can't always guarantee total control over the generated HTML, but this is not necessarily a problem for most pages and applications. As a matter of fact, there's growing demand for more control over HTML; but the demand for the high level of productivity that server controls can offer has not decreased yet.

If you look at the future of ASP.NET 4.0, you see that Microsoft is investing a lot in a powerful JavaScript framework to bind incoming data to existing HTML elements. This prefigures future server-side pages as being dense with JavaScript and plain HTML.

If you look at what independent software vendors (ISVs) are doing, you see products that are essentially libraries of server controls that emit both HTML and JavaScript. Each control has its own client-side object model that talks to the server by asynchronous postbacks similar to partial rendering operations or, in other cases, via direct calls to Web or WCF services.

Microsoft seems to be focused on building a robust and powerful JavaScript framework; subsequently, third-party vendors seem to be focused on building server controls on top of that.

Have server controls definitely been surpassed? It's hard to say.

For sure, we need some sort of tool to help write HTML and JavaScript. I doubt that we'll end up back where we were in the early days of Web, handcrafting HTML and JavaScript in pages. Large applications with hundreds of pages just can't afford this model.

For the past five years or so, server controls have been the primary tool used to help developers write the HTML presentation layer. In the future, we will certainly have a new generation of server controls that emit HTML and JavaScript, as well as HTML helpers like those you find today in the view objects of ASP.NET MVC Framework applications.

Inside the HTTP Façade

The HTTP façade is the collection of public HTTP endpoints you can invoke from within Web pages via JavaScript. There are two main categories of endpoints: service endpoints and page endpoints.

Service endpoints refer to Web or WCF services that expose some server-side logic to the client.

Page endpoints refer to some client-callable logic exposed by the page itself. Page endpoints are just the *Page Methods* presented in the previous chapter. Using page methods saves you from the burden of creating a JSON-enabled Web service or a WCF service. At the same time, though, it limits the scope of the method to the sole page where it's defined. When you use page methods, the page itself operates as the service and the page method is just the publicly callable operation.

Let's examine the format of requests placed to HTTP endpoints.

Anatomy of an HTTP Request

A request made to a Web or WCF service has a well-defined format. It sets the content-type header to *application/json* and points to the URL of the service method of choice. Input parameters are embedded in the body of the request as a JSON string. In Figure 3-3, you can see the details of a request made to a WCF service. In particular, the method invoked is *GetQuotesFromConfig* and the service endpoint is *livequotes.svc*.

The request body is a plain JSON string, such as the one shown here:

```
{"isOffline":true}
```

The *GetQuotesFromConfig* method takes just one Boolean parameter, whose formal name is *isOffline*. The JSON string just describes an object with one property named *isOffline* that stores a value of *true*.

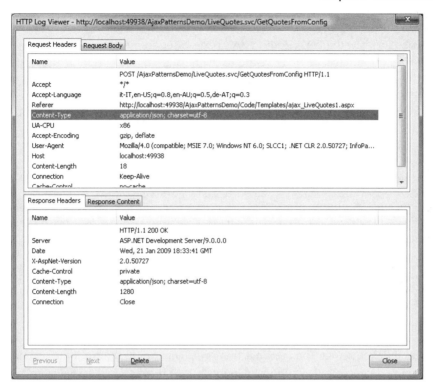

FIGURE 3-3 Internals of an AJAX request to a WCF service

The response is always a JSON string; in particular, it's the JSON serialization of the value returned by the invoked method. If the method returns an array of *StockInfo* objects, here's some possible output:

```
{"d":
  [{"__type":"StockInfo:#Samples.Services.FinanceInfo",
    "Change":"+8.87%",
    "Day":"12\/16\/2008",
    "ProviderName":"Unknown Provider",
    "Quote":"57.549",
    "Symbol":"CONTOSO",
    "Time":"8:53 PM"},
   {"__type":"StockInfo:#Samples.Services.FinanceInfo",
    "Change":"-5.62%",
    "Day":"12\/16\/2008",
    "ProviderName":"Unknown Provider",
    "Quote":"30.793",
    "Symbol":"NANCY DAVOLIO INC",
    "Time":"8:53 PM"}
  ]
}
```

Let's see what's required to write WCF services to be invoked via AJAX calls.

WCF Services

To be invoked from within an ASP.NET AJAX page, a service must meet a number of requirements, the strictest of which relate to the location of the endpoint and underlying platform. AJAX-enabled services must be hosted in the same domain from which the call is made. If we consider using WCF services to back an AJAX front end, the service must be hosted in an Internet Information Services (IIS) application on the same Web server as the ASP.NET application.

> **Important** By default, AJAX-enabled WCF services run side by side with the ASP.NET application in the same AppDomain. Requests for an *.svc* resource are first dispatched to the ASP.NET runtime, but then the WCF hosting infrastructure intercepts these requests and routes them out of the HTTP pipeline. ASP.NET doesn't participate in the processing of WCF requests past the *PostAuthenticateRequest* event in the request life cycle. At that point, in fact, the WCF infrastructure intercepts the request and starts processing that in total autonomy. In the default configuration, the WCF service method has no access to ASP.NET intrinsics, ASP.NET impersonation and URL authorization settings are ignored, and HTTP modules interested in filtering the WCF request past the *PostAuthenticateRequest* event never get a chance to do their work.

To expose WCF services to an ASP.NET AJAX client, you need the .NET Framework 3.5 running on the Web server. The reason is that some changes to the run-time engine of the WCF platform are necessary to support AJAX calls; and these changes have been made only with the .NET Framework 3.5.

In particular, to support AJAX calls you need to be able to expose service methods through HTTP requests and subsequently map methods to URLs. This is just what the WCF Web programming model has to offer. The WCF Web programming model enables services to support plain-old XML (POX) style messaging instead of SOAP, which is the key step to enabling the JSON calls typical of ASP.NET AJAX clients.

The following code snippet shows how to use the new *WebGet* attribute in the definition of a service contract:

```
[ServiceContract]
public interface ICalculator {
  [OperationContract]
  [WebGet]
  long Add(long x, long y);

  [OperationContract]
  [WebGet(UriTemplate="Sub?p1={x}&p2={y}")]
  long Subtract(long x, long y);
}
```

The *WebGet* attribute qualifies a method as a retrieval operation and enables callers to use the HTTP GET verb to invoke it. The *WebGet* attribute also features the *UriTemplate* property. You use this property to specify which URL format is accepted to invoke the method. If not otherwise specified via an explicit *UriTemplate* property, the URI template for a *WebGet* method like the aforementioned *Add* is the following:

```
theService.svc/Add?x=1&y=2
```

The service name is followed by the method name, and formal parameters follow in order, each with its own actual value. You can change this standard URI template by changing the method name and formal parameter names.

The *WebInvoke* attribute indicates that a given method has to be considered as a logical invoke operation that can be invoked using any HTTP verb, but typically the POST verb is called upon:

```
[ServiceContract]
public interface ICalculator {
  [OperationContract]
  [WebInvoke(Method="Post",
    RequestFormat=WebMessageFormat.Xml,
    ResponseFormat=WebMessageFormat.Json)]
  long Add(long x, long y);
}
```

Through the *WebInvoke* attribute, you can set the URI template, the method to be used to invoke the method, as well as the format for the request and response text.

To be invoked from an AJAX client, a WCF service must be configured with a new binding model—the *webHttpBinding* model. The *webHttpBinding* model is a basic HTTP binding except that it doesn't use SOAP. In addition, the scriptable endpoints must feature a behavior where Web scripting is explicitly enabled. Here's an excerpt from a sample configuration script for an AJAX-enabled WCF service:

```
<system.serviceModel>
  <behaviors>
    <endpointBehaviors>
      <behavior name="ajaxBehavior">
        <enableWebScript />
      </behavior>
    </endpointBehaviors>

    <serviceBehaviors>
      <behavior name="metadataBehavior">
        <serviceMetadata httpGetEnabled="true" />
      </behavior>
    </serviceBehaviors>
  </behaviors>

    ⋮

</system.serviceModel>
```

Attached to an endpoint behavior, the *enableWebScript* element enables the runtime to generate the JavaScript proxy for the service. In addition, you might also want to publish service metadata for retrieval using an HTTP GET request.

The services hosted by the Web application must be configured especially to use the Web HTTP-specific binding model, as shown here:

```
<system.serviceModel>
    ⋮
  <services>
    <service name="Samples.TimeService"
             behaviorConfiguration="metadataBehavior">
      <endpoint contract="Samples.ITimeService"
                binding="webHttpBinding"
                behaviorConfiguration="ajaxBehavior" />
    </service>
  </services>
</system.serviceModel>
```

The configuration of a WCF service specifies key pieces of information—the binding model (mandatory), contract, and behavior. For AJAX-enabled services, the only possible binding scheme is *webHttpBinding*. The *contract* attribute indicates which contract the endpoint is exposing. If the service class implements a single contract type, the *contract* attribute can be omitted in the endpoint section. Finally, the *behaviorConfiguration* attribute contains the name of the behavior to be used in the endpoint.

> **Note** In some particular scenarios, you can also resort to a simplified configuration scheme for AJAX-enabled WCF services. In the service endpoint file—the *.svc* file—you use the *Factory* attribute in the *@ServiceHost* directive and make it point to a system-provided class that supplies default settings for binding and endpoint behaviors. Here's the code for the *.svc* endpoint file:
>
> ```
> <%@ ServiceHost
>     Factory="System.ServiceModel.Activation.WebScriptServiceHostFactory"
>     Service="Samples.Services.TimeService" %>
> ```
>
> Note that you can use simplified configuration only for service classes that implement one contract only.

The definition of the service contract for an AJAX-enabled WCF service is not different from that of any other WCF services. You use the *OperationContract* attribute to qualify a method as a public service method, and you use the optional *WebGet* and *WebInvoke* attributes to configure the URL template. Here's an example:

```
[ServiceContract(Namespace="Samples.Services", Name="TimeService")]
public interface ITimeService
{
    [OperationContract]
    DateTime GetTime();

    [OperationContract]
    string GetTimeFormat(string format);
}
```

```
public class TimeService : ITimeService
{
    public DateTime GetTime()
    {
        return DateTime.Now;
    }
      .
      .
      .
}
```

You should be sure to give meaningful values to the *Namespace* and *Name* properties of the *ServiceContract* attribute. The reason is that the concatenation of those values determines the name of the JavaScript proxy class used to access the WCF service. If you leave them blank, the JavaScript proxy for the preceding service will be named *tempuri.org.ITimeService*. Not really a nice or helpful name!

For AJAX-enabled WCF services, the data contract—namely, the agreement between the service and client that describes the data to be exchanged—also is defined in the canonical way. You use an implicit contract for serialization, and deserialization is used for collections, primitive types, dates, enumerations, and the GUID; an explicit contract is required for custom complex types. In this case, you use the *DataContract* and *DataMember* attributes on class members to determine which members go into the serialization stream.

For more information on WCF services, you might want to refer to Juval Lowy's excellent book *Programming WCF* (O'Reilly, 2008).

Important The configuration of a WCF service is different if the client is a Silverlight application. In such a case, in fact, you are not allowed to use *webHttpBinding* and must resort to the *basicHttpBinding* model, which executes the method call over a SOAP 1.1 channel.

ASP.NET Web Services

The primary reason for choosing ASP.NET Web services instead of WCF as the technology for building your HTTP façade is that ASP.NET Web services don't require ASP.NET 3.5 or newer versions. You can call ASP.NET Web services from AJAX clients as long as your Web server runs the .NET Framework 2.0 plus AJAX Extensions 1.0.

A Web service made to measure for an ASP.NET AJAX application is similar to any other ASP.NET Web service you might write for whatever purposes. Just one peripheral aspect, though, marks a key difference. You must use a new attribute to decorate the class of the Web service that is not allowed on regular ASP.NET Web services—the *ScriptService* attribute. Here's how to use it:

```
namespace Samples.WebServices
{
    [ScriptService]
    [WebService(Namespace = "urn:webarch.book/")]
    public class TimeService : System.Web.Services.WebService, ITimeService
    {
        [WebMethod]
```

```
public DateTime GetTime()
{
    return DateTime.Now;
}
      .
      .
      .
    }
}
```

Note that the *ScriptService* attribute simply enables AJAX callers to connect to the service; it doesn't prevent SOAP callers from sending their packets. As a result, an ASP.NET AJAX Web service might have a double public interface: the JSON-based interface consumed by the hosting ASP.NET AJAX application, and the classic SOAP-based interface exposed to any clients, from any platforms, that can reach the service URL.

How can the ASP.NET runtime handle .*asmx* requests properly?

To enable Web service calls from within AJAX applications, you need to add the following script to the application's *web.config* file. It removes any ASMX handler you might have and registers a special new HTTP handler factory to service incoming .*asmx* requests:

```
<httpHandlers>
    <remove verb="*" path="*.asmx" />
    <add verb="*" path="*.asmx"
        type="System.Web.Script.Services.ScriptHandlerFactory" />
      .
      .
</httpHandlers>
```

This setting is included in the default *web.config* file that Microsoft Visual Studio 2008 creates for you when you create an AJAX-enabled Web project.

A handler factory determines which HTTP handler is in charge of serving a given set of requests. The specialized handler factory for .*asmx* requests distinguishes JSON calls made by script code from ordinary Web service calls coming from SOAP-based clients, including ASP. NET and Windows Forms applications. JSON-based requests are served by a different HTTP handler (informally known as the REST handler), whereas regular SOAP calls take the usual route in the ASP.NET pipeline. (See Figure 3-4.)

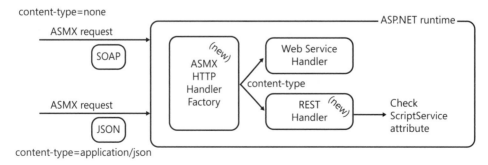

FIGURE 3-4 How ASP.NET handles incoming .*asmx* requests

The handler factory determines the handler to use by looking at the *content-type* header of the incoming request. The REST handler uses .NET reflection to specifically check whether the Web service class is decorated with the *ScriptService* attribute. If it is not, it refuses the call.

You can disable SOAP clients by entering the following configuration script into the *web.config* file of the ASP.NET application that hosts the Web service:

```
<system.Web>
    ⋮

    <webServices>
        <protocols>
            <clear />
        </protocols>
    </webServices>

    ⋮

</system.Web>
```

This simple change disables any protocols defined for ASP.NET Web services (in particular, SOAP) and lets the service reply only to JSON requests. Note that with these settings on, you can no longer call the Web service through the browser's address bar for a quick test. Likewise, you can't ask for the WSDL by adding the *?wsdl* suffix to the URL.

When you write an AJAX-enabled ASP.NET Web service, you have no need for a contracted interface as with WCF services. However, extracting an interface from the service class is rarely a bad idea.

```
public class TimeService : System.Web.Services.WebService, ITimeService
{
    [WebMethod]
    public DateTime GetTime()
    {
        return DateTime.Now;
    }

    ⋮

}
```

Public methods of the Web service class decorated with the *WebMethod* attribute can be invoked from the AJAX page. Any method is invoked using the HTTP POST verb and returns any value as a JSON object. You can change these default settings on a per-method basis by using an optional attribute—*ScriptMethod*. In particular, through the *ScriptMethod* attribute you can enable HTTP GET calls and use XML instead of JSON as the serialization format.

Enabling the use of the HTTP GET verb opens security holes: the service method can be invoked through a cross-site scripting attack that attaches external script to the *<script>* or *<img>* HTML tags. These HTML elements are the sole elements allowed to access resources from outside the current domain. However, they always operate through a GET verb. This means that by keeping the HTTP GET verb disabled on your Web service method you prevent at the root any possible cross-site scripting attacks. More in general, my opinion is that you should have very good reasons to use the *ScriptMethod* attribute, anyway.

Finally, deriving the Web service class from *System.Web.Services.WebService* is not mandatory either. If you use that class as a parent, all that you gain is that you enable the service to access ASP.NET intrinsics directly without using the *HttpContext.Current* object as an intermediary.

> **Important** By default, AJAX-enabled WCF services process requests for method execution outside the ASP.NET pipeline. Requests for ASP.NET Web services methods, conversely, are treated as standard ASP.NET requests. In other words, *.asmx* requests flow through the classic request life cycle whereas *.svc* requests are routed out of the pipeline at some point.
>
> By switching WCF services to ASP.NET compatibility mode, you ensure that *.svc* requests are treated identically to *.asmx* requests with respect to ASP.NET intrinsics, URL authorization, and impersonation. However, the ASP.NET compatibility mode for WCF services breaks the WCF ability to behave consistently across hosting environments and transports. Compatibility mode is an option only for WCF services that will always operate over HTTP and be hosted by IIS, which is just what the majority of AJAX-enabled WCF services do.

Custom Services

Nothing prevents you from connecting your AJAX or Silverlight page to a custom HTTP handler exposed by your ASP.NET application. A call to a custom HTTP handler requires that you manage the HTTP request from start to finish. To call an HTTP handler, you need to write JavaScript code that uses *XMLHttpRequest* and, on the server, you need to parse any input data, execute your action, and serialize any output data to a valid format that the AJAX caller can understand.

Calling HTTP handlers is definitely something that can be done. However, compared to the native machinery in place for ASP.NET Web services and WCF services, it's just a little bit more work that you could otherwise avoid. It's definitely doable, and it gives you total control over the request. And, among other things, it gives you a chance for exchanging data that is not JSON.

ADO.NET Data Services

Introduced with the .NET Framework 3.5 SP1, ADO.NET Data Services are a framework to create and consume data services via a flexible, RESTful interface. But what's a RESTful interface for data, exactly?

Essentially, it's a programming interface to refer to data as any other resource representation available over HTTP. Data is treated as a representation of a resource, and HTTP methods are used to act on the resource via its representation. You use the GET verb to query data, POST to create, PUT to update, and DELETE to delete data.

Data is wrapped up with a special service that you work with using HTTP verbs via a uniform URL syntax. The URL syntax allows you to address every piece of information. Here are some sample URLs you can use against a data service:

```
/Customers
/Customers('ALFKI')
/Customers('ALFKI')/ContactName
/Customers?$orderby=Country
```

An ADO.NET data service incorporates an entity data model created with Entity Framework (EF). The operations you execute via HTTP target the data modeled by the EF model. An ADO.NET data service is an *.svc* resource that AJAX and Silverlight applications can freely access to receive JSON data.

The Visual Studio 2008 environment for Silverlight 2 provides some facilities to consume ADO.NET Data Services. Facilities consist essentially of the automatic creation of all required entity classes for the model wrapped by the service. Here's how you consume an ADO.NET data service:

```
// Get a reference to the data context class
Uri svc = new Uri("Northwind.svc", UriKind.Relative);
DataServiceContext ctx = new DataServiceContext(svc);

// Run a query. OnLoaded is the callback to update the UI.
Uri query = new Uri("Customers?$orderby=Country", UriKind.Relative);
ctx.BeginExecute<Customer>(query, OnLoaded, ctx);
```

The *DataServiceContext* class is a Silverlight class whose assembly (named *System.Data.Services.Client*) is automatically linked to the project as soon as you add an ADO.NET Data Services reference.

What about ASP.NET AJAX?

In ASP.NET AJAX, you call an ADO.NET data service via *XMLHttpRequest*. However, more facilities are coming with ASP.NET 4.0. In particular, the next version of ASP.NET will offer classes and methods to support typical operations such as insert, query, update, and delete, plus a programming interface to make client-side data binding easy and effective.

The AJAX Presentation Layer

From an ASP.NET AJAX perspective, differences between Web and WCF services are definitely blurred. All that an AJAX client expects from Web and WCF services is to execute some code and return some data. Most of the other extraordinary capabilities of the WCF platform are of little interest to an AJAX client.

Also from an ASP.NET AJAX perspective, the biggest difference between Web and WCF services and plain HTTP handlers is that the former two provide automatic data marshaling between the .NET space and the JSON format. However, this occurs only if proper proxy classes are employed to drive the call to a remote service.

Getting a Proxy for the HTTP Façade

When you add a Web or WCF service to a classic Web application project or to a Windows Forms project, you go through a Visual Studio 2008 wizard, indicate the URL of the service, specify the desired namespace, and finally have the wizard generate a proxy class and add it in the folds of the project solution.

When you add a reference to Web or WCF services to an ASP.NET AJAX page, no Visual Studio 2008 wizard will be there to silently invoke an SDK tool that automagically creates the proxy class. In the first place, you don't add a service reference through the Web project. Instead, you programmatically add the service reference to the ASP.NET page, as shown here:

```
<asp:ScriptManager ID="ScriptManager1" runat="server">
    <Services>
        <asp:ServiceReference Path="appAjaxLayer.svc" />
        :
    </Services>
</asp:ScriptManager>
```

The script manager emits the following markup:

```
<script src="appAjaxLayer.svc/js" type="text/javascript"></script>
```

If you're testing your page and have debug mode set in the *web.config* file, the suffix to the service URL will be */jsdebug* instead of */js*.

The */js* suffix is the magic word that instructs the service infrastructure to generate a JavaScript proxy class for the page code to call into the service. The ability to generate a JavaScript proxy class is built into the REST handler that was shown in Figure 3-4 for ASMX Web services and into the AJAX-enabled Web programming model of WCF. In particular, for WCF services the *enableWebScript* attribute of the endpoint behavior enables the generation of the proxy; subsequently, it enables the service to be scripted from an AJAX client.

The JavaScript proxy class is named according to different rules for Web and WCF services. For Web services, the proxy gets the exact fully qualified name of the class behind the *.asmx* endpoint. As mentioned earlier, for WCF services the name of the proxy class is determined by the concatenation of the *Namespace* and *Name* properties specified in the *ServiceContract* attribute you're targeting. Note, therefore, that when you call a WCF service method you're actually calling a method defined on a contract. To invoke a WCF service, it's the contract that matters, not the class that implements it. In fact, the same service class can implement multiple contracts.

Using the Proxy

After you have the JavaScript proxy, invoking the Web or WCF service is nearly the same thing. The proxy object comes as a singleton and exposes the same set of contracted methods you have on the original service. The communication model is asynchronous and requires you to specify at least a callback function to use in case of successful execution. Here's an example:

```
// Async call of method GetQuotes with a callback
Samples.Services.FinanceInfoService.GetQuotes(symbols, onDataAvailable);
```

The code can refer to a Web service as well as a WCF service. If it refers to a Web service, the Web service class is named *Samples.Services.FinanceInfoService*; if it refers to a WCF service, the namespace of the service contract might be *Samples.Services* and the name of the contract might be *FinanceInfoService*. The preceding code snippet invokes the method *GetQuotes*.

In addition to the regular list of parameters for the service method, each proxy method can take up to three extra parameters. The first extra parameter is mandatory and represents the callback to invoke if the method execution is successful. The second and third optional parameters indicate, respectively, the callback to use in case of failure and a state object to pass to both callbacks. In the code snippet just shown, the *onDataAvailable* parameter refers to a JavaScript callback to call only if the method executes successfully.

The signature of the success and failure callbacks is similar, but the internal format of the *results* parameter can change quite a bit. Here's the callback signature:

```
function method(results, context, methodName)
```

Table 3-1 provides more details about the various arguments.

TABLE 3-1 Arguments for a JavaScript Proxy Callback Function

Argument	Description
results	Indicates the return value from the method in the case of success. In the case of failure, a JavaScript *Error* object mimics the exception that occurred on the server during the execution of the method.
context	The state object passed to the callback.
methodName	The name of the service method that was invoked.

The JavaScript proxy exposes a number of properties and methods for you to configure. The list is presented in Table 3-2.

TABLE 3-2 Static Properties on a JavaScript Proxy Class

Property	Description
path	Gets and sets the URL of the underlying Web service
timeout	Gets and sets the duration (in seconds) before the method call times out
defaultSucceededCallback	Gets and sets the default JavaScript callback function to invoke for any successful call to a method
defaultFailedCallback	Gets and sets the default JavaScript callback function, if any, to invoke for a failed or timed-out call
defaultUserContext	Gets and sets the default JavaScript state object, if any, to be passed to success and failure callbacks

If you set a "default succeeded" callback, you don't have to specify a "succeeded" callback in any successive call as long as the desired callback function is the same. The same holds true for the failed callback and the user context object. The user context object is any JavaScript object, filled with any information that makes sense to you, that gets automatically passed to any callback that handles the success or failure of the call.

> **Note** The JavaScript code injected for the proxy class uses the *path* property to define the URL to the Web service. You can change the property programmatically to redirect the proxy to a different URL.

The JavaScript Model-Controller Pattern

Compared to the Web pages we were writing only five or six years ago, today's Web pages contain much more JavaScript. It's hard to predict the future evolution of the Web but, as of today, the role of server controls is diminishing. Fewer and fewer developers are satisfied with pieces of server code that churn out all the HTML for the page.

A few years ago, only very simple JavaScript functions were added to Web pages to optimize very specific features and smooth bottlenecks. With the growing amount of JavaScript that is being added to pages, organizing that code in a readable and serviceable way becomes a must.

Recently, a number of people in the developer community started considering the implications of bringing the Model-View-Controller (MVC) pattern to JavaScript. Personally, I believe that anything that looks like MVC in JavaScript requires an ad hoc framework and an appropriate programming style. In other words, the final JavaScript will probably look like a brand new language—which is not necessarily a bad thing.

Even without reaching the lofty heights of a complete implementation of MVC in JavaScript, I recommend that you consider the creation of a "controller" object in every page with a good amount of JavaScript code. The controller will be merely a container of methods associated with user-clicking events.

Any of the methods would then talk to the "model"—whatever that means to you. I tend to consider the "model" in an MVC pattern as just the server side of an application—the middle tier in a layered system. In an ASP.NET AJAX context, the "model" can also be the topmost part of the middle tier—the service layer.

By rethinking your client-side page code in terms of a *controller* and a *model*, you automatically make it easier to read and more practical to write because you essentially establish a discipline for developers to follow.

> **Note** What about the view, then? In an ASP.NET AJAX page, the view is just HTML. I don't see the point of having an additional layer of JavaScript code that creates the view—perhaps via the HTML DOM. In an MVC architecture, the "view" creates the user interface; here, instead, the view is already hardcoded in HTML. In my opinion, all a "view" layer can possibly do is update the entire user interface to make it reflect the current status of the page.

Security Considerations

Services in the HTTP façade are called by two groups of users—legitimate users and outsiders. Legitimate users connect through a regular Web front end, be it ASP.NET AJAX or Silverlight 2. Outsiders reach the URL using any platform they can—usually a custom, full-trust application.

Any Web presentation layer runs over HTTP, and HTTP wasn't designed with security in mind. HTTP was designed to be stateless and was kept simple overall to make it easy for engineers to provide an implementation for just about every platform. On the other hand, the problem of Web security arose only after the Web became public and millions of people all over the world started using it.

HTTPS is only a layer of cryptography applied at the gate on both sides of the communication. It guarantees confidentiality and integrity; it can't do much as far as authentication and authorization are concerned. HTTPS doesn't transport user credentials, but at least it does ensure through digital certificates that the two communicating parties are who they claim to be.

It's realistic to estimate that at least a few of the services in the HTTP façade are business-critical services and thus require protection from unauthorized access. Let's see what you can do about it.

> **Note** As baffling as it might sound, you read it right. Yes, HTTP has no native security features in it. What about HTTPS, then?
>
> As commonly defined, HTTPS is a uniform resource identifier that combines HTTP with a cryptography engine, such as Secure Sockets Layer (SSL) or Transport Layer Security (TLS). HTTPS is like HTTP except that it uses a different port (port 443 instead of port 80) and adds a cryptography mechanism down the stack between TCP and HTTP. In this regard, HTTP even with the final *S* is not a technologically secure protocol if you're looking for authentication and authorization. You need HTTP authentication on top of it or something like ASP.NET support (cookies and such). Authorization is, of course, up to the individual application. If you still find this statement hard to accept, consider that when HTTP is used, WCF leverages its own infrastructure and bindings to ensure security and authentication.

The HTTP Façade Is Not Your Middle Tier

To design an effective ASP.NET AJAX architecture, you must fully understand a key fact. The HTTP façade and business application services—the services that can raise your application to the level of a service-oriented application—are different things.

In an ASP.NET AJAX (or Silverlight) application, the HTTP façade exposes a few hosted services that are, conceptually speaking, an internal part of the application. However, for technical reasons, these services are exposed through public endpoints over IIS. Everything you have in the HTTP façade is private by design but public by deployment.

As mentioned, for AJAX-enabled WCF services you can't use the *wsHttpBinding* binding model and all of its security options. From an ASP.NET AJAX client, you must resort to the *webHttpBinding* scheme, which is much simpler from a security perspective. It supports only the following options: no security, transportation security (HTTPS), and clear text credentials.

A service that enables Silverlight clients is forced to the *basicHttpBinding* scheme, instead. As you can see in Figure 3-5, the *basicHttpBinding* scheme doesn't offer a Silverlight client the same security options a full-trust client would get. Security options for WCF services are limited to HTTPS and default to no security at all.

```
ServiceReferences.ClientConfig*

 <configuration>
    <system.serviceModel>
        <bindings>
            <basicHttpBinding>
                <binding name="BasicHttpBinding_StockService" maxBufferSize="2147483647"
                    maxReceivedMessageSize="2147483647">
                    <security mode="None" />
                </binding>            None
            </basicHttpBinding>      Transport
        </bindings>
        <client>
            <endpoint address="http://localhost:4565/ServiceFun_Web/StockService.svc"
                binding="basicHttpBinding" bindingConfiguration="BasicHttpBinding_StockService"
                contract="Samples.StockService" name="BasicHttpBinding_StockService" />
        </client>
    </system.serviceModel>
 </configuration>
```

FIGURE 3-5 Security modes for *basicHttpBinding* in Silverlight

Should such a simple security model in AJAX and Silverlight scenarios be surprising at all? Well, AJAX and Silverlight are Web clients that have one main interest in services: craft a request and then look at the response. REST embodies this approach, and it's all about simplicity. If you need to protect sensitive data while it's being transmitted, you have HTTPS as an option. If you need authentication, you have to look elsewhere, as we'll see in a moment.

> **Important**   SOAP vs. REST is an ongoing debate that essentially comes down to a developer's love for standards vs. a developer's love for simplicity. After having spent years wishing for Web standards, developers and architects have discovered the weight that support for standards adds to development. So REST emerged as the lightweight alternative to services.
>
> People like REST because overall it's simple, cheap, and easy to implement. REST is standardless in the sense that there's no standard to dictate the format of the data being exchanged; with REST you can return whatever you want, formatted as you like. I'm not so sure that simplicity all the way through is always a good argument. There are scenarios where simplicity is king and makes it really cheaper and faster without side effects. And there are scenarios where the certainty of standards (message envelope, data types, constructs) is the real added value.

Built-in Security Countermeasures

The scaffolding for AJAX-enabled Web and WCF services contains some measures to raise the security bar and hinders outsiders from crashing the party. For example, by default HTTP GET calls are disabled and a particular content type is required—the *application/json* type.

Thanks to these measures, cross-site scripting can't reach the service through the *<script>* tag. The *<script>* tag (as well as the *<img>* tag) certainly can accept a cross-domain URL that points to the service, but it can invoke it only via an HTTP GET and without specifying a particular request header and content type. Unless you change the default settings, an AJAX-enabled service is immune from cross-site scripting.

Built-in countermeasures, though, do not resolve the problem of offering services only to authenticated and authorized users.

Replay Attacks

Although it's safe from cross-site scripting, an AJAX-enabled service is still vulnerable to replay attacks. A *replay attack* occurs when an attacker intercepts a message that two parties legitimately exchange and replays it on behalf of one of the parties.

Because services in the HTTP façade are connected to the middle tier of the application, a replay attack can produce bad consequences. Unless mitigated, the services would process the message as a legitimate message, thus opening the door of the middle tier to unauthorized users.

To perpetrate a basic replay attack against an AJAX-enabled service, you don't even have to be an expert hacker. All that you need is some expertise with the classes in the *System.Net* namespace of the .NET Framework to craft a Web request from a full-trust Windows Forms or console application.

Services in the HTTP façade are exposed, and you have to defend them. The first rule to apply is this: Do not expose in the HTTP façade any critical business logic. The second rule is this: Find a way to discriminate between legitimate users and outsiders.

Discriminate Against Outsiders

Any security barrier you place around the HTTP façade at the network level (for example, a firewall) to filter outsiders would likely stop legitimate calls too. When all calls come from a plain Web browser and from the Internet place, you need a reliable way to welcome legitimate users and reject outsiders.

To do so, you have to identify a piece of information that only legitimate users can easily provide. The simplest and most effective piece of information is an authentication cookie generated by the ASP.NET forms authentication.

To protect critical services in the HTTP façade, you isolate in a reserved area of the site any ASP.NET pages that invoke a sensitive service method and any services to protect. After pages and services are placed in a protected area of the site, access to them requires that users go through a login page.

The login page gets credentials from the user and verifies whether the user is authorized to visit the page. If all is fine, the request is authorized and an authentication cookie is generated and attached to the response. From now on, any requests the user makes to the application, including requests directed at services in the HTTP façade, will bring the cookie. (See Figure 3-6.)

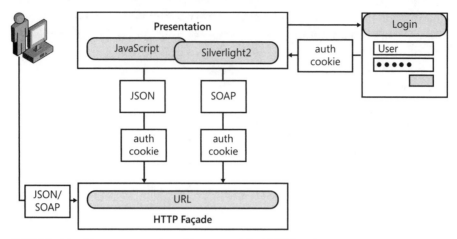

FIGURE 3-6 Legitimate users and outsiders around the HTTP façade

In ASP.NET, login pages require that forms authentication be turned on. Furthermore, anonymous users should be denied access to any resources within the protected area. Here's a sample configuration script you can use:

```
<location path="ProtectedAreaOfTheSite">
    <system.web>
        <authorization>
            <deny users="?" />
        </authorization>
    </system.web>
</location>
```

If necessary, login pages can be placed on a different server and work over HTTPS. This solution, however, has no impact on the security of the HTTP façade.

Outsiders can still try to access the services via the public URL. In this case, though, because the service IIS endpoint is also placed behind an authorization section, they will receive an HTTP 401 error code (unauthorized access). The outsider call will pass only if the outsider can show a valid authentication cookie. But this can happen only if a cookie theft has occurred previously. However, this is all another problem that relates to the security of the Web site rather than to the security of the services in the HTTP façade.

The only viable alternative to using cookies and ASP.NET Forms authentication are client certificates installed on all client machine.

Trusting the HTTP Façade

Should WCF and Web services do something on their own to keep outsiders off the site? If you place service endpoints behind a protected area of the site, you're as safe as with any other ASP.NET pages based on Forms authentication. To give you an idea, if you combine Forms authentication with HTTPS you have the same security level currently used by online banking applications and payment sites.

It's therefore safe for the middle tier to trust the upper HTTP façade and accept any calls coming down the way. However, nothing prevents you from implementing an extra check for authorization within the body of service methods. In this case, though, you need to access credentials information from within the service.

AJAX-enabled services can carry this information only via the authentication cookie or client certificates. Programmatically, a service gets user credentials via intrinsic objects of the run-time platform. ASP.NET XML Web services live within the ASP.NET runtime and have full access to the ASP.NET intrinsics, including the *User* object.

By default, instead, WCF service calls are processed by the WCF runtime, which lives side by side with ASP.NET, but it's not a part of it. As a result, a WCF service method can't access the HTTP request context and put its hands on the *User* object. The only possible workaround is running all the WCF services hosted by the site in ASP.NET compatibility mode.

You turn compatibility mode on in the configuration file, as shown here:

```
<system.serviceModel>
    <serviceHostingEnvironment aspNetCompatibilityEnabled="true" />
    ⋮
</system.serviceModel>
```

In addition, each service is required to express its explicit approval of the model. A service does this by decorating the service class—not the service contract—with the *AspNetCompatibilityRequirements* attribute, as shown here:

```
[AspNetCompatibilityRequirements(
        RequirementsMode = AspNetCompatibilityRequirementsMode.Allowed)]
public class TimeService : ITimeService
{
    ⋮
}
```

Note that, by default, a WCF service has the *RequirementsMode* property set to *NotAllowed*. If this value is not changed to either *Allowed* or *Required*, you get a run-time exception as you attempt to make a call to the service.

> **Note** WCF services have been designed to be independent from binding and transportation. By turning on ASP.NET compatibility mode, you break this rule because you make the service dependent on IIS as the host and HTTP as the transportation protocol. On the other hand, services in the HTTP façade are just AJAX-specific services so, in this regard, enabling ASP.NET compatibility is actually a natural choice.

The AJAX Server Pages Pattern

AJAX Server Pages indicates the working style of pages that employ a new generation of AJAX-enabled server controls. These controls work over the classic postback model of ASP.NET, except they use asynchronous requests and exchange a mix of script and markup.

In the AJAX Server Pages pattern, AJAX capabilities of a page mostly result from the individual AJAX capabilities of constituent controls. Awaiting for ASP.NET 4.0, these special controls today exist only in ad hoc commercial libraries.

> **Important** On a more emphatic note, I believe that many of the most popular suites of controls currently available in the marketplace are implementing their own framework on top of the AJAX Server Pages architectural pattern. I wouldn't say the same for the Microsoft's ASP.NET AJAX framework as of version 3.5 Service Pack 1. As you'll see in the rest of the chapter, Microsoft's partial rendering is an effective, but relatively rudimentary, approach to AJAX server pages.
>
> The gist of AJAX Server Pages is that it uses server controls and postback as usual. It's about allowing you to continue writing code-behind classes that talk to the middle tier, oblivious of the AJAX factor. It's about completely integrating AJAX in the ASP.NET platform so that everything is different under the hood even though it looks, walks, and quacks the same on the surface. Fully implementing the AJAX Server Pages pattern means that you don't even realize AJAX is a special flavor of the application and keep on doing the same thing, but over asynchronous requests. And where the classic ASP.NET platform was shielding you only from generation of HTML, the AJAX Server Pages pattern on top of ASP.NET also shields you from details of asynchronous requests. As mentioned, today this is possible only if you pick up a commercial library. With ASP.NET 4.0, things might be a bit different. Time will tell.

Architectural Overview

Today, server controls are experiencing hard times, but for different reasons. Not always is the generated markup easy to style via cascading style sheets (CSS). And, more importantly, not always do server controls let developers gain full control over the generated markup. This means that getting XHTML, text encoding, and the desired syntax is harder than it should be.

AJAX requires that more and more work be done (and subsequently programmed) on the client using HTML and JavaScript. This requirement allows you to better manage situations involving the preceding points and overall weakens the role of server controls.

But with ASP.NET server controls, developers can reach a level of productivity that is currently unmatched by other approaches. In addition, with server controls developers can leverage most of their existing skills and learn to use new features with surprisingly short learning curves.

Classic ASP.NET Server Controls

Officially released in early 2002 after two years of experimentation, ASP.NET marked a watershed and changed the world of Web development forever. ASP.NET was an improvement over the existing model of Active Server Pages (ASP), which was already a milestone in Web development itself. ASP.NET reinforced the point of developing HTML markup on the server and added composable black boxes known as *server controls*.

Server controls didn't exist before ASP.NET. And if my memory serves me, any attempt to use server-side blocks of code in classic ASP page was not very heartily welcomed at the time. Before ASP.NET arrived, the world of Web development on the Microsoft platform was ruled by *design-time controls,* which were especially popular in Visual InterDev 6.0. A design-time control runs only within the development environment to help create a finished combination of HTML and script. When the page is run, the script executes just like a handwritten script, without any extra costs on the server side.

> **Note** As a personal anecdote, I like to recall that I wrote a sort of prototype of what we would call a server control today while flying home from my first ever conference in the United States. It was the late summer of 1999. (By the way, the control I tested was, guess what, a data grid.) Only two months later, I would have my initial exposure to ASP.NET, still named ASP+ at the time.

The independently developed idea of server-side controls didn't really get rave reviews from the circle of my peers—too much pressure on the server and subsequent poor performance. However, server controls became a worldwide standard in just a few months with the first public builds of ASP.NET.

In classic ASP.NET, server controls are merely black boxes that output markup and some sparse chunks of JavaScript code. Such server controls usually have no client-side object model and leverage the view state to rebuild their own state across successive requests. Furthermore, very few such server controls control their own postbacks. Only button controls, therefore, post back, in addition to the few controls that expose an autopostback property. When the postback occurs, the response covers the entire page and not just the modified delta.

Increasing JavaScript Emissions in the Page

The biggest difference between classic ASP.NET controls and AJAX-enabled server controls is in the amount of JavaScript code emitted. Whereas only the smartest among classic ASP.NET controls (for example, validation controls) emit small chunks of JavaScript code, AJAX-enabled server controls link a full client-side object model realized in JavaScript.

For example, an AJAX-enabled *Label* control will group in a JavaScript function a set of methods for client code to refresh the rendered markup. Here's a brief excerpt written using the Microsoft AJAX Library. (I'll cover the library in the next chapter.)

```
Samples.Label = function Samples$Label(domElement)
{
    Samples.Label.initializeBase(this);
    this._element = domElement;
}
function Samples$Label$get_text()
{
    if (arguments.length !== 0) throw Error.parameterCount();
    return this._element.innerHTML;
}
function Samples$Label$set_text(value)
{
    var e = Function._validateParams(arguments, [{name: 'value', type: String}]);
    if (e) throw e;
    this._element.innerHTML = value;
}
```

A client-side object model for each control is essential in an AJAX application that uses server controls. An AJAX-enabled control differs from a classic ASP.NET control because it emits markup *and* JavaScript. However, the emission of JavaScript is not limited to just the few lines required to support a specific feature (such as quick validation checks on user input); instead, they cover the entire behavior of the control, including the interaction with the user and the postback.

As discussed in Chapter 2, "The Easy Way to AJAX," an AJAX postback doesn't return the entire new page, just an updated delta of it. In the AJAX Server Pages pattern, an AJAX control that governs its own postbacks returns the updated delta of its markup and perhaps that of other controls in the page. The updated markup is then easily applied on a per-control basis if each control has its own client object model.

Having a JavaScript model for each control also makes it easier to arrange data binding and updates that integrate into the page DOM data calculated by server methods. Realistically, to have a JavaScript model for each control you need to pick up a commercial library.

Code-Behind and Service Layer

In a model where server controls are used to produce the user interface and JavaScript is mostly used to refresh the DOM and trigger asynchronous requests, do you really need an HTTP façade?

If you adopt the AJAX Server Pages pattern, you *can* have an HTTP façade, but you *aren't* forced to have one in your applications.

The AJAX Server Pages pattern requires you to write all (or at least most) of your Web application in managed code, thus abstracting away JavaScript and AJAX machinery. Don't misunderstand me, though: you will still need *a lot* of JavaScript code to do AJAX, but you delegate the underlying framework to managing most or all of it. You write JavaScript yourself only if it's necessary to achieve a particular feature (for example, simultaneous calls or polling).

With AJAX Server Pages, most of your application is still written in code-behind classes, which are better if they're enriched with a pattern that adds testability and separation of concerns. My favorite is the Model-View-Presenter (MVP) pattern. (For more information about patterns in layered applications, check out my book *Microsoft .NET: Architecting Applications for the Enterprise*, Microsoft Press, 2008.)

With AJAX Server Pages, you don't really need an AJAX service layer; however, on the server, from the code-behind class you directly call the application services in the middle tier.

The Classic Postback Model Revisited

The AJAX Server Pages pattern doesn't introduce a different application model. It's still based on the classic postback model. More exactly, it's a revisitation of the postback model and has similarities with the partial rendering model in ASP.NET AJAX.

It's Always a Postback

Figure 3-7 shows graphically the difference between classic ASP.NET partial rendering and the AJAX Server Pages pattern.

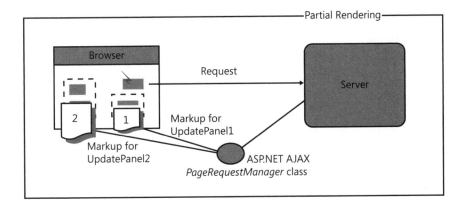

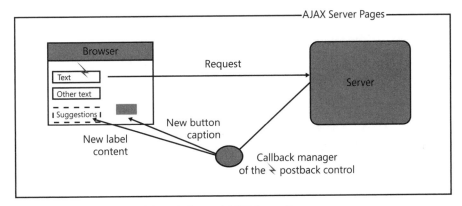

FIGURE 3-7 Comparing partial rendering and AJAX Server Pages

The difference is in the granularity of the postback event (entire page vs. control), the content of the returned delta, and the behavior of the manager component that updates the page. Overall, the AJAX Server Pages pattern is an improved and smarter form of partial rendering. Let's dig out more.

A Smarter Form of Partial Rendering

As we saw in Chapter 2, ASP.NET partial rendering works by installing a centralized handler for the form's *submit* event. Whenever a form in the page submits its content through the browser, a smart piece of JavaScript code kicks in and invokes the request to the ASP.NET AJAX client framework.

The body of the request is slightly modified to include extra data. Next, the request executes asynchronously. When the response is received, the ASP.NET AJAX client framework manages to update the user interface. The response is organized in update-panels. An update-panel is a fraction of the page that includes multiple controls and implicit or explicit postback triggers. The update-panel is a mere container that exists for the convenience of update. It's not responsible for triggering the postback and updating the page.

As the upper part of Figure 3-7 shows, partial rendering replaces parts of the page over a postback. The overall page is a patchwork of update-panels that, in turn, are a patchwork of individual controls.

The AJAX Server Pages pattern requires a much more sophisticated scheme. Each control might be able to post back and carry markup back to the client. The response takes different formats depending on the framework, so it's the framework code that actually applies it to the DOM.

A framework that fully embraces the AJAX Server Pages pattern will also likely enhance two aspects of classic partial rendering that are often recognized as weak points of the technology: view state transmission and simultaneous calls. For example, the framework callback manager—either implemented as a global component or incorporated in the client object model of each control—can manage partial view state and implement a queue to support concurrent requests while serving them strictly sequentially.

Libraries in Action

In an AJAX Server Pages scenario, server controls emit markup and JavaScript. The JavaScript code they emit uses functionalities from a framework library, where typically you find an object model for each of the controls plus some general facilities.

Common facilities include a callback manager to prepare asynchronous requests and parse-related responses, possibly a queue to serialize concurrent calls, maybe a client cache, and client-side cross-cutting aspects such as drag-and-drop, resizability, and modality.

Let's see how three popular commercial libraries implement the AJAX Server Pages pattern.

> **Note** This section of the chapter is not intended to be a comprehensive cheat sheet about various commercial products. I focus only on how libraries arrange the communication between the client page and the server environment. Put another way, I limit my discussion to considering what controls each library offers, what is downloaded to the client, and how the callback manager works. The purpose is not to argue which library is preferable.

Telerik's RadControls for ASP.NET AJAX

This library offers a range of controls that abstract away from low-level ASP.NET and HTML capabilities to offer more high-level components aligned with what developers commonly need to do within a Web page. You find enhanced versions of common controls such as text and combo boxes, as well as rich controls such as grids, tree views, and toolbars. In particular, you have date, numeric, and masked text boxes, as well as a templated combo box.

RadControls for ASP.NET AJAX is fully integrated with the Microsoft ASP.NET AJAX framework, and internally it uses the partial rendering engine to generate some of its output. In a typical RadControls page, you find the ASP.NET *ScriptManager* control as well as the in-house *RadAjaxManager* control. Here's an example of a page that handles a combo box item selection on the server:

```
<asp:ScriptManager runat="server" ID="ScriptManager1" />
<telerik:RadComboBox ID="RadComboBox1" runat="server"
        EnableLoadOnDemand="true"
        DataTextField="CompanyName"
        OnItemsRequested="RadComboBox1_ItemsRequested">
   <HeaderTemplate>
      :
   <HeaderTemplate>
   <ItemTemplate>
      :
   </ItemTemplate>
</telerik:RadComboBox>
<telerik:RadAjaxManager ID="RadAjaxManager1" runat="server">
   <AjaxSettings>
      <telerik:AjaxSetting AjaxControlID="i0">
         <UpdatedControls>
            <telerik:AjaxUpdatedControl ControlID="RadComboBox1" />
         </UpdatedControls>
      </telerik:AjaxSetting>
   </AjaxSettings>
</telerik:RadAjaxManager>
```

The page doesn't contain any explicit *UpdatePanel* controls, but it's still heavily based on built-in partial rendering. In addition, a bunch of script code is downloaded to the client that contains Telerik's client-side library.

In the sample page, the *RadComboBox* control fires a postback event using an injected click handler and uses the code in the internal JavaScript library to perform an asynchronous postback. On the server, the following code is employed:

```
public partial class DefaultCS: XhtmlPage
{
   void RadComboBox1_ItemsRequested(object o, RadComboBoxItemsRequestedEventArgs e)
   {
      // e.Text refers to the currently selected content of the combo box
         :
   }
      :
}
```

The server-side event handler does its own work and then yields to the page's rendering engine. As we saw in Chapter 2, the *ScriptManager* in the page hooks up the rendering process and proceeds through the list of *UpdatePanels* registered for updates.

The content of the *RadAjaxManager* control determines how many *UpdatePanel* regions will be silently created on the server to produce markup. In the code snippet, it's the same *RadComboBox1* control to be updated, as stated by the *AjaxSetting* element.

The RadControls library is smart enough to distinguish calls for on-demand data from page updates. In the former case, a proprietary text format is used to return markup. In the latter case, full partial rendering markup is returned, including view state.

The code discussed here can be seen in action at *http://demos.telerik.com/aspnet-ajax/ComboBox*.

Gaiaware's Gaia AJAX

The Gaia AJAX library features server controls whose level of abstraction is really close to that of standard ASP.NET controls. Most of the Gaia Ajax controls inherit from their ASP.NET counterparts. This means, for instance, that every single property you have in, say, *System.Web.UI.WebControls.Button* is also available in the Gaia AJAX *Button* control.

In a certain way, Gaia AJAX doesn't simply provide a library to do some good AJAX programming—it really replaces ASP.NET basic controls with new controls that support AJAX from the ground up. The library provides out-of-the-box advanced controls, such as *TabControl*, *FishEye*, *Toolbar*, and *Window*, but it also includes simpler controls such as *Label*, *Button*, and *CheckBox*, as well as ASP.NET-specific controls, such as *CheckBoxList* and *RadioButtonList*.

All of these controls fire a server-side event when their state is changed on the client. The connection with the server is obviously asynchronous and nearly identical to a classic ASP.NET postback. As a developer, you don't need to write a single line of JavaScript code, and no markup is explicitly returned to the client.

Asynchronous postbacks and no markup returned? Where's the magic?

Quite simply, Gaia AJAX controls record their server changes and have an internal component to serialize changes through JavaScript code to run on the client. Here's an example:

```
<form id="form1" runat="server">
    <gaia:Label ID="Label1" runat="server" />
    <br />
    <gaia:Button ID="Button1" runat="server"
        OnClick="Button1_Click" Text="Click me" />
</form>
```

When you click the button, the following managed code is run:

```
protected void Button1_Click(object sender, EventArgs e)
{
    Label1.Text = "Hello Gaia AJAX";
}
```

Is this really AJAX? Isn't it plain ASP.NET, instead?

Sure, ASP.NET partial rendering also puts forth a similar application model, but it requires *ScriptManager* and *UpdatePanel* controls. The beauty of Gaia AJAX is that you need no *ScriptManager*, no updatable panels, no Web services, and no (explicit) JavaScript. You write code as you would in ASP.NET, except that you can take advantage of some richer controls and—a fairly unique feature—AJAX aspects. But before I get into AJAX aspects, a look at the request payloads is in order.

The response you get from the server when you execute the preceding code is shown here:

```
$G('Label1').setText('Hello Gaia AJAX');
$FChange('__VIEWSTATE', 43,
    'EHgtIYXNSZW5kZXJlZGceBFRleHQFFEhlbGxvIEFqYXggV29ybGQQgMi4wZGQCAw8
    PFgIfAGdkZGSLlpkbOd1wQuK4M9lMGeOIWhPkMA==');
Gaia.Control.setUpdateControl(null, true);
```

The *$G* function comes from the Gaia JavaScript library and is equivalent to *document.getElementById*. It simply retrieves the element modified on the server and updates its displayed text. Next, the view state is also updated to reflect server changes. Any controls updated during the postback will add their own update script to the response to update each control's client-side object model.

A rather unique feature of Gaia AJAX is that it returns partial view state. The *$FChange* function gets the modified portion of the view state and recomposes it with what's on the client. The number in the call to *$FChange* indicates the position where the changes to the client view state must be inserted.

As mentioned, aspects are another feature of Gaia AJAX that deserves attention. An aspect is a behavior you might want to get from a variety of controls such as modality, resizability, or draggability. Every Gaia AJAX control has a special *Aspects* collection property. By adding aspects into this collection, the control will render appropriate client-side code, thus modifying the actual behavior of the control. Let's consider the following *Window* control:

```
<gaia:Window ID="Window1" runat="server"
      Caption="Summary"
      Height="480px"
      Width="600px"
      Visible="false"
      CssClass="gaiax">
   ⋮
</gaia:Window>
```

By adding the modal aspect, you make the window display with modality, as shown here:

```
protected override void OnLoad(EventArgs e)
{
  // The window is now modal, movable, and resizable
  Window1.Aspects.Add(new AspectModal());
  Window1.Aspects.Add(new AspectDraggable());
  Window1.Aspects.Add(new AspectResizable());
}
protected void Button1_Click(object sender, EventArgs e)
{
  // Display the window (with all of its configured aspects)
  Window1.Visible = true;
}
```

Aspects can be added to any Gaia controls, but not to standard ASP.NET controls. Likewise, the optimized JavaScript rendering after a postback applies only to Gaia controls. If you use non-Gaia controls, the library will emit plain markup for the control.

For more information, pay a visit to *http://www.gaiaware.net*.

> **Note** Another popular suite of controls, ComponentArt's WebUI, can be seen as the representative of the other AJAX pattern we covered earlier in the chapter—the AJAX Service Layer. ComponentArt hosts a white paper on their Web site that explains the motivation of their innovative approach to ASP.NET AJAX programming. The white paper can be obtained from *http://www.componentart.com/webui/ajax.aspx*.
>
> In summary, the idea is that server controls generate JavaScript code and storage arrays containing the minimum data and style information required to display the user interface. Next, developers are required to write JavaScript logic for event handlers. In doing so, developers find available a full client object model nearly identical to the object model of a server control. Some controls are also capable of connecting to configured (custom) Web services and get data autonomously. Directly bindable to control elements, these Web services clearly form the AJAX Service Layer.

The Tough Call

A *pattern* is a known and well-established core solution applicable to a family of concrete design points. A pattern is a core solution and, as such, it might need adaptation to a specific context.

If two patterns exist for a given design problem, therefore, it's not because of redundancy. If two patterns exist for a given design problem, it's because they offer a different perspective on the problem and in the end provide different solutions with different pros and cons. If you compare two similar patterns, you'll rarely ever have an absolute winner. Instead, you'll have one pattern that might adapt better than the other to a given context.

This said, when is *AJAX Service Layer* preferable over *AJAX Server Pages*? And when is the opposite true?

In the past few years, I've changed my mind many times about what would be the most effective way to get AJAX in ASP.NET applications. And I'm still not entirely committed to a particular answer. I feel that the most effective way shouldn't force you too far away from the classic ASP.NET programming model. Of the two patterns, AJAX Server Pages is clearly the closest to this definition.

AJAX Server Pages propose a model that is easier to learn and apply, and it builds on the skills that a development team might already have. In this regard, it works great for large applications. In my humble opinion, this would have been the perfect approach for evolving the ASP.NET platform. On the flip side, it realistically requires a commercial library to supply the scaffolding.

The two libraries mentioned here (Gaia AJAX and RadControls) are, to my knowledge, excellent implementations of the AJAX Server Pages pattern. RadControls offer more sophisticated controls; Gaia, on the other hand, really blurs the distinction between ASP.NET and ASP.NET AJAX. It looks like ASP.NET, but it does AJAX.

AJAX Service Layer is more of an architectural pattern. It requires a bit more design work on the presentation and business layers. You have to extract functionalities from the existing middle tier and craft a new tier of AJAX-enabled services. In addition, the presentation layer requires much more JavaScript. However, the JavaScript you need in this context is not always code that a server control can automatically generate.

The AJAX Service Layer forces you to write much of the presentation logic in JavaScript. ASP.NET is evolving in this direction. ASP.NET already provides an excellent framework to invoke services, and in the next version it's expected to strengthen the abstraction level of JavaScript to make it a more modern language. A good point in favor of the AJAX Service Layer is that the same server architecture serves well both an ASP.NET AJAX and a Silverlight client. The same doesn't hold true for the AJAX Server Pages pattern. A good commercial product to consider to power up the presentation of AJAX and Silverlight clients in a service layer scenario is the aforementioned ComponentArt's WebUI.

 Note A bunch of other products, from a completely different category, exist to build AJAX front ends: Google Web Toolkit, Backbase, and Visual GUI, to name a few. And more will undoubtedly be available over time. The products mentioned here such as Telerik and Gaia were mentioned because they most closely fit the AJAX Server Pages pattern with the least impact to the ASP.NET developer. Other viable options cause you to write more code in support or change the way ASP.NET pages are developed in some way.

Summary

AJAX burst into the Web world only a few years ago, and it's revolutionizing the infrastructure of Web applications. Are ASP.NET and AJAX destined to remain separate things, to be combined only when you need them to be?

My (way too easy?) forecast is that in five years we'll forget that there ever was a time when AJAX was just an option rather than the standard. AJAX is an "option" today for two main reasons. First, it's a relatively new approach that is a true paradigm shift for mature and consolidated technologies. Second, applying AJAX is currently a bit expensive. However, five years from now AJAX will become a standard part of nearly all contemporary Web development tools. It might even become harder to build Web applications that *do not* incorporate AJAX.

But keep in mind that today, to make developing AJAX solutions smooth and effective, you need to get (and pay for) a commercial product. If you stick to the Microsoft platform as it exists today, AJAX development becomes expensive because of limited productivity.

Overall, two main architectures exist to add AJAX to a Web application. You can drive the presentation layer using manual or injected JavaScript and direct calls to an AJAX service layer. Alternatively, you can keep using the same ASP.NET application model and adopt improved or perfected versions of partial rendering.

In any case, as you move toward AJAX you can't save yourself from the JavaScript learning curve. Even though many libraries promise to keep you away from JavaScript, I suggest that you still come to grips with JavaScript programming. In the end, you'll find yourself working not with the classic JavaScript application, but rather with a modified JavaScript library designed for the AJAX framework you decide to use. This is exactly the topic we'll cover in the next chapter.

Part II
Power to the Client

Chapter 4
A Better and Richer JavaScript

Language is the source of misunderstandings.

—Antoine de Saint-Exupery

Aside from the social implications of it, the Web 2.0 from a technology viewpoint is mostly about running more JavaScript code on the client. You can't just take the standard JavaScript language that most browsers support today and ask any developer to write immensely capable applications using it. As a projectwide approach, it just doesn't scale and work the way you might expect. JavaScript is not like, say, C#. JavaScript is a very special type of language; it's probably not the language everybody would choose to use today to power up the client side of the Web. However, it's the only common language we have, and we have to stick to it to reach the largest audience.

So what if you want (or more likely need) more power on the client?

Be ready to write more JavaScript code; more importantly, be ready to import more JavaScript code written by others. Either of these two ways of using JavaScript is OK, as they are not mutually exclusive options.

JavaScript is not the perfect language, and, amazingly, it was not designed to be the super language to rule the Web. JavaScript is popular, and this is its major strength and most significant weakness. It's a strength because it allows you to reach virtually every browser and every user; it's a weakness because its widespread use makes implementing any important change or extension painful in terms of achieving compatibility.

In summary, I firmly believe that for the time being you can't just transform JavaScript into something else that is radically different from what the language is today. However, the Web has repeatedly proven to be a surprisingly dynamic and agile environment; so who really knows what could happen in five years? Giving a judgment today, I would say that a winning approach needs to evolve the language without breaking compatibility with all of today's browsers. It ultimately means creating new libraries that add new features to the language. However, these libraries must be created using the same core language and, ideally, they should also be stacked up and composed together in a recipe that suits any given application.

In this chapter and the next, I'll review two JavaScript libraries that work well together today and that will probably evolve together in the near future: the Microsoft AJAX library and the jQuery library.

JavaScript Today

AJAX would not be possible without JavaScript. And this happens not because JavaScript is such a powerful language, but because JavaScript is so popular and built in nearly the same form in virtually all browsers released in the past five years.

Three ingredients, combined in the right doses, almost spontaneously originated the AJAX paradigm shift: a standard browser-hosted programming language (JavaScript), a standard object model to fully represent the document being viewed (the W3C's Document Object Model), and a sufficiently rich browser object model that includes the key *XMLHttpRequest* object.

Separating these elements is almost impossible nowadays. JavaScript is more than a simple programming language and, as you'll see later in the chapter, modern libraries reflect that.

The Language and the Browser

JavaScript is a language tailor-made for the Web and, more specifically, for the browser. In fact, there's no compiler currently available that allows you to create binaries from a bunch of JavaScript source files.

The only exception I'm aware of is the Managed JScript compiler for the .NET Framework. However, I don't recall ever meeting someone who used it concretely to build applications and not simply as a proof of some concepts.

I won't stray too far from the truth by saying that there's no life for JavaScript outside the realm of a Web browser. Of course, this is largely due to where JavaScript originated and the purpose it fulfilled at the time. Let's briefly recall the origins of the language.

Original Goals of the Language

The first appearance of JavaScript as a browser-hosted language dates back to late 1995, when the first beta of Netscape Navigator 2 was released. JavaScript was introduced to give authors of Web documents the ability to incorporate some logic and action in HTML pages. Before then, a Web page was essentially a static collection of HTML tags and text. Historically, the first significant enhancement made to the syntax of HTML was the support for tags to include script code.

JavaScript was not designed to be a classic and cutting-edge programming language—not even by the standards of 15 years ago. The primary goal of its designers was to create a language that resembled a simpler Java that could be used with ease by nonexpert page authors.

To some extent, the design of JavaScript was influenced by many languages, but the predominant factor was simplicity. It was named JavaScript because the language was essentially meant to be a powerful language (like Java) but focused on scripting. No other relationships, beyond the deliberate reference in the name, exist between Java and JavaScript.

As a result, JavaScript is an interpreted and weakly typed language that also supports dynamic binding and objects. JavaScript, however, is not a fully object-oriented language.

Note Originally developed at Netscape by Brendan Eich, JavaScript was first named *LiveScript*. The name was changed to JavaScript when Netscape added support for Java technology in its Navigator browser. The *script* suffix was simply meant to be the script version of an excellent programming language like Java. In no way was the language supposed to be a spinoff of Java.

Later, Microsoft created a similar language for its Internet Explorer browser and named it JScript to avoid trademark issues. In 1997, JavaScript was submitted to the European Computer Manufacturers Association (ECMA) International for standardization. The process culminated a couple of years later in the standardized version of the language named ECMAScript.

The Scripting Engine

Being an interpreted language, JavaScript requires an ad hoc run-time environment to produce visible effects from the source code. The run-time environment is often referred to as the browser's *scripting engine*. As such, the JavaScript's run-time environment can be slightly different from one browser to the next. The result is that the same JavaScript language feature might provide a different performance on different browsers and might be flawed on one browser while working efficiently on another one.

This fact makes it hard to write good, cross-browser JavaScript code and justifies the love/hate relationship (well, mostly hate) that many developers have developed with the language over the years.

The diagram in Figure 4-1 shows the overall structure of a scripting engine.

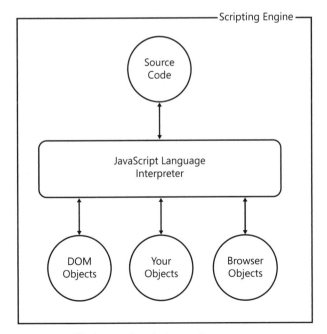

FIGURE 4-1 The browser's scripting engine

The engine is a component that is hosted in the browser and receives the source code to process. Armed with language knowledge, the engine can resolve any name in the source code that can be mapped to a syntax element—keywords, variables, local functions, and objects.

In addition, the source code processed within a Web browser is likely populated with specific objects coming from a variety of sources. For example, you can find DOM objects to access the content being displayed in the page as well as browser-specific objects such as *XMLHttpRequest* and *window*. Furthermore, any libraries you reference from the page are also published to the engine. After the script has been loaded, the browser runs the script through the engine. This action results in the functionality defined by the commands in the code.

As mentioned, although JavaScript is definitely a stable language that hasn't faced significant changes for 10 years now, virtually any broadly used library is packed with forks in code to distinguish the behavior of different browsers and ensure the same overall interface.

One of the first rules—if not the first rule—you should follow to write good AJAX applications is get yourself a powerful JavaScript library that adds abstraction and features to the JavaScript language and that works in a cross-browser manner.

Note As far as the ASP.NET platform is concerned, the good news is that you have neither to reinvent the wheel nor to invent your own wheel to proceed. In fact, the AJAX extensions to ASP.NET include a cross-browser core library that you can use as the foundation for any JavaScript code you might need beyond ready-made objects and functionalities.

Recognized Flaws

As you'll see in a moment, JavaScript has a number of drawbacks, both technical and infrastructural. In spite of all these factors, though, JavaScript works just great for the majority of Web applications. And nothing any better has been invented yet.

All things considered, the limitations of JavaScript can be summarized as two elements: it is an interpreted language, and it is not fully object oriented. The former drawback makes the language significantly slower than a compiled language. The latter makes it harder for developers to write complex code.

These were not limitations in the beginning, about 10 years ago. Nonetheless, they are now limitations that become more evident every day. Replacing JavaScript, however, is not something that can happen overnight.

JavaScript is so popular and widely used that making any breaking changes to it would break too many applications. Yet the direction that JavaScript is taking in light of AJAX addresses the two aforementioned limitations.

The Google Chrome browser (which you can read more about at *http://www.google.com/chrome*) comes with an open-source JavaScript engine that compiles source code to native machine code before executing it. As a result, Chrome runs JavaScript applications at the speed of a compiled binary, which is significantly better than any bytecode or interpreted code.

The Microsoft AJAX library, as well as other popular JavaScript libraries, such as Prototype, offers some built-in features to add inheritance to JavaScript objects and flavors of object orientation.

> **Note** Chrome and its V8 JavaScript engine are taking an innovative approach to dealing with the growth in size and complexity of JavaScript code in AJAX applications. Other libraries are trying to offer more powerful instruments to raise the abstraction level of the original JavaScript language. We are not seeing either a brand new language or an improved core language, but something is happening on the client side to make JavaScript code more effective.

Pillars of the Language

In more than 10 years of existence, JavaScript has never been as central a technology in the world of Web computing as it is today following the arrival of AJAX. JavaScript code in the average Web page has grown from just a few lines of trivial code that just scripts page elements to hundreds of kilobytes of code providing rich object models, if not true frameworks.

Because it was not created to be a spinoff of a true compiled programming language, JavaScript supports all the syntax elements of a common structured programming language, such as *if, switch, for,* and *while* statements. Types are not strongly enforced and are associated with values rather than with variables. Let's briefly review the pillars of the JavaScript language.

> **Note** Any piece of source code written in JavaScript and completely delivered to a browser is immediately executable. Clearly, this provides the potential for malicious code to be downloaded and run on the client computer. To contain the risk, the browser runs any script within a *sandbox*. A sandbox is a virtual environment where hosted programs can perform only controlled actions and are typically not granted permissions to operate on the file system and the local hardware.
>
> In addition, browsers also commonly restrict scripts from accessing any information from an external site. This is known as a *same origin policy.* Violating the same origin policy may result in a cross-site scripting attack.

Objects as Dictionaries

The JavaScript language allows you to use objects, but it doesn't natively support all principles of object-oriented programming (OOP), such as inheritance, encapsulation, and polymorphism. To some extent, some of these principles can be recognized here and there in the language's capabilities; however, JavaScript can't be described as a fully object-oriented (OO) language.

The primary reason for not cataloging JavaScript as an OO language is that the definition of an *object* you get from JavaScript is different from the commonly accepted idea of an object you get out of classic OO languages such as C++ or C#.

In C# and C++, you create new objects by telling the runtime which *class* you want to instantiate. A *class* is a fixed template used for the object creation. A class defines the properties and methods an object will have, and these properties and methods are forever fixed. In C# and C++, you can't manipulate the structure of an object by adding or removing properties and methods at runtime.

In JavaScript, objects are essentially dictionaries of values or associative arrays. An object is a container of name/value pairs that can be added at any time, and especially at runtime. In an attempt to express a JavaScript object via a C# notation, you would probably resort to something similar to the following:

```
Dictionary<string, object>
```

The property name is a string that acts as the key in the dictionary, as shown here:

```
var obj = new YourJavaScriptObject();
obj["Property"] = "Hello";
```

You can also use an alternate syntax based on the *dot* notation. The effect is the same:

```
obj.Property = "Hello";
```

JavaScript objects contain more than just a dictionary of values. In particular, they contain the *prototype* object. The prototype is like a directory that defines the public interface of the object. By acting on the prototype, you can augment the capabilities of the object in a fully dynamic manner.

Functions as Objects

Another fundamental characteristic of JavaScript is that functions are first-class language elements and objects themselves. In other words, functions might have properties and can be passed around and interacted with as you would do with any other object.

You can use the *new* operator with a function. When you do so, you get an entirely new object and can reference it internally using the *this* keyword. Just like any other object, the function has its own *prototype* property that determines the public interface of the new object:

```
MyPet = function (name, isDog)
{
    this._name = name;
    this._isDog = isDog;
}
MyPet.prototype = {
    get_Name = function() {return this._name;},
    get_IsDog = function()  {return this._isDog;}
}
```

Given the preceding code, you can use the *new* operator on the *MyPet* function and invoke the members in the prototype.

Dynamic Typing

The nature of objects and functions makes JavaScript a very dynamic language. Types are not an exception and don't force developers to follow strict rules as in a classic programming language.

Like many other scripting languages, JavaScript recognizes a few primitive types (string, number, date, Boolean) but doesn't let you declare a variable of a given, fixed type. Variables are untyped on declaration and can hold values of different types during their lifetime. As mentioned, in JavaScript types are associated with values rather than with variables.

```
x = "1";    // It is a string
x = 1;      // It is a number
```

For this reason, equality operators work in a slightly different manner. Given the following lines of code, what would be the result of the expression *x == y*?

```
x = "1";
y = 1;
```

If you look at the code from an OO perspective, you can have only one answer: *false*. Quite surprisingly, instead, in JavaScript *x==y* returns *true* because the comparison is made on the value, not the type. To get the expected result, you must switch to the === operator, which checks value *and* type.

JavaScript provides the *typeof* built-in function to test the type of an object. Another approach is *duck typing*. Duck typing basically consists of providing the freedom of invoking on an object any methods it *seems* to have. If it does not have a particular method, you just get a run-time exception. Duck typing originates from the statement: *If it walks like a duck and quacks like a duck, I would call it a duck.*

Closures and Prototypes

The three pillars of object orientation can be implemented in JavaScript to various degrees. For example, encapsulation is easy to get via the *var* keyword in a *closure* model. Encapsulation is impossible to achieve if you are working with a *prototype* model. The prototype model makes it easy to build inheritance, and polymorphism can be obtained via a combination of functions and duck typing.

There are two main models for designing classes in JavaScript: closures and prototypes. The models are not entirely equivalent, so choosing one over the other is a matter of evaluating the tradeoffs. Also, the performance you get for both models in the major browsers is not the same. Let's learn more about the closure model.

In the closure model, a custom object is a single function where all members are defined together within the same (closed) context, as shown here:

```
// The Person object is entirely defined here
Person = function()
{
    var _firstName;    // private member
    var _lastName;     // private member
    this.get_FirstName = function() { return this._firstName; }
    this.get_LastName = function() { return this._lastName; }
}
```

The use of the *var* keyword keeps a member declaration local to the context and ensures data encapsulation. Accessing *_firstName* and *_lastName* members from outside the closure is impossible, as is the case when accessing a private member from outside a class definition in C# or C++. Members not tagged with the *var* keyword are meant to be public. The object declaration occurs in a single place and through a unique constructor. Using objects built as closures can be memory intensive because a new instance is required for any work—just like in C# or C++.

The prototype model defines the public structure of the class through the built-in *prototype* object. The definition of an object, however, is not centered around a single point of scope. Here's how the object definition changes if you opt for the prototype model:

```
Person = function (firstName, lastName)
{
    this._firstName = firstName;
    this._lastName = lastName;
}
Person.prototype = {
    get_FirstName = function() {return this._firstName;},
    get_LastName = function()  {return this._lastName;}
}
```

As you can see, the object constructor and members are clearly separated. Members are shared by all instances and are private only by convention. Using the *var* keyword in the definition of, say, *_firstName* would make it private and inaccessible. On the other hand, not using the *var* keyword keeps the member public and therefore visible from the outside.

Because members of the *prototype* are global and static, the prototype model reduces the amount of memory required by each instance of the object and makes object instantiation a bit faster.

 Note Prototypes have a good load time in nearly all modern-day browsers, and load times are excellent in Firefox. On the other hand, closures are faster than prototypes in all recent versions of Internet Explorer.

JavaScript (If Any) of the Future

Two pillars carry the whole weight of the Web: HTML and JavaScript. Neither of them seems to be entirely appropriate in the age of AJAX. And neither can be blissfully dismissed and replaced for compatibility and interoperability reasons. Regarding JavaScript, what can we do?

Like HTML, JavaScript is very efficient in doing the few and relatively simple things it was originally designed to do. The point is that the community of developers needs much more—more programming power and more performance.

Personally, I value programming power and language expressivity more than performance. To some extent, performance and JavaScript still sound to me like incompatible concepts.

Performance is especially relevant in a scenario where an ounce of performance lost in some task might be automatically multiplied by some factor, such as the growing number of requests. With JavaScript, frankly, there are no such risks. The JavaScript code runs on the client and on a computer that serves a single user at a time. There's no bad performance multiplier around.

JavaScript performance can become an issue—but not really a showstopper—only when you have so many lines of code (something like several hundred kilobytes) that it just takes too much to produce a user-friendly result.

Improving JavaScript might be desirable. But if so, how should that be done? There are two main schools of thought, plus a clever ploy.

Overhauling the Language

The specification for JavaScript 2.0 is currently being discussed and defined. You can find more details at *http://www.mozilla.org/js/language/evolvingJS.pdf*. JavaScript 2.0 is expected to be a significant overhaul of the language.

The most radical change that will come with JavaScript 2.0 is support for real classes and interfaces. The following syntax should be acceptable in the next version:

```
class Person
{
  this.FirstName = "dino";
  this.LastName = "esposito";
}
var p = new Person();
```

Compile-time type checking is another aspect waiting for improvement. A component that requires *strict* mode will have static type checking and a number of other checks performed before execution, such as verification that all referenced names are known and that only comparisons between valid types are made.

Namespaces and packages complete the set of hot features slated for the next JavaScript. A package is a library of code that is automatically loaded only on demand.

It's All About Security

Another camp sees the future of JavaScript in a different manner. This camp is well represented by Douglas Crockford—one of the creators of JSON. According to Douglas, security is the biggest concern for JavaScript developers. So by simply making JavaScript a more secure programming environment, we would make JavaScript a better environment.

Douglas suggests adding a *verifier* to analyze the source and spot unsafe code and a *transformer* to add indirection and run-time checks around critical instructions. More in general, the vision put forth by Douglas is centered on the idea of improving the language by making today's de facto standard solutions a native part of the language.

Google's V8 Engine

As mentioned, a new approach to JavaScript programming is coming out with Google's Chrome browser—the V8 engine. V8 is a new JavaScript engine specifically designed for optimized execution of *large* JavaScript applications.

The basic idea is that the browser operates as a just-in-time JavaScript compiler, wrapping functions into memory objects and turning them into machine code. In addition to dynamic machine-code generation, the increment of improved performance is the result of a couple of other factors: fast property access and efficient garbage collection. For more information, check out *http://code.google.com/p/v8*.

The Microsoft AJAX Library

A truly powerful JavaScript library today can't ignore the dependencies existing between the language itself and the Document Object Model (DOM) and Browser Object Model (BOM). Subsequently, a modern JavaScript library is made of three fundamental pieces: a flavor of object orientation, facilities for visual effects, and a network stack.

It is not coincidental that this is also the recipe for the Microsoft AJAX library—one of the pillars of the Microsoft strategy for AJAX. Initially developed to back up the ASP.NET AJAX Extensions 1.0, and successively integrated in ASP.NET 3.5, the library is still being improved and enhanced for ASP.NET 4.0.

The next release of ASP.NET is expected to ship a stronger and more powerful client platform that results from the integration of the newer AJAX library and the newest version of another quite popular and largely complementary library—the jQuery library.

Overview of the Library

The Microsoft AJAX library is written in JavaScript, although with a strong sense of object orientation. ASP.NET AJAX takes the JavaScript language to the next level by adding some type-system extensions, the notion of namespace and interface, plus facilities for inheritance. In addition, the ASP.NET AJAX JavaScript supports enumerations and reflection, and it has a number of helper functions to manipulate strings and arrays.

Constituent Files

The Microsoft AJAX library is coded using the base set of instructions that characterize the core JavaScript language, and it is persisted to a set of *.js* files. These *.js* files are not installed as distinct files on the Web server when you install ASP.NET. They are embedded as resources into the ASP.NET AJAX assembly—*system.web.extensions*. If you want them available as distinct files (for example, for your home perusal), go to *http://msdn2.microsoft.com/en-us/ asp.net/bb944808.aspx*, check the license agreement, and get them as a single downloaded compressed file.

We already hinted at it in Chapter 2, "The Easy Way to AJAX," but let's briefly review in Table 4-1 the files that make up the library.

TABLE 4-1 Files That Form the Microsoft AJAX Library

Script	Description
MicrosoftAjax.js	A core part of the library, this file contains object-oriented extensions, the network stack, and a number of facilities, such as those for tracing and debugging.
MicrosoftAjaxWebForms.js	This file contains script functions to support ASP.NET partial rendering. In particular, it defines the client-side engine and programming interface for partial rendering.
MicrosoftAjaxTimer.js	This file contains the client-side programming interface of the *Timer* server control, a built-in control that comes with ASP.NET AJAX. The control creates a timer on the client and makes it post back upon timeout.

As you can see, these are plain JavaScript files that can be linked from any sort of Web page regardless of the technology it is written for—PHP, classic ASP.NET, ASP, or even plain HTML.

Linking the Microsoft AJAX Library

In ASP.NET 3.5 pages, you don't need to load files from the Microsoft AJAX library explicitly. This is a viable option when you don't have a customized version of the files to load. If you embed a *ScriptManager* control in your pages, the control will automatically recognize the Microsoft AJAX library files you need and will download them as required.

By default, script files will be extracted from the resources of the *system.web.extensions* assembly. If you hold your own copies of the scripts and want to reference them instead, you use the *ScriptManager* control as shown here:

```
<asp:ScriptReference Name="MicrosoftAjax.js"
                     Path="./MyScripts/MicrosoftAjax.js" />
```

You need the *Name* property to identify the name of the embedded resource that contains the client script file. The *Path* property can optionally be used to specify the physical server location where the named script file has to be loaded from.

When both *Name* and *Path* are specified, *Path* is the winner. Does it really make sense to specify both? Sure it does. When both properties are specified, you actually *replace* the standard *MicrosoftAjax.js* with the specified script.

Tip This trick can be used to take advantage of the script-related services of the *ScriptManager* control and also in scenarios where your pages are not dependent on the Microsoft AJAX library. By setting the *Name* property to *MicrosoftAjax.js* and the *Path* property to, say, *jquery.js*, you load *jQuery* instead of *Microsoft AJAX* while taking advantage of all the extra facilities of the *ScriptManager* control that we reviewed in Chapter 2. Read the full story at *http://weblogs.asp.net/ bleroy/archive/2008/07/07/using-scriptmanager-with-other-frameworks.aspx*.

> **Note** As general advice, I suggest that to reference a script file you don't strictly need the *ScriptManager* control. However, you should always consider using the *ScriptManager* control because of the handy services it provides, such as its ability to detect script duplicates and its free compression and localization.

No Bells and Whistles

As you'll see in greater detail in a moment, the Microsoft AJAX library provides core JavaScript services such as type extensions, OOP flavors, and an AJAX-enabled network stack. It doesn't provide any facilities for adding visual effects to your pages.

The integration between Microsoft AJAX library and jQuery that is coming out with the next version of ASP.NET will make up for this. You'll have a script framework that offers a richer JavaScript with advanced and commonly used widgets such as those provided by jQuery.

Let's dig out now the key capabilities of the Microsoft AJAX library.

JavaScript Language Extensions

The JavaScript language features a set of built-in objects, including *Function, Object, Boolean, Array, Number,* and *String.* All intrinsic objects have a read-only property named *prototype.* The *prototype* property provides a base set of functionality shared by any new instance of an object of that class.

New functionality can be added to each object by extending and improving its prototype. This is exactly what the Microsoft AJAX library does.

Primitive Types

The Microsoft AJAX library contains code that defines new objects and extends existing JavaScript objects with additional functionality. Table 4-2 lists the main global objects defined in the library and explains how they relate to original JavaScript types.

TABLE 4-2 Top-Level Objects in the Microsoft AJAX Library

Object	Description
Array	Extends the native *Array* object. This object groups static methods to add, insert, remove, and clear elements of an array. It also includes static methods to enumerate elements and check whether a given element is contained in the array.
Boolean	Extends the native *Boolean* object. This object defines a static *parse* method to infer a *Boolean* value from a string or any expression that evaluates to a *Boolean* value.
Date	Extends the native *Date* object with a couple of instance methods: *localeFormat* and *format*. These methods format the date using the locale or invariant culture information.

TABLE 4-2 Top-Level Objects in the Microsoft AJAX Library

Object	Description
Error	Defines a static create method to wrap the JavaScript *Error* object and add a richer constructor to it. This object incorporates a couple of properties—*message* and *name*—to provide a description of the error that occurred and identify the error by name. A number of built-in error objects are used to simulate exceptions. In this case, the *name* property indicates the name of the exception caught.
Function	Extends the native *Function* object. This object groups methods to define classes, namespaces, delegates, and a bunch of other object-oriented facilities.
Number	Extends the native *Number* object. This object defines a static *parse* method to infer a numeric value from a string or any expression that evaluates to a numeric value. In addition, it supports a pair of static formatting methods: *localeFormat* and *format*.
Object	Extends the native *Object* object. This object groups methods to read type information, such as the type of the object being used.
RegExp	Wraps the native *RegExp* object.
String	Extends the native *String* object. This object groups string manipulation methods, such as trim methods and *endsWith* and *startsWith* methods. In addition, it defines static *localeFormat* and *format* methods that are close relatives of the *String.Format* method of the managed *String* type.

After the Microsoft AJAX library has been added to an application, the following code will work just fine:

```
var s = "Dino";
alert(s.startsWith('D'));
```

The native JavaScript *String* object doesn't feature either a *startsWith* or an *endsWith* method; the extended AJAX *String* object, instead, does.

New Types

As mentioned, it's only in a future version of JavaScript that you can start creating new complex and custom types as you do today in classic object-oriented languages. The Microsoft AJAX library, though, provides its own application programming interface (API) to let you register new objects—essentially custom JavaScript functions—with the library and use them as classes with an object-oriented flavor.

No new keyword is added for compatibility reasons, but a couple of new methods must be used to wrap the definition of a new type, as shown next for the sample *MyClass* type:

```
Type.registerNamespace("Samples");
Samples.MyClass = function ()
{
    :
}

// Other blocks of code here for class members
:

Samples.MyClass.registerClass("Samples.MyClass");
```

Enumerations are a special breed of a new type in JavaScript. As in the .NET Framework, an enumeration represents an easily readable alternative to integers. Here's a sample definition for an enumerated type in JavaScript:

```
Type.registerNamespace("Samples");

// Define an enumeration type and register it.
Samples.Color = function() {};
Samples.Color.prototype =
{
    Red:     0xFF0000,
    Blue:    0x0000FF,
    Green:   0x00FF00,
    White:   0xFFFFFF
}
Samples.Color.registerEnum("Samples.Color");
```

To register an enumerated type, you use a tailor-made registration function—the *registerEnum* function.

Shorthand Functions

I would find it hard to believe that most of you reading this book have never made the mistake of using the name of the HTML element in a page as a shortcut to get the corresponding DOM reference. Suppose you have a text box element named *TextBox1* in the client page. The following script code won't work on all browsers:

```
alert(TextBox1.value);
```

The correct form ratified by the World Wide Web Consortium (W3C) paper for the HTML DOM standard is shown here:

```
alert(document.getElementById("TextBox1").value);
```

The correct form is clearly more verbose and bothersome to write over and over again. The Microsoft AJAX library comes to the rescue with the *$get* global function. Simply put, the *$get* function is a shortcut for the *document.getElementById* function. If the Microsoft AJAX library is in use, the following expression is fully equivalent to the one just shown:

```
alert($get("TextBox1").value);
```

The *$get* function has two overloads. If you call *$get* passing the sole ID, the function falls back into *document.getElementById*. Alternatively, you can specify a container as the second argument, as shown here:

```
var parent = $get("Div1");
$get("TextBox1", parent);
```

If the container element supports the *getElementById* method, the function returns the output of *element.getElementById*; otherwise, the *$get* function uses the DOM interface to explore the contents of the subtree rooted in the element to locate any node with the given ID.

Although *$get* is only an alias for a regular JavaScript function, it is often mistaken for a new language element. Other similar shortcuts exist in the library to create objects and add or remove event handlers.

> **Note** The *$get* function has a lot in common with jQuery's *$* root object. To be precise, early builds of the Microsoft AJAX library were still using the same *$* expression that was renamed later to avoid collisions. The *$get* object in the Microsoft AJAX library is merely a direct DOM selector that just filters by ID. The *$* object in jQuery, instead, is a full selector that supports a much richer CSS-based syntax to filter DOM elements to return.

Object-Oriented Extensions

In JavaScript, the *Function* object is the main tool you use to combine code with properties and forge new components. In the Microsoft AJAX library, the *Function* object is extended to incorporate type information, as well as namespaces, inheritance, interfaces, and enumerations.

Namespaces and Classes

A namespace provides a way of grouping and classifying the types belonging to a library. Not a type itself, a namespace adds more information to the definition of each type in the library to better qualify it.

All custom JavaScript functions belong to the global space of names. In the Microsoft AJAX library, you can associate a custom function with a particular namespace, for purely organizational reasons. When declaring a custom type in the Microsoft AJAX library, you can do as follows:

```
Type.registerNamespace("Samples");
Samples.Person = function Samples$Person(firstName, lastName)
{
    this._firstName = firstName;
    this._lastName = lastName;
}

// Define the body of all members
function Samples$Person$ToString()
{
    return this._lastName + ", " + this._firstName;
}
.
.
.
// Define the prototype of the class
Samples.Person.prototype =
{
    ToString:       Samples$Person$ToString,
    get_FirstName: Samples$Person$get_FirstName,
    set_FirstName: Samples$Person$set_FirstName,
```

```
        get_LastName:   Samples$Person$get_LastName,
        set_LastName:   Samples$Person$set_LastName
}

// Register the class
Samples.Person.registerClass("Samples.Person");
```

The *Type.registerNamespace* method adds the specified namespace to the run-time environment. In a way, the *registerNamespace* method is equivalent to using the *namespace {...}* construct in C#. The *Samples.Person* function defined following the namespace declaration describes a *Person* type in the *Samples* namespace. Finally, the newly defined function must be registered as a class with the Microsoft AJAX library framework. You use the *registerClass* method on the current function.

The *registerClass* method takes a number of parameters. The first parameter is mandatory, and it indicates the public name that will be used to expose the JavaScript function as a class. Additional and optional parameters (not shown in the preceding code) are the parent class, if there is any, and any interface implemented by the class. We'll get into this in just a moment.

The Microsoft AJAX library follows the prototype model (as opposed to closures) to define its own custom types. The goal of the ASP.NET AJAX team was to deliver a model that provided the best quality and performance on the largest number of browsers. Prototypes have a good load time in all browsers; and indeed, they have excellent performance in Firefox. Furthermore, prototypes lend themselves well, more than closures do, to debugging as far as object instantiation and access to private members are concerned.

> **Note** In the definition of a new class, you can use an anonymous function or a named function. In terms of syntax, both solutions are acceptable. The convention, though, is that you opt for named functions and name each function after its fully qualified name, replacing the dot symbol (.) with a dollar symbol ($). The convention is justified by the help this approach provides to IntelliSense in Microsoft Visual Studio 2008.

Inheritance and Polymorphism

Let's now define a new class, *Citizen*, that extends *Person* by adding a new property: a national identification number. Here's the skeleton of the code you need:

```
// Declare the class
Samples.Citizen = function Samples$Citizen(firstName, lastName, id)
{
    :
}

// Define the prototype of the class
Samples.Citizen.prototype =
{
    :
}
```

```
// Register the class
Samples.Citizen.registerClass("Samples.Citizen", Samples.Person);
```

Note that the first argument of *registerClass* is a string, but the second one has to be an object reference. The second argument indicates the object acting as the parent of the newly created object. Let's flesh out this code a bit.

In the constructor, you'll set some private members and call the base constructor to initialize the members defined on the base class. The *initializeBase* method (defined on the revisited *Function* object you get from the library) retrieves and invokes the base constructor:

```
Samples.Citizen = function Samples$Citizen(firstName, lastName, id)
{
    Samples.Citizen.initializeBase(this, [firstName, lastName]);
    this._id = id;
}
```

You pass *initializeBase* the reference to the current object as well as an array with any parameters that the constructor to call requires. You can use the *[...]* notation to define an array inline. If you omit the *[...]* notation, be ready to handle a parameter count exception.

Quite often, developers derive a class because they need to add new members or alter the behavior of an existing method or property. Object-oriented languages define a proper keyword to flag members as overridable. How is that possible in JavaScript?

Any member listed in the prototype of an object is automatically public and overridable. Here's the prototype of the *Citizen* class:

```
Samples.Citizen.prototype =
{
    ToString:    Samples$Citizen$ToString,
    get_ID:      Samples$Citizen$get_ID
}
```

The class has a read-only *ID* property and overrides the *ToString* method defined in the parent class. Let's have a look at the implementation of the overriding method:

```
function Samples$Citizen$ToString()
{
    var temp = Samples.Citizen.callBaseMethod(this, 'ToString');
    temp += "  [" + this._id + "]";
    return temp;
}
```

You use *callBaseMethod* to invoke the same method on the parent class. Defined on the *Function* class, the *callBaseMethod* method takes up to three parameters: the instance, the name of the method, plus an optional array of arguments for the base method.

As mentioned earlier, the *ToString* method on the *Person* class returns a *LastName, FirstName* string. The *ToString* method on the *Citizen* class returns a string in the following format: *LastName, FirstName [ID]*.

> **Note** When the prototype model is used, JavaScript has no notion of private members because no common closure can be provided for all methods contributing to the same object. As a result, private members are conventionally indicated by the underscore symbol (_) prefixing their names. They're still public and accessible, though.

Interfaces

An interface describes a group of related behaviors that are typical of a variety of classes. In general, an interface can include methods, properties, and events; in JavaScript, it contains only methods.

Keeping in mind the constraints of the JavaScript language, to define an interface you create a regular class with a constructor and a prototype. The constructor and each prototyped method, though, will just throw a not-implemented exception. Here's the code for the sample *Sys.IDisposable* built-in interface:

```
Type.registerNamespace("Sys");
Sys.IDisposable = function Sys$IDisposable()
{
    throw Error.notImplemented();
}
function Sys$IDisposable$dispose()
{
    throw Error.notImplemented();
}
Sys.IDisposable.prototype =
{
    dispose: Sys$IDisposable$dispose
}
Sys.IDisposable.registerInterface('Sys.IDisposable');
```

The following statement registers the *Citizen* class, makes it derive from *Person*, and implements the *IDisposable* interface:

```
Samples.Citizen.registerClass('Samples.Citizen',
        Samples.Person, Sys.IDisposable);
```

To implement a given interface, a JavaScript class simply provides all methods in the interface and lists the interface while registering the class:

```
function Samples$Citizen$dispose
{
    this._id = "";
}

Samples.Citizen.prototype =
{
    dispose: Samples$Citizen$dispose
    :
    :
}
```

Note, though, that you won't receive any run-time error if the class that claims to implement a given interface doesn't really support all the methods. You will receive an error if a caller happens to invoke an interface function your class didn't implement, so by convention all interface methods should be implemented.

If a class implements multiple interfaces, you simply list all required interfaces in the *registerClass* method as additional parameters. Here's an example:

```
Sys.Component.registerClass('Sys.Component', null,
    Sys.IDisposable,
    Sys.INotifyPropertyChange,
    Sys.INotifyDisposing);
```

As you can see, in this case you don't have to group interfaces in an array.

Framework Facilities

Many layers of code form the Microsoft AJAX library, including a layer specifically created to smooth the creation of rich UI controls with AJAX capabilities. (See *http://www.codeplex.com/ AjaxControlToolkit* for example controls.) This particular aspect of the library, though, is expected to evolve significantly in the next release of ASP.NET.

Let's focus instead on other core facilities you find in the library, such as event handling, debugging, and networking. To start out, let's attack with reflection capabilities.

Reflection

While debugging some JavaScript code, isn't it a bit frustrating when you need to know the actual type of a variable and cannot get it exact? In general, *reflection* refers to the ability of a function to examine the structure of an object at runtime. When it comes to reflection, the JavaScript language doesn't offer much. The Microsoft AJAX library largely makes up for this.

In plain JavaScript, the built-in *typeof* operator returns information about the type of the variable you are dealing with. The operator, though, is limited to the core set of JavaScript types. Let's consider the following code snippet:

```
Samples.Citizen = new function() {
    :
    :
}
var c = new Samples.Citizen();
alert(typeof c);
```

As expected, the displayed string is a generic *object*.

Adding a thick object-oriented infrastructure, the Microsoft AJAX library makes it easy to track the exact name of the pseudo-type of a given object. The following code returns a more precise message, as shown in Figure 4-2.

```
// Returns "Samples.Citizen"
var c = new Samples.Citizen();
alert(Object.getTypeName(c));
```

FIGURE 4-2 The "real" type name of a JavaScript object

Whenever a new object is registered with the Microsoft AJAX framework, its name and pseudo-type are added to an internal list. Reflection functions just look up these internal dictionaries and return what they read.

> **Note** I use the expression *pseudo-type* to indicate a type that has its own fully qualified name according to the Microsoft AJAX library, such as *Person* in the preceding code snippet. It should be noted, though, that at the lower level of the JavaScript engine there remains a plain *object* type.

In the Microsoft AJAX library, reflection capabilities are offered as extensions of the *Type* object. These methods enable you to collect information about an object, such as what it inherits from, whether it implements a particular interface, and whether it is an instance of a particular class. Note that the *Type* class aliases the built-in JavaScript *Function* object. Therefore, many of the methods exposed through the general interface of the *Type* object are also available through the instance of any custom type (that is, function) you create.

Table 4-3 lists the members of the *Type* object, which is also a compendium of the reflection capabilities of the Microsoft AJAX library.

TABLE 4-3 Members of the *Type* Object

Member	Description
callBaseMethod	Invokes a base class method with specified arguments
getBaseMethod	Gets the implementation of a method from the base class of the specified instance
getBaseType	Gets the base type of the specified instance
getInterfaces	Returns the list of interfaces that the type implements
getName	Gets the name of the type of the specified instance
implementsInterface	Indicates whether a given instance implements the specified interface
inheritsFrom	Indicates whether the type inherits from the specified base type
initializeBase	Invokes the base constructor of a given type
isClass	Indicates whether the specified type is a Microsoft AJAX library class
isImplementedBy	Indicates whether the specified interface is implemented by the object
isInstanceOfType	Indicates whether the object is an instance of the specified type
isInterface	Indicates whether the specified type is an interface

TABLE 4-3 **Members of the *Type* Object**

Member	Description
isNamespace	Indicates whether the specified object is a namespace
Parse	Returns an instance of the type that is specified by a type name
registerClass	Registers an object as a Microsoft AJAX library class
registerEnum	Registers an object as a Microsoft AJAX library enumeration
registerInterface	Registers an object as a Microsoft AJAX library interface
registerNamespace	Creates a namespace

Finally, here's a brief example of how to use reflection in practice:

```
var t = Samples.Components.Timer;
var obj = new Samples.Components.Timer();
if (obj.isInstanceOfType(t))
{
    alert(t.getName() + " is a " + obj.getName() + ".");
}
```

The Application Object

The execution of each Web page that links the Microsoft AJAX library is controlled by an application object. This object is an instance of a private class—the *Sys._Application* class. An instance of the application object is created in the body of the library, specifically in the *MicrosoftAjax.js* file:

```
// Excerpt from MicrosoftAjax.js
Sys.Application = new Sys._Application();
```

If properly initialized, the application object invokes a pair of page-level callbacks with fixed names—*pageLoad* and *pageUnload*:

```
function pageLoad(sender, args)
{
   // sender is the Sys.Application instance
   // args   is of type Sys.ApplicationLoadEventArgs
     :
     :
}
function pageUnload(sender, args)
{
   // sender is the Sys.Application instance
   // args   is of type Sys.ApplicationLoadEventArgs
     :
     :
}
```

In particular, *pageLoad* is a good place for the page to perform any initialization tasks that require the Microsoft AJAX library. This is more reliable than using the *window*'s *onload* event.

The *pageLoad* callback receives a *Sys.ApplicationLoadEventArgs* data structure packed with the list of Microsoft AJAX library components already created and a Boolean flag to indicate that the callback is invoked within a regular postback or a partial rendering operation.

Beyond page loading events, the *Sys.Application* object serves one main purpose: providing access to client-side page components. Generally, the term *component* denotes an object that is reusable and can interact with other objects in the context of a framework. In the Microsoft AJAX framework, a component is a JavaScript object that inherits from the *Sys.Component* class. These objects are tracked by the library infrastructure and exposed via methods on the *Sys.Application* object.

In particular, the *findComponent* method scrolls the run-time hierarchy of Microsoft AJAX components for the current page until it finds a component with a matching ID. The method has two possible prototypes:

```
Sys.Application.findComponent(id);
Sys.Application.findComponent(id, parent);
```

The former overload takes the ID of the component, uses it to look up the component, and then navigates the hierarchy all the way down from the root. When a non-null *parent* argument is specified, the search is restricted to the subtree rooted in the context object. The *id* parameter must be a string; the *parent* parameter must be a Microsoft AJAX library object. The method returns the object that matches the ID, or it returns null if no such object is found.

The Microsoft AJAX library also supports a shortcut for retrieving run-time components—the *$find* method. The *$find* method is an alias for *findComponent*:

```
var $find = Sys.Application.findComponent;
```

You can use this method to locate all components created by server controls that use the Microsoft AJAX library (for example, extenders in the AJAX Control Toolkit and new controls in ASP.NET 4.0), as well as by your own JavaScript code. You can't use *$find* to locate DOM elements; for DOM elements, you must resort to *$get*.

String Manipulation

The *Sys.StringBuilder* class adds advanced text manipulation capabilities to Web pages based on the library. As the name suggests, the class mimics the behavior of the managed *StringBuilder* class defined in the .NET Framework.

When you create an instance of the builder object, you specify initial text. The builder caches the text in an internal array by using an element for each added text or line. The *Sys.StringBuilder* object doesn't accept objects other than non-null strings. You add text using the *append* and *appendLine* methods. The *toString* method composes the text by using the join method of the JavaScript array class.

```
// Build an HTML table as a string
var header = "<table><thead> ... </thead>";
var footer = "<tfoot> ... </tfoot></table>";
var builder = new Sys.StringBuilder(header);
:
builder.append(footer);
alert(builder.toString());
```

The Microsoft AJAX library *String* class is also enriched with a format method that mimics the behavior of the *Format* method on the .NET Framework *String* class:

```
alert(String.format("Today is: {0}", new Date()));
```

You define placeholders in the format string using *{n}* elements. The real value for placeholders is determined by looking at the *n*.th argument in the format method call.

Debugging

Another class that is worth mentioning is the *Sys._Debug* class. An instance of this internal class is assigned to the *Sys.Debug* global object:

```
Sys.Debug = new Sys._Debug();
```

In your pages, you use the *Sys.Debug* object to assert conditions, break into the debugger, or trace text. For example, the *traceDump* method writes the contents of the specified object in a human-readable format in the Microsoft AJAX library trace area. The trace area is expected to be a *<textarea>* element with a mandatory ID of *traceConsole*. You can place this element anywhere in the page:

```
<textarea id="traceConsole" cols="40" rows="10" />
```

The *traceDump* method accepts two parameters, as shown here:

```
Sys.Debug.traceDump(object, name)
```

The *name* parameter indicates descriptive text to display as the heading of the object dump. The text can contain HTML markup. Figure 4-3 shows the output of a trace dump.

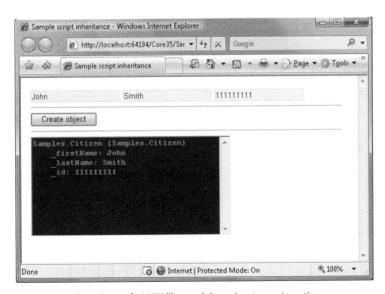

FIGURE 4-3 The Microsoft AJAX library debugging tracer in action

You use the *clearTrace* method to clear the output console. The *fail* method breaks into the debugger and the method *assert* displays a message if the specified condition is false.

The Network Stack

The most relevant feature of an AJAX library is the ability to execute out-of-band Web requests from the client browser. In particular, AJAX extensions to ASP.NET let you invoke Web service methods without dismissing the currently displayed page. This ability leverages the networking support built into the Microsoft AJAX library.

In the Microsoft AJAX library, a remote request is represented by an instance of the *Sys.Net.WebRequest* class. Table 4-4 lists the properties of the class.

TABLE 4-4 Members of the *Sys.Net.WebRequest* Object

Member	Description
body	Gets and sets the body of the request
executor	Gets and sets the Microsoft AJAX library object that will take care of executing the request
headers	Gets the headers of the request
httpVerb	Gets and sets the HTTP verb for the request
timeout	Gets and sets the timeout, if any, for the request
url	Gets and sets the URL of the request

The *WebRequest* class defines the *url* property to get and set the target URL and the *headers* property to add header strings to the request. If the request is going to be a POST, you set the body of the request through the *body* property. A request executes through the method *invoke*. The *completed* event informs you about the completion of the request.

Each Web request is executed through an internal class—the Web request manager—that employs an "executor" to open the socket and send the packet. All executors derive from a common base class—the *Sys.Net.WebRequestExecutor* class.

The Microsoft AJAX library defines just one HTTP executor—the *Sys.Net.XMLHttpExecutor* class. As the name suggests, this executor uses the popular *XMLHttpRequest* object to execute the HTTP request.

The *Sys.Net.WebRequest* class is essentially a framework class that other higher level classes use, but page authors hardly ever use it. I've seen this class used only a few times in real-world JavaScript code. As you saw in Chapter 2, the ASP.NET AJAX framework makes it so easy to invoke a Web service method or perhaps a static method on a page that you hardly feel the need to invoke another type of HTTP endpoint.

If you need to download a resource such as a JavaScript file, you need quite a bit of code if you go through this class.

```
var endpoint = "ondemand.js";
var request = new Sys.Net.WebRequest();
request.set_url(endpoint);
request.add_completed(function() {...});
request.invoke();
```

With other AJAX libraries—for instance, jQuery—this code reduces to just one line. I'll return
to jQuery in the next chapter.

> **Note** All AJAX libraries are associated with the *XMLHttpRequest* browser object. So what else
> could an executor be other than a reference to the *XMLHttpRequest* browser object? In general,
> an HTTP executor is any means you can use to carry out a Web request. An alternative executor
> might be based on HTTP frames. The idea is to use a dynamically created inline frame to
> download the response of a given request and then parse that result into usable objects.

The Eventing Model

Building cross-browser compatibility for events is not an easy task. Internet Explorer has its
own eventing model, and so do Firefox and Safari. For this reason, the event model of the
Microsoft AJAX library is a new abstract API that joins together the standard W3C API and
the Internet Explorer model. The new API is closely modeled after the standard W3C API.

In addition to using different method names (*add/removeEventListener* is for Firefox, and
attach/detachEvent is for Internet Explorer), browsers differ in the way they pass event data
down to handlers. In Internet Explorer, an event handler receives its data through the global
window.event object; in Firefox, the event data is passed as an argument to the handler.
In the Microsoft AJAX library, event handlers receive a parameter with proper event data.

Another significant difference is in the way mouse and keyboard events are represented. The
Microsoft AJAX library abstracts away any differences between browsers by providing ad hoc
enumerated types, such as *Sys.UI.Key* and *Sys.UI.MouseButton*. Here's some sample code:

```
function Button1_Click(e)
{
  if (e.button === Sys.UI.MouseButton.leftButton)
  {
    :
  }
}
function keyboard_EnterPressed(e)
{
  if (e.keyCode === Sys.UI.Key.enter)
  {
    :
  }
}
```

The Microsoft AJAX library provides a shorthand notation to create DOM event hookups and removal. For example, you can use the *$addHandler* and *$removeHandler* aliases to add and remove a handler. Here's the syntax:

```
$addHandler(element, "eventName", handler);
$removeHandler(element, "eventName", handler);
```

In many cases, you'll want to hook up several handlers to a DOM event for a component. Rather than manually creating all the required delegates and related handlers, you can use a condensed syntax to add and remove multiple handlers:

```
initialize: function()
{
    var elem = this.get_element();
    $addHandlers(
        elem,
        {[
            'mouseover': this._mouseHoverHandler,
            'mouseout': this._mouseOutHandler,
            'focus', this._focusHandler,
            'blur', this_blurHandler
        ]},
        this);
}
```

The *$clearHandlers* alias, conversely, removes all handlers set for a particular DOM element in a single shot.

If you write a component and wire up some events, it's essential that you clear all handlers when the component is unloaded, or even earlier, if you don't need the handler any longer. For example, you should do that from the component's *dispose* method to break circular references between your JavaScript objects and the DOM. Correctly applied, this trick easily prevents nasty memory leaks.

Summary

JavaScript is one of the pillars of the Web. Now that the arrival of AJAX is shaking the foundation of the Web, what about JavaScript? Is JavaScript going to change in the near future?

For years, the JavaScript language has remained very stable, and this stability created the environmental conditions for AJAX to flourish and thrive. AJAX means more and more code hosted and running within the client browser. This code can only be written in JavaScript.

The perception of a language is different when you have only a few lines of code to write as opposed to when you have to use it to write large sections of the application. For this more exacting job, JavaScript seems more inadequate every day. And JavaScript 2.0 is slowly but steadily emerging. JavaScript 2.0 is not a thing of the immediate future, though.

For now, a better and richer JavaScript is possible only through libraries that cover the parts of client-side programming that the language doesn't natively cover. Classes, networking, static type checking, and a common and cross-browser model for managing events and exploring the document are all features required in modern JavaScript code. Popular libraries, such as the Microsoft AJAX library, provide just this.

The key trait of the Microsoft AJAX library is the set of extensions to transform JavaScript into an object-oriented language. JavaScript is not a true OOP language even though it always has supported objects and also provides a rudimentary mechanism for prototyping classes and derived classes. The Microsoft AJAX library builds on top of this basic functionality to add namespace and interface support in addition to a number of helpful facilities.

In the next chapter, I'll cover another extremely popular library that addresses UI enhancements and makes it so easy and effective to add AJAX capabilities to Web pages. This library is jQuery.

Chapter 5
JavaScript Libraries

You can't wait for inspiration. You have to go after it with a club.

—Jack London

If you look back at the events that have characterized the past five years of Web programming, you see that server controls have been welcomed as a powerful productivity tool since the advent of ASP.NET but are being belittled as AJAX gains wider acceptance. Although server controls often boost your productivity, the HTML they generate usually can't be modified to any great extent, and sometimes they don't work well (if at all) with partial page updates. Developers today are instead turning to frameworks such as the Microsoft AJAX library and creating their own client applications that embrace AJAX, even at the cost of increased JavaScript development on their part. AJAX is that powerful.

The fact is, in addition to enabling partial page updates, AJAX also allows us to view the use of JavaScript in Web pages in a different—and largely positive—light. As you read in the previous chapter, Web developers are turning their attention to JavaScript. But JavaScript is nothing new; it's not the hot new Web technology that enables features to be used that were impossible or impractical to use before. JavaScript was there before AJAX arrived on the scene, and it's a building block of the whole Web experience.

At first glance, this renewed interest in JavaScript can be seen as the resurgence of a technology that was pushed aside maybe too hastily. A more thoughtful look, however, reveals a key fact that makes the initial impression inaccurate. The new wave of interest for JavaScript originates from a different category of professionals—the people who authored so many ASP.NET pages in the past five years and established the Web as a common element of our everyday life.

These people are looking for a valid and reliable set of client-side programming tools. JavaScript is there and works, although it's not perfect. It's natural, then, that JavaScript is the starting point for any experiment aimed at increasing the interactivity and responsiveness of Web pages. But as we clearly saw in Chapter 4, "A Better and Richer JavaScript," today's JavaScript is not entirely up to the task. Extensions are required, and they are being built. One extremely popular extension to JavaScript and Web pages is the jQuery library.

In this chapter, I'll describe the main characteristics of the jQuery library and focus in particular on CSS selectors, function chaining, and wrapped sets. I'll also cover more specific topics such as using jQuery to enhance ASP.NET controls, eventing, effects, browser-side caching, AJAX capabilities, plug-ins, and the user interface.

Before going any further, though, it's helpful to take a detailed look at the ongoing evolution that is moving server controls into the background in favor of JavaScript widgets—precisely an area where jQuery excels.

From Server Controls to JavaScript Widgets

The advent of ASP.NET shifted the focus of Web development to the server side. For a few years, Web pages contained only the smallest possible amount of JavaScript that could make the page minimally functional. In ASP.NET, in particular, JavaScript was mostly used to do some preliminary, client-side validation of input data and to trigger a postback from HTML elements such as hyperlink and list elements not natively enabled for form submission.

With ASP.NET, a new category of professionals started coding for the Web. Prior to ASP.NET, Web developers were typically not individuals trained in computer engineering or science, but rather free-thinking and creative individuals who simply made it work. Today, we see trained developers bringing their skills to the Web, and this changes everything. These developers started their Web careers using ASP.NET with a very limited knowledge of basic Web client-side technologies such as JavaScript, CSS, and the Document Object Model (DOM). Although not necessarily creative in a layout and artistic sense, the new wave of Web developers are strong in the engineering sense, and the nature of how applications work today is vastly different than how they worked even five or six years ago. Now these professionals are discovering the client side of the Web, and they are demanding better and richer tools.

These new tools aren't necessarily tools that dumb down the artistic side because of skill limitations; rather they are tools that enhance the developer's ability to engineer the applications while making the other necessary parts (markup, CSS) more accessible and less developed by hand.

The ASP.NET Factor

ASP.NET pages are made of code, markup tags, literal text, and server controls. Based on the request, the server controls generate the right markup language. The ASP.NET runtime combines the output of all controls and serves the client a page to display in a browser.

The programming richness of ASP.NET springs from an unlimited library of server controls that covers the basic tasks of HTML interaction—for example, collecting text through input tags—as well as more advanced functionalities such as calendaring, menus, tree views, and grid-based data display.

Why Was ASP.NET a Milestone?

ASP.NET was a winner because it combined an effective programming model with high-level and object-oriented programming languages. No special skills other than classic software development skills were required for getting started with ASP.NET. This fact did more to lure

C++, Java, and Pascal developers into developing ASP.NET solutions than any other reason. ASP.NET was a milestone in the history of Web programming because it opened up Web programming to virtually all developers.

When the ASP.NET platform was introduced, server controls looked like a panacea for all evils. They were perfect because they were a convenient tradeoff between performance and productivity.

Server controls made it very easy to generate complex markup for pages. With the help of a powerful integrated development environment (IDE) such as Visual Studio, developers could drag one control from the toolbox and drop it on the Web Form drawing surface. Developers could then select some of the control's properties and set values declaratively. Finally, developers only had to point the browser to the page to see the result. Easy, effective, and especially quick.

Books and tons of articles have been written in the past few years to illustrate how to create custom ASP.NET server controls and how to effectively use existing controls. Now, all of a sudden, server controls seem to have lost all of their sex appeal. Why is this?

The Wind Is Changing for Server Controls

The initial enthusiasm for server controls was mostly because of the productivity they could guarantee. Now, a few years later, other factors are being considered and seem to be prevailing.

Server controls are black boxes of markup. Using them is similar to carrying on a conversation while using only predefined sentences from a vocabulary list. You can choose how to combine sentences and pick out one of many similar sentences, but you do not have total freedom of expression. You can't craft the sentence yourself; you can't control every word, verb, and preposition you use in the sentence.

This is the major strength and weakness of the server controls. Out-of-the-box output was their strength until now. Today, it's turning into a major weakness because the application's users are demanding increased complexity and server interaction, which are things that can't be backfilled into existing server controls.

Styling server controls is critical, too. Despite the fact that Microsoft enriched ASP.NET with features such as themes, skins, and CSS adapters, to gain total control of the user interface appearance you need to resort to CSS over raw HTML.

Finally, server controls are necessarily bound to view state and the classic page life cycle triggered by the ASP.NET HTTP runtime. View state results in a few KBs of extra stuff added to the page. Although it's not as large as it was in the first version of ASP.NET, the view state is still an unnecessary burden added to the page download that is useful only for restoring the state of the control once it's back on the server. In an AJAX model where the paradigm moves toward direct data-for-data calls (as discussed in Chapter 1, "Under the Umbrella of AJAX"), the view state is a legacy item; and a heavy legacy item, indeed.

What's the future (if any) of server controls?

Server controls are still a formidable and largely unparalleled instrument of productivity. Pages are getting richer in terms of client code, but writing client code manually is error prone, even if you use advanced JavaScript libraries. My forecast—or simply my guess—is that server controls will be used more as black boxes to generate JavaScript code based on some JavaScript libraries—including the Microsoft AJAX library and jQuery.

The Widget Factor

The current re-emergence of JavaScript in Web programming is the result of a new quest for interactivity now being conducted by ASP.NET developers—that is, a category of professionals with a strong programming background and not necessarily skilled in scripting and HTML.

The answers to the demand for more interactivity are not so different from the answers found by the first Web page authors 10 or more years ago. The popularity of the Web and the programming frameworks are different, though.

More JavaScript is required, and it must be better organized. This raises the need for libraries, possibly object-oriented libraries. Another factor is the effectiveness and speed of potential solutions. At the end of the day, through JavaScript you need to manipulate the DOM, manipulate the style elements, add some effects, and provide a richer user interface. Working in a cross-browser manner is also a key requirement. These are common tasks that must be automated to be effective and provide concrete added value while speeding up the development of AJAX-based applications.

In one word, these are *widgets*—that is, ad hoc JavaScript components to make the Web user interface more attractive and easier to use. Widgets are the foundation of the enhanced user experience AJAX applications deliver to users.

Most Popular Libraries

The rush to making the client side of the Web as rich and appealing as possible started a few years ago and produced quite a few libraries, all reasonably describing themselves with the same set of words: unique, easy-to-use, intuitive, extensible, high-performance, rich Internet application. I don't think I'm oversimplifying it if I say that the differences between all these JavaScript libraries are quite blurry. You can pick any one of them and be relatively satisfied with it. Table 5-1 lists some of these libraries.

TABLE 5-1 Popular JavaScript Libraries

Library	URL
Dojo	*http://www.dojotoolkit.org*
Ext JS	*http://www.extjs.com*
jQuery	*http://jquery.com*
Prototype JS	*http://www.prototypejs.org*
Script.aculo.us	*http://script.aculo.us*
Yahoo! UI	*http://developer.yahoo.com/yui*

The list of available libraries doesn't end here, of course. A more comprehensive, but hardly exhaustive, list can be found on Wikipedia at the following address: *http://en.wikipedia.org/ wiki/Comparison_of_JavaScript_frameworks*.

Libraries are all cross-browser products and offer various licensing models. The memory required to run in the browser and the download time also vary based on the core characteristics of the library and the optional features you choose to download. The overall range is between 20 KB and 300 KB.

Let's dig out some more information about these libraries. As you'll note, some of these libraries are just specializations of another library that have grown to be an independent product at some point.

The Dojo Library

In Dojo, you find prepackaged components for common user interface elements such as menus, tabs, tooltips, date-picker, time-picker, treeview with drag-and-drop, ready-made forms, and input validation.

Dojo also offers sortable tables, 2D vectorial graphics, and animated effects such as fades and wipes. It also abstracts the popular *XMLHttpRequest* object to a custom component. Dojo's *XMLHttpRequest* component automatically falls back to using an IFRAME element when this is convenient.

Dojo also provides local data storage that extends cookies and leverages any browser's capabilities. The abstract model works with Internet Explorer, Firefox, and Safari.

The ExtJS Library

The ExtJS library was originally built as an add-on to the Yahoo! UI library. Now available as version 2.0, ExtJS is a totally independent library, although it's fully interoperable with jQuery and Prototype.

ExtJS is built around a set of widgets, including a variety of input controls (text and numeric fields, date-pickers, lists, sliders), panels, trees, and grids. In addition, ExtJS features some application-level capabilities such as modal dialog boxes and interactive validation message boxes that pop up when invalid content is entered into a field.

A DOM component is available to select page elements that match a filter, along with a page-level data store acting as a local cache for data that can be in JSON and XML formats.

The PrototypeJS Library

The PrototypeJS library is available as a single JavaScript file, or it can be distributed as part of larger projects in combination with Ruby on Rails and Script.aculo.us.

The library offers an abstraction over *XMLHttpRequest* that is two-fold. In particular, you find a function to receive raw data from a remote HTTP endpoint and a function to receive a chunk of HTML to be injected as-is into the existing DOM. In terms of AJAX patterns, the

Ajax.Request function implements the *Browser-Side Template (BST) pattern*, which leaves on the client the burden of producing HTML from the raw endpoint response.

```
var url = "...";
var call = new Ajax.Request(
    url,
    { parameters: { ... },
        onSuccess: onCompleted,
        onFailure: onFailed
    }
);
```

The *Ajax.Updater* function, on the other hand, implements the *HTML Message (HM) pattern* and receives HTML from the HTTP endpoint. The received HTML response is then automatically injected inside a specified DOM object.

```
var url = "...";
var domElement = document.getElementById("...");
var call = new Ajax.Updater(
    domElement,
    url
);
```

In addition to providing an abstraction over *XMLHttpRequest*, PrototypeJS offers an emulation of classes and, thus, a flavor of object orientation. As with the Microsoft AJAX library, there's no magic behind the feature—the core JavaScript *prototype* property is used. Here's a quick example of the syntax that is supported to define a new class:

```
var Person = Class.create(
    baseClass,
    {initialize: function (first, last)
        {
            this.FirstName = first;
            this.LastName = last;
        }
    }
);
```

The first argument, if specified, is the parent class. If no parent class is required, you just skip the parameter. Finally, the *initialize* method serves as a constructor for the new class.

The Script.aculo.us Library

The Script.aculo.us library is built on top of PrototypeJS and adds cool visual effects to DOM elements in the page. The library is articulated in a bunch of distinct JavaScript files, each providing a specific skill—effects, drag-and-drop, sliders, or controls.

One single file—the *scriptaculous.js* file—governs the loading of any necessary JavaScript files for the requested features. If you just need a specific subset of features, you explicitly list them using the following syntax:

```
<script src="scriptaculous.js?load=effects,dragdrop" type="text/javascript"></script>
```

The scripts available on demand are *builder*, *effects*, *dragdrop*, *controls*, and *slider*. It should be noted that some of the scripts might have a dependency on others. In this case, the loading engine will manage extra downloads.

The library is especially known for its visual effects, which are quick and easy to set up. Here's a brief example:

```
<script type="text/javascript" language="javascript">
  // <![CDATA[
  $('panel_ExtraInfo').appear({duration: 3.0});
  // ]]>
</script>
```

The sample script takes three seconds to switch the CSS *display* attribute of the specified DOM element to *visible*. The *$* function is shorthand for *document.getElementById*.

The Yahoo! UI Library

The Yahoo! UI library is articulated in four types of components: core, utilities, UI controls, and CSS components, plus developer and build tools such as a logger and profiler.

The library's core block is made of a set of tools for event management and DOM manipulation along with the Yahoo! *Global* object, which contains several utilities such as methods for type-checking and user agent detection, a class model, and behaviors to augment the DOM element's capabilities.

The library offers facilities to access browser events such as mouse and keyboard events, and it also provides its own object to publish custom events and subscribe to other components' custom events.

The Yahoo! UI library comes with a set of predefined CSS files to automatically style all default elements of a page in a consistent manner. You use the *Reset* CSS file to fix any inconsistent styles of HTML elements and the *Base* CSS file to apply consistent settings instead. For example, one of the CSS files in the Base suite is designed to style common HTML elements so that they fit in a 100 percent wide page.

A few UI controls exist out of the box that address most common necessities for Web pages—buttons, a calendar, a color-picker, menus, various types of panels, a slider, and tabstrips. Such components are entirely client-side components created and commanded using JavaScript code.

The Yahoo! UI library also has an optional (and free) library of ASP.NET controls—the YUIAsp.Net library. By means of this library, you can actually use the YUI widgets even if you have limited knowledge of JavaScript. The following code snippet shows how to emit a JavaScript-based link button component from the Yahoo! UI library through an ASP.NET server control:

```
<yui:Button ID="btnLink" runat="server"
    Text="Hooked by ASP.NET?"
    Target="_blank"
    ButtonType="Link"
    NavigateUrl="http://www.asp.net"
/>
```

For more information on Yahoo! UI server controls, have a look at *http://www.yuiasp.net*.

In the category of utilities, you find functions to add various capabilities such as AJAX connectivity, downloads, history, and cookies management.

> **Important** As mentioned, the size of JavaScript libraries ranges from 20 KB to 300 KB. However, these numbers depend on the actual features you download and are subject to further reduction because of *minification*—the equivalent of compilation for JavaScript interpreted code. Minification consists of removing unnecessary characters from JavaScript code, such as white spaces, newlines, comments, and block delimiters. All of these characters add readability to the code, but they are not strictly required for execution. The average savings is in the order of 40 percent.
>
> This savings can be further increased by applying GZIP compression to the minified JavaScript file. Experiments demonstrate that the combination of minifying and GZIP produces a better result than using only minification or GZIP-ping alone. Not all minifiers produce the same code, and this affects the subsequent performance of GZIP. As a rule of thumb, you can expect to get about half the size from minification and up to one-third of the input size from GZIP. This would make for a final (and ideal) one-sixth of the original size.
>
> Some of the aforementioned libraries have their own minifier, such as the Yahoo! UI Compressor and the JS Dojo Minifier. Most minifiers are based on JSMin, developed by Douglas Crockford, which is available at *http://www.crockford.com/javascript/jsmin.html*. Building your own team-based minifier is not difficult, as the engine can be easily wrapped in a Windows Forms or an ASP.NET tailor-made front end.

Libraries and the Process of Natural Selection

As you can see, all JavaScript libraries have a lot in common. In addition, you can synthesize the content of a JavaScript library with three macro features:

- UI widgets and effects
- Flavors of object orientation
- Programming utilities such as AJAX, downloads, caching, and history

When all the libraries look sort of the same, which one should you choose?

> **Note** In the mid-1970s, two technologies for video recording vied to conquer the market: JVC's VHS and Sony's Betamax. The winner was VHS in spite of the fact that, with good reason, many people considered Betamax to be the superior technology. So the best technology is not necessarily the one that is best received by the marketplace. The success of a particular technology often depends on a mix of factors.
>
> Ancient Romans used to say that the voice of the people was the voice of the gods. Applied to this discussion, this saying means that if users establish the success of a particular technology, you are probably better off going with that technology, too—unless you have strong reasons and good evidence to do otherwise. For JavaScript libraries, the winner seems to be jQuery, and jQuery is the one I feel most comfortable recommending—unless you have valid reasons for picking up another (mostly equivalent) one.

If all the libraries look the same to you, I suggest you start with jQuery. This library is simple to use and powerful at the same time. This said, choosing jQuery, PrototypeJS, or maybe Yahoo! UI is ultimately a matter of personal preference.

As a developer, you need a higher level tool to focus on for client-side coding than the raw JavaScript language. Libraries exist to raise the level of abstraction and provide a significantly more powerful set of functions. You and your team, though, decide what really makes you more powerful.

This said, the reasons why more and more developers are using jQuery, and the reasons why in this book I am presenting jQuery as the winner, can be summarized as follows:

- With jQuery, you tend to write far fewer lines of code than with other libraries.

- It has a common-sense API and is easy to understand.

- The extensible architecture of jQuery has triggered the creation of a large number of plug-ins that will likely satisfy any need you might have.

For us .NET people, another good reason for picking jQuery is the fact that it is now distributed with ASP.NET MVC and probably will be also when ASP.NET 4.0 is rolled out.

If I had to mention only one reason to look at jQuery I'd pick the *chaining* of queries. As you'll see in the rest of the chapter, jQuery is mostly about selecting DOM elements, placing them into groups, and applying functions and effects to all of them. Because most jQuery functions return another jQuery object, you can easily build intuitive statements that are surprisingly easy to chain together to create intricate but understandable effects. Here's a brief example that shows you how to disable all input elements in a page:

```
// For each DOM element of class <input>, set the disabled attribute to "disabled".
$("input").attr("disabled", "disabled");
```

Isn't this code similar to the code snippet listed earlier based on Script.aculo.us? Sure, it is because we're talking about the same kind of object. You just need to make your choice of libraries.

The jQuery Library

Like many other JavaScript libraries, jQuery offers DOM and CSS manipulation and navigation, event handling, nice user interface effects, and AJAX capabilities. However, the main trait of the library is *call chaining*. Most methods, after execution, return the same jQuery object they have been called from. In this way, you can chain new commands to the object, thus building an effective workflow.

As mentioned, Microsoft is now fully supporting jQuery and, among other things, distributes it with the ASP.NET MVC framework. Furthermore, extensions have been developed to fully integrate jQuery IntelliSense in Microsoft Visual Studio 2008 SP1. Starting with the next version of .NET, jQuery will become a constituent part of the ASP.NET platform. As such, it will be fully supported by Microsoft Product Support Services in a 24/7 modality. (Microsoft Product Support Services is the group that answers the phone when you call technical support for help.) The library, though, will continue to be developed independently by the same group of people who made it so successful.

The Library at a Glance

Written by John Resig, the jQuery library consists of a single *.js* file, which is available from *http://docs.jquery.com/Downloading_jQuery*. At the time of this writing, the latest available version is numbered 1.3 and was released in the winter of 2009.

Size of the Library

The download site offers three versions of the library: uncompressed, packed, and minimized. The size of the uncompressed version measures nearly 100 KB and contains completely uncompressed and un-minified code that is full of comments and written in a human-readable way. This is definitely the version to pick up for debugging and for your own perusal.

The minified version is about 50 KB. With all extra characters removed from the source, the code is impractical, if not impossible, to read for humans. However, it works just fine for computers. (At the end of the day, JavaScript minification is also a form of obfuscation.) Once GZIPped, the minified version of the library is only 15 KB and takes only a few moments to download.

> **Note** If you are not able to use GZIP for downloading, you might want to consider the *packed* version of jQuery, which is about 30 KB in size. The packed version, though, requires more initialization time on the client. The packed version consists of the *eval()* of a string of code, where the public names of functions and common segments of text have been replaced with shorter strings that need to be restored before execution. The jQuery official site recommends you evaluate the packed version very carefully because it might have unexpected performance issues. In general, the best option is the minified version, possibly with GZIP to speed up downloading. Note, though, that some old versions of Internet Explorer may be unhappy with GZIP. See *http://support.microsoft.com/kb/823386* for more information.

Fundamental Traits

The whole set of jQuery functionality can be divided into four main areas: DOM query and manipulation, visual effects and animation, AJAX, and core functions to work with arrays, filter data, and detect browser capabilities.

A separate leg of the jQuery library is *jQuery UI*—a library of visual components and widgets. The project home page is located at *http://ui.jquery.com*. All the widgets form a comprehensive library to install separately from the core library. It's possible to use components individually, but you might need to download other widgets because of dependencies. To smooth the whole process, the jQuery UI site supplies a builder component that assembles the proper JavaScript file for your own needs.

The jQuery library is extensible through the mechanism of plug-ins. A jQuery plug-in consists of a bunch of new methods and functionality grouped in a new file. A plug-in is not like a new class; it has more to do with adding methods to the prototype of the jQuery root object. As a result, adding new capabilities is as easy as writing a few new JavaScript functions. Once you create a plug-in, using the newly added plug-in functionality is as easy as using a built-in jQuery method.

Extensibility and chainability are two fundamental traits of jQuery, and they are probably the key to its wide and growing adoption.

Using the Library in Visual Studio 2008

As mentioned, Microsoft is now committed to fully supporting jQuery. As we await the next major release of the .NET Framework, the first step that demonstrates Microsoft's commitment to jQuery is the release of the documentation file created to enable IntelliSense when the jQuery library is used within an ASP.NET project.

From *http://docs.jquery.com/Downloading_jQuery*, you can download the file *jquery-1.3.vsdoc.js* and enable IntelliSense within Visual Studio 2008. You also need a Visual Studio 2008 Service Pack 1 patch (as described in Knowledge Base article 958502) for the documentation file to be correctly processed, as shown in Figure 5-1.

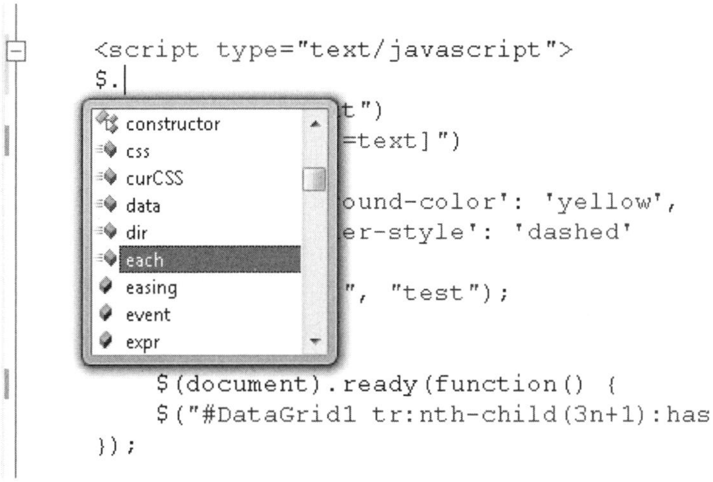

FIGURE 5-1 IntelliSense in action on jQuery objects within Visual Studio 2008

In ASP.NET, you can either use a plain *<script>* tag to link the library or you can list it in the *Scripts* section of the *ScriptManager* control, as shown here:

```
<asp:ScriptManager id="ScriptManager1" runat="server">
    <Scripts>
        <asp:ScriptReference path="jquery-1.3.min.js" />
    </Scripts>
</asp:ScriptManager>
```

Obviously, you don't need to deploy the Visual Studio documentation file to the server. The file must simply be available in your Visual Studio 2008 project and, if the aforementioned patch is installed, Visual Studio 2008 will automatically check and consume the documentation file.

> **Note** The Visual Studio 2008 SP1 patch for the script documentation file is not specifically intended for the jQuery library, but it's valid for all JavaScript files. Visual Studio 2008 SP1 looks for documentation files related to any script file. In particular, Visual Studio searches for *xxx-vsdoc.js* in the same folder that contains the *xxx* script file. If the *vsdoc* file is not found, Visual Studio searches for an *xxx.debug.js* file, and finally it looks for the *xxx.js* file. If you already have a fully documented debug script file, there's no strict need for you to create a *vsdoc* file.

The Core Library

The word *query* in the library's name says it all—the jQuery library is primarily designed for running (clever) queries over the DOM. The library supplies a powerful interface to select DOM elements that goes far beyond the simple search for all elements that match a given ID. For example, you can easily select all elements that share a given CSS class, have certain attributes, or appear in a given position in the tree. More importantly, you can chain multiple clauses together and prepare complex queries.

The $ Function

The root of the jQuery library is the *jQuery* function. The function is defined as an extension to the browser's *window* object and is aliased with the popular *$* function. Here's the function definition as it comes from the source:

```
var jQuery = window.jQuery = window.$ = function( selector, context )
{
    return new jQuery.fn.init( selector, context );
};
```

Every time you reference the *jQuery* or *$* function, you end up creating a new function that accepts two parameters—a selector and a context. The selector indicates the query expression to run over the DOM; the context indicates the portion of the DOM from which to run the query. If no context is specified, the *jQuery* function looks for DOM elements within the entire page DOM.

> **Note** In the definition of the *jQuery* object, you can recognize an instance of the Builder design pattern. The pattern recommends separating the construction of a complex object from its representation. You use an internal helper object as the builder and isolate in that helper all the required building logic. In this way, the constructor focuses on the expected behavior to provide the internal implementation and logic. The *init* function is the builder of the *jQuery* object.

From the preceding definition, four initialization options are available for you to use:

```
jQuery( expression, [context] )
jQuery( html, [ownerDocument] )
jQuery( elements )
jQuery( callback )
```

The first option takes a selector string and returns an array of matching HTML elements. The second one accepts an HTML string, creates the related subtree, and appends it to the specified owner documents, if any. The third overload picks up the specified DOM element or elements. Finally, the fourth option just takes a callback function and runs it on the entire document as soon as the page's document is fully loaded.

The return value you get can be a single DOM element, including the whole document or, more often, a new *jQuery* object.

Wrapped Sets

The *jQuery* object incorporates an initially empty JavaScript array. When the *jQuery* object is returned from a query, the array is packed with references to selected DOM elements. For this reason, any returned *jQuery* object is often referred to as a *wrapped set*.

A wrapped set is never null, even though no matching elements have been found. You check the actual size of the wrapped set by looking at the *length* property of the *jQuery* object, as shown here:

```
// All IMG tags in the page
var wrappedSet = new jQuery("img");
if (wrappedSet.length == 0)
    alert("No IMG tags found.");
else
{
    // The String.format function comes from the Microsoft AJAX library
    alert(String.format("{0} IMG tags found.", wrappedSet.length));
}
```

The *wrapped set* is not a special data container; rather, it's a jQuery-specific term to indicate the results of a query. However, once you hold all the elements you were looking for, you need to process them. To start off, let's see which methods are available on the root *$* function.

Helper Methods of the *$* Function

The root *jQuery* object is augmented with a bunch of helper methods that perform some common tasks, such as enumerating the content of the wrapped set. Helper methods are listed in Table 5-2.

TABLE 5-2 Helper Methods on the *jQuery* Object

Method	Description
each(callback)	This method loops over the entire list of DOM elements in the wrapped set and executes the specified JavaScript callback.
length	This method gets the number of DOM elements contained in the wrapped set.
eq(position)	This method gets rid of all elements in the wrapped set except the one at the specified position. The index of the sole element to preserve ranges from 0 to *length*–1. After the method, property *length* equals 1.
get()	This method extracts the wrapped set from the *jQuery* object and returns it as a JavaScript array of DOM elements.
get(index)	This method returns the DOM element found at the specified 0-based position in the wrapped set.
	This method is provided for compatibility reasons. It sort of violates the rule of chainability of jQuery because it returns a DOM object rather than a jQuery object. It isn't possible to continue another jQuery chain given a DOM object.
index(element)	This method loops over the wrapped set looking for the specified DOM element. If a match is found, the current 0-based index is returned. The method returns –1 if the object wasn't found.

These methods form only the core set of jQuery accessors. Many more operations are available on wrapped sets, and many others can be added through plug-ins. I'll return to the topic of operations that are possible on a wrapped set later in the chapter, right after discussing the syntax used to arrange queries.

jQuery Selectors

In the jQuery library, a *selector* is an expression used to select DOM elements to return. In a way, the selector is the jQuery counterpart of an SQL statement used to select rows from a database table.

The selector expression is driven by the CSS 3.0 syntax and can reach a nontrivial level of complexity. In addition to basic CSS selectors, the library features a few predefined selectors named *filters*.

CSS Selectors

Table 5-3 lists the CSS selectors supported by the *jQuery* object.

TABLE 5-3 Supported jQuery Selectors

Selector	Description
#id	Returns the first element in the DOM with a matching ID. An empty wrapped set is returned otherwise. Periods and colons in the ID must be escaped with a backslash.
element	Returns all DOM elements with a matching tag name.
.class	Returns all DOM elements with a matching CSS class.

TABLE 5-3 Supported jQuery Selectors

Selector	Description
*	Returns all DOM elements in the page.
selector1, ..., selectorN	Applies all given basic selectors, and returns the combined results. A selector can be any of the preceding selectors.
ancestor descendant	Given an ancestor selector, returns the collection of all descendant elements that match the descendant selector. For example, *"div p"* returns all *<p>* elements within a *<div>*.
parent > child	Given a selector, returns the collection of all child elements that match the child selector.
previous + next	Given a selector, returns the collection of all sibling elements that match the *next* selector and are located next to the *previous* selector.
previous ~ sibling	Given a selector, returns the collection of all sibling elements that match the sibling selector and follow the *previous* selector.

To retrieve a DOM element by ID, you need the following code:

```
var domElement = $("#DataGrid1");
```

The # symbol doesn't belong to the ID string. It's just a prefix for the *$* function to disambiguate ID strings, CSS classes, and HTML tag names. The # symbol comes from the CSS 3.0 syntax.

The preceding code snippet is functionally equivalent to the following standard DOM statement:

```
var domElement = document.getElementById("DataGrid1");
```

The similarity between classic DOM methods and the *$* function ends here. The *$* function is much more powerful because it returns a wrapped set for you to perform further operations.

Note The HTML DOM standard allows you to have multiple elements named in the same way. If multiple elements match the ID, the method *getElementById* returns only the first match. On the other hand, the *getElementsByName* method returns the entire collection. In jQuery, you don't have a direct counterpart to *getElementsByName*, even though you can easily simulate that by using an attribute filter.

CSS Selectors in Action

It's worth showing some quick examples of selectors, such as those listed in Table 5-3.

The following selector selects all *<input>* elements in the current *<form>*:

```
form input
```

You can also select all *<input>* elements within a particular form by switching to the following syntax. In this case, *Form1* is the ID of the form you want to search within:

```
#Form1 input
```

Given a selector, such as *input*, you can further restrict the query to all such elements having a given CSS class—say, *MyTextBox*:

```
input.MyTextBox
```

Things can be even more sophisticated, such as when you want to get all *<span>* elements whose CSS class is *appHeader* located within any *<div>* in the page:

```
div span.appHeader
```

The search can be limited to child or sibling elements. Let's consider the following:

```
h2 + p
```

The query returns all *<p>* elements that are next to an *<h2>* element. Being *next* to an element means sharing the same parent and coming immediately after the element. As an example, consider the following markup:

```
<p id="Header">Samples</p>
<h2>Welcome</h2>
<p id="First">Hello</p>
<p id="Second">Dino</p>
```

Only the *<p>* named *First* is selected with an *h2+p* selector because it's the only one next to an *<h2>* element and sibling.

Filters

Selectors can be further refined by applying filters on position, content, attributes, and visibility. A filter is a sort of built-in function applied to the wrapped set returned by a basic selector. Table 5-4 lists positional filters in jQuery.

TABLE 5-4 Positional Filters

Positional Filters	Description
:first	Returns the first DOM element that matches
:last	Returns the last DOM element that matches
:not(selector)	Returns all DOM elements that do not match the specified selector
:even	Returns all DOM elements that occupy an even position in a 0-based indexing
:odd	Returns all DOM elements that occupy an odd position in a 0-based indexing
:eq(index)	Returns the DOM element in the wrapped set that occupies the specified 0-based position
:gt(index)	Returns all DOM elements that occupy a position in a 0-based indexing greater than the specified index
:lt(index)	Returns all DOM elements that occupy a position in a 0-based indexing less than the specified index

TABLE 5-4 Positional Filters

Positional Filters	Description
:header()	Returns all DOM elements that are headers, such as H1, H2, and the like
:animated()	Returns all DOM elements that are currently being animated via some functions in the jQuery library

What's the difference between the *get(index)* we met in Table 5-2 and the *eq(index)* we just found in Table 5-4? The definition is nearly the same, but the role is radically different. The *get(index)* is a function on the *jQuery* object and applies to a wrapped set; the *eq(index)* is a filter and applies to a selector. Let's consider the two statements shown next:

```
// Both queries select the first DIV with a CSS class different from infoPanel
var elem1 = $("div:not(.infoPanel):eq(0)");    // returns a jQuery object
var elem2 = $("div:not(.infoPanel)).get(0);    // returns a DOM element
```

The variable *elem1* is a *jQuery* object. The variable *elem2* is a plain DOM element; in particular, it's a reference to a *<div>* element.

Table 5-5 lists all supported filters through which you can select elements that are children of a parent element.

TABLE 5-5 Child Filters

Child Filters	Description
:nth-child(expression)	Returns all child elements of any parent that match the given expression. The expression can be an index or a math sequence (for example, 3n+1), including standard sequences such as odd and even.
:first:child	Returns all elements that are the first child of their parent.
:last-child	Returns all elements that are the last child of their parent.
:only-child	Returns all elements that are the only child of their parent.

A particularly powerful filter is *nth-child*. It supports a number of different input expressions, as shown here:

```
:nth-child(index)
:nth-child(even)
:nth-child(odd)
:nth-child(sequence)
```

The first format selects the *n*.th child of all HTML elements in the source selector. All child elements placed at any odd or even position in a 0-based indexing are returned if you specify the *odd* or *even* filter instead.

Finally, you can pass the *nth-child* filter a mathematical sequence such as *3n* to indicate all elements in a position that are a multiple of 3. The following selector picks up all rows in a table (labeled *Table1*) that are on the positions determined by the sequence 3n+1—that is, 1, 4, 7, and so forth:

```
#Table1 tr:nth-child(3n+1)
```

Table 5-6 lists expressions to filter elements by content.

TABLE 5-6 Content Filters

Content Filters	Description
:contains(text)	Returns all elements that contain the specified text
:empty	Returns all elements with no children
:has(selector)	Returns all elements that contain at least one element that matches the given selector
:parent	Returns all elements that have at least one child

As far as content filters are concerned, you should note that any text in an HTML element is considered a child node. So elements selected by the :empty filter have no child nodes and no text as well, like <br/>.

A popular and powerful category of filters are attribute filters. Attribute filters allow you to select HTML elements where a given attribute is in a given relationship with a value. Table 5-7 lists all attribute filters supported in jQuery.

TABLE 5-7 Attribute Filters

Attribute Filters	Description
[attribute]	Returns all elements that have the specified attribute. This filter selects the element regardless of the attribute's value.
[attribute = value]	Returns all elements where the specified attribute (if present) is set to the specified value.
[attribute != value]	Returns all elements whose specified attribute (if present) has a value different from the given one.
[attribute ^= value]	Returns all elements whose specified attribute (if present) has content that starts with the given value.
[attribute $= value]	Returns all elements whose specified attribute (if present) has content that ends with the given value.
[attribute *= value]	Returns all elements whose specified attribute (if present) has content that contains the given value.

Attribute filters can also be concatenated by simply placing two or more of them side by side, as in the following example:

```
var elems = $("td[align=right][valign=top]");
```

The returned set includes all <td> elements where the horizontal alignment is right and the vertical alignment is top.

The next expression, which is much more sophisticated, demonstrates the power and flexibility of jQuery selectors, as it combines quite a few of them:

```
#Table1 tr:nth-child(3n+1):has(td[align=right]) td:odd
```

It reads as follows:

> *Within the body of element* Table1, *select all <tr> elements at positions 1, 4, 7, and so forth. Next, you keep only table rows where a <td> element exists with the attribute* align *equal to the value of* right. *Furthermore, of the remaining rows you take only the cells on columns with an odd index.*

The result is a wrapped set made of *<td>* elements. Let's consider the following HTML table and apply the preceding selector to it:

```
<table id="Table1" border="1">
    <tr>
        <td></td>
        <td>Country</td>
        <td>Capital</td></tr>
    <tr>
        <td>1</td>
        <td>Norway</td>
        <td align="right">Oslo</td></tr>
    <tr>
        <td>2</td>
        <td>Italy</td>
        <td align="right">Rome</td></tr>
    <tr>
        <td>3</td>
        <td>Spain</td>
        <td align="right">Madrid</td></tr>
    <tr>
        <td>4</td>
        <td>UK</td>
        <td>London</td></tr>
    <tr>
        <td>5</td>
        <td>France</td>
        <td>Paris</td></tr>
    <tr>
        <td>6</td>
        <td>Greece</td>
        <td>Athens</td></tr>
    <tr>
        <td>7</td>
        <td>Belgium</td>
        <td>Brussels</td></tr>
</table>
```

Only the fourth row (including the header) matches both the *:nth-child* and *:has* filters. Of the three cells, only the one in the middle has an even index in a 0-based indexing. In Figure 5-2, you see the output that results, with some extra CSS styling applied to the wrapped set:

```
<script type="text/javascript">
  $("#Table1 tr:nth-child(3n+1):has(td[align=right]) td:odd")
   .css("background", "yellow");
</script>
```

	Country	Capital
1	Norway	Oslo
2	Italy	Rome
3	Spain	Madrid
4	UK	London
5	France	Paris
6	Greece	Athens
7	Belgium	Brussels

FIGURE 5-2 Only matching table cells have their background color turned to yellow.

Finally, a couple more filters exist that are related to the visibility of elements. The *:visible* filter returns all elements that are currently visible. The *:hidden* filter returns all elements that are currently hidden from view. The wrapped set also includes all input elements of type *hidden*.

Form Filters

A special family of filters exists for HTML input elements. Table 5-8 lists all of them.

TABLE 5-8 Form Filters

Form Filters	Description
:input	Returns all elements that have a role in collecting input data
:text	Returns all input elements whose *type* attribute is *text*
:password	Returns all input elements whose *type* attribute is *password*
:checkbox	Returns all input elements whose *type* attribute is *checkbox*
:radio	Returns all input elements whose *type* attribute is *radio*
:submit	Returns all input elements whose *type* attribute is *submit*
:reset	Returns all input elements whose *type* attribute is *reset*
:image	Returns all input elements whose *type* attribute is *image*
:button	Returns all input elements whose *type* attribute is *button*
:file	Returns all input elements whose *type* attribute is *file*
:hidden	Returns all input elements whose *type* attribute is *hidden*
:enabled	Returns all input elements that are currently enabled
:disabled	Returns all input elements that are currently disabled
:checked	Returns all input elements that are currently checked
:selected	Returns all input elements that are currently selected

The *:input* filter, in particular, refers to all logical input elements you might find within a page form and is not limited solely to the *<input>* elements. In fact, it also picks up *<textarea>* and *<select>* elements used to display multiline text boxes and lists. The filters in Table 5-8 provide handy shortcuts for selecting homogeneous elements and are functionally equivalent to the other legal jQuery selectors. For example, *:checkbox* is equivalent to the following:

```
form input[type=checkbox]
```

Other nice helpers are available to grab all input elements in a page form that are currently enabled or disabled and all check boxes and radio buttons currently selected.

Working on Wrapped Sets

The jQuery library is great at selecting DOM elements that match a given expression. But how would you process elements? The simplest possible approach entails that you set up a loop and run a function over each item in the wrapped set:

```
var expression = "...";
var wrappedSet = $(expression);
for(i = 0; i< wrappedSet.length; i++)
{
    processElement(wrappedSet.get(i));
}
function processElement(domElement)
{
    :
}
```

In such a manual iteration, you access DOM elements directly, as usual in classic JavaScript programming. The jQuery library, though, offers a couple of alternate routes that are functionally equivalent to manual iteration. And, nicely enough, they also result in more compact and even more readable code.

Looping over Wrapped Sets

To loop over a wrapped set, the first option to consider is the *each* method. (See Table 5-2.) Here's a code snippet that shows the method in action that turns the foreground color of all *<input>* tags in a form to blue, plus some other work on background color and border style:

```
$("form input").each(
    function(i) {
        // this is already mapped to the element being processed
        this.style.color = "blue";
        this.style.background-color = "yellow";
        this.style.border-style = "dashed";
    }
);
```

The difference between *each* and a manual JavaScript loop lies in the fact that the function *each* automatically maps the *this* object to the element being processed. The callback function, however, received an integer parameter that is the 0-based index of the iteration—the "i" in *function(i)*.

The jQuery *each* function executes a user-defined callback on any element associated with the wrapped set. This is definitely the option to choose whenever you have custom code to run on each selected element.

Some Predefined Operations

A fairly large number of operational methods exist to make it even quicker and easier for you to execute common operations on the content of the wrapped set. The predefined operations belong to four functional groups: to traverse the DOM, manipulate the DOM, work with attributes, and work with CSS.

The list of individual operations is fairly long and variegated and deserves a book of its own. In this book, I'll briefly skim through some of the operations to give you an idea of the power of jQuery. For more details, you can either refer to the online documentation at *http://docs.jquery.com* or pick up a book such as *jQuery in Action*, by Bear Bibeault, Yehuda Katz, and John Resig (Manning Publications, 2008).

For example, you can use the *css* function to apply some CSS settings to the wrapped set. Here's an example that rewrites the previous example using the *css* function:

```
$("form input").css(
    {'color' : 'blue',
     'background-color' : 'yellow',
     'border-style' : 'dashed'}
);
```

Likewise, you can add, remove, and even toggle a CSS class on the elements in the wrapped set. You do this via the *addClass*, *removeClass*, and *toggleClass* functions.

The *attr* function, on the other hand, allows you to set one or multiple attributes on all elements in a wrapped set. For example, here's how to disable all input elements in a single shot:

```
$("form input").attr(
    {'disabled' : 'disabled'}
);
```

The *html* function sets the HTML content of a given element. The *html* function uses the *innerHTML* property internally. To set the inner text of an element, instead, you use the *text* function and pass the text to set as the argument.

> **Note** This is a good place to comment on the benefits of having a cross-browser library. Although it's not part of the standard DOM, the property *innerHTML* is supported by all browsers and works anywhere in the same way. The same can't be said for the analogous property that only sets the text. This property is *innerText* in Internet Explorer and, for instance, *textElement* in Firefox. The *text* function hides differences and provides the same functionality across all browsers.

You also have a method to wrap each matched element with the specified HTML content (the *wrap* method) and a method to replace all matched elements with the specified HTML or DOM elements (the *replaceWith* method).

Chaining Methods

As mentioned, almost every method within the library returns the query object itself. This allows for building chains of calls. In this way, you express the desired behavior with just one line of code. Consider the following:

```
$("a").addClass("Hyperlink").attr(alt, "Click me").show();
```

All individual methods return the *jQuery* object, thus making it possible for you to execute a new operation on the resulting wrapped set. Each new operation generates a new wrapped set, and so forth.

Among the set of predefined operations, there are some that let you add or remove elements from the selection. For example, the following code first selects all *<span>* elements and then adds all *<p>* elements. The final wrapped set is styled using the *css* function:

```
$("span").add("p").css( ... );
```

Likewise, you can remove all elements from the wrapped set that do not match a specified function:

```
// Get all <span> and <p>, style them, and then remove those
// that don't match the function
$("span").add("p").css( ... ).filter(
   function(index) {
      // Must return a Boolean
      return this.attr("width") > 300;
   }
);
```

There's no limit to the chains of methods you can create. You will find this provides for maximum flexibility and expressivity.

jQuery Utilities

Among the countless methods available on jQuery objects, I'd like to select and further discuss a few more that fall into popular functional areas, such as visual effects, AJAX, caching, and events. Let's start with event handling and manipulation.

Event Handling

As discussed in Chapter 4, normalizing event handling to a cross-browser API is a necessary but nontrivial task for any serious JavaScript library. The jQuery library is no exception.

The event-handling API is organized into two groups of functions: general event functions plus a long list of helpers. General functions provide the foundation for helpers to work; helpers do the magic of making jQuery programming easy and effective.

Table 5-9 lists basic functions to binding and unbinding handlers to HTML element events.

TABLE 5-9 Core Event-Handling API

Function	Description
bind	Binds a handler to one or more events for each element in the wrapped set
one	Binds a handler to one or more events to be executed once for each element in the wrapped set
trigger	Triggers a given event for each element in the wrapped set
triggerHandler	Triggers all bound handlers on an element for a specific event, and cancels the default browser actions
unbind	Removes bound events from each element in the wrapped set

The *bind* function attaches a handler to a given event on all elements in a wrapped set. Here's a brief example that attaches a handler to the *click* event of a button. The handler simply changes the button's caption once it is clicked:

```
$("#btnProcess").bind("click",
    function(e) {
      $("#btnProcess").text("Processing ... ");
    }
);
```

The complete signature of the *bind* method is shown here:

```
bind(eventName, eventData, eventHandler)
```

The event name is a string that contains the name of the event (or events) to bind. You can register the same handler for multiple events by simply separating event names with a blank space. The following example toggles a CSS style when the mouse enters or leaves an input button:

```
$("input[type=button]").bind("mouseenter mouseleave",
    function(e) {
        $(this).toggleClass("hovered");
    }
);
```

The second argument of *bind*—the event arguments—is optional. If specified, it indicates user-defined data to be passed to the handler:

```
$("#btnProcess").bind("click", {newText: "Processing..."}, handler)
```

The handler then retrieves this data through the *data* property of the function's argument:

```
function handler(e)
{
    $("#btnProcess").text(e.data.newText");
}
```

Each event handler receives an object with a few predefined properties, as described in Table 5-10.

TABLE 5-10 **Properties of the Event Object**

Property	Description
type	Gets the name of the event, such as "click".
target	Gets a reference to the DOM element that issued the event. It can be the same element that registered the handler or one of its children.
pageX	Gets the *x* mouse coordinate relative to the document.
pageY	Gets the *y* mouse coordinate relative to the document.

The event object also features a couple of methods: *preventDefault* and *stopPropagation*. The *preventDefault* method cancels the default action the browser would take after the event. It doesn't stop, though, the bubbling of the event through the object's stack. The method *stopPropagation* stops the bubbling but doesn't prevent the browser's action. To do both things, you need not call any of these methods; you just return *false* from the event handler.

Any handlers attached through the *bind* method can be detached using the *unbind* method. The method takes two optional parameters: the names of the event and handler. If none is specified, all handlers are removed from all elements in the wrapped set. By specifying parameters, you can unbind all handlers from certain events and only certain handlers for certain events.

The *one* method is similar to *bind* except that it runs any bound handlers only once and removes them all after that.

Finally, the *trigger* method causes the library to invoke any handlers registered with the specified event. The following shows how to programmatically trigger a *click* event on a button:

```
$("#btnProcess").trigger("click");
```

The *triggerHandler* function differs from *trigger* in two respects: it prevents the browser's default action, and it affects only one element in the wrapped set. If the wrapped set contains multiple matching elements, only the first has handlers triggered for the specified event:

```
// No browser-led focus on the first <input> tag in the page
$("input").triggerHandler("focus");
```

Before we look at event helpers built using the core eventing API, let's look at three special event functions that are commonly used: *ready*, *hover*, and *toggle*.

The *ready* function takes a function and runs it when the document is ready to be traversed and manipulated. The *hover* function accepts two handlers. The first is run when the mouse hovers over an element in the wrapped set. The second runs when the mouse leaves the element's area. The *toggle* function performs an even smarter task: it takes two or more handlers and runs them alternately as the user clicks. In other words, the first click on a matching element runs the first handler, the second click runs the second handler, and so on. When the bottom of the handler list is reached, all subsequent clicks run back from the first function in the list.

Table 5-11 shows some helpers built to make it easier for you to bind handlers to commonly used DOM events.

TABLE 5-11 Event Helpers

Helper	Description
blur blur(fn)	Triggers the *blur* event on the wrapped set. If a function is specified, it binds that to the *blur* event of matching elements.
change change(fn)	Triggers the *change* event on the wrapped set. If a function is specified, it binds that to the *change* event of matching elements.
click click(fn)	Triggers the *click* event on the wrapped set. If a function is specified, it binds that to the *click* event of matching elements.
dblclick dblclick(fn)	Triggers the *dblclick* event on the wrapped set. If a function is specified, it binds that to the *dblclick* event of matching elements.
error error(fn)	Triggers the *error* event on the wrapped set. If a function is specified, it binds that to the *error* event of matching elements.
focus focus(fn)	Triggers the *focus* event on the wrapped set. If a function is specified, it binds that to the *focus* event of matching elements.
keydown keydown(fn)	Triggers the *keydown* event on the wrapped set. If a function is specified, it binds that to the *keydown* event of matching elements.
keypress keypress(fn)	Triggers the *keypress* event on the wrapped set. If a function is specified, it binds that to the *keypress* event of matching elements.
keyup keyup(fn)	Triggers the *keyup* event on the wrapped set. If a function is specified, it binds that to the *keyup* event of matching elements.
load(fn)	Binds a function to the *load* event of matching elements in the wrapped set.
mousedown(fn)	Binds a function to the *mousedown* event of matching elements in the wrapped set.
mousemove(fn)	Binds a function to the *mousemove* event of matching elements in the wrapped set.
mouseout(fn)	Binds a function to the *mouseout* event of matching elements in the wrapped set.
mouseover(fn)	Binds a function to the *mouseover* event of matching elements in the wrapped set.
mouseup(fn)	Binds a function to the *mouseup* event of matching elements in the wrapped set.
resize(fn)	Binds a function to the *resize* event of matching elements in the wrapped set.
scroll(fn)	Binds a function to the *scroll* event of matching elements in the wrapped set.
select select(fn)	Triggers the *select* event on the wrapped set. If a function is specified, it binds that to the *select* event of matching elements.
submit submit(fn)	Triggers the *submit* event on the wrapped set. If a function is specified, it binds that to the *submit* event of matching elements.
unload(fn)	Binds a function to the *unload* event of matching elements in the wrapped set.

Helpers come in two forms: with and without a parameter. The parameter, if any, is a function to execute when the event is fired. If no parameter is specified, the method triggers the given event on any element in the wrapped set. For example, the following code registers a *click* event for a given button. The binding executes as soon as the document is fully loaded and ready to be manipulated programmatically.

```
$(document).ready( function() {
    $("#btnProcess").click(
        function(e) {
            $("#btnProcess").text("Processing ... ");
        }
    );
});
```

The internal implementation of events in the jQuery library is largely based on the standard DOM model. The helpers listed in Table 5-11 all refer to standard DOM events.

Visual Effects

One of the renowned characteristics of the jQuery library is its set of visual effects. The library defines a few effects out of the box, plus a simple but effective engine for custom animations.

Predefined effects act on the visibility, height, and opacity of elements in the wrapped set. Table 5-12 lists available effects.

TABLE 5-12 Predefined Visual Effects

Function	Category	Description
show	*Visibility*	Turns on the visibility of any elements in the wrapped set.
hide	*Visibility*	Turns off the visibility of any elements in the wrapped set.
toggle	*Visibility*	Toggles the visibility of any elements in the wrapped set.
slideDown	*Sliding*	Displays any matching elements by adjusting their height so that the display happens by revealing the element progressively.
slideUp	*Sliding*	Hides any matching elements using the same algorithm as the *slideDown* function.
slideToggle	*Sliding*	Slides all matching elements down or up, inverting the current setting.
fadeIn	*Fading*	Displays any matching elements by adjusting their opacity so that the display happens to fade in the element.
fadeOut	*Fading*	Hides any matching elements using the same algorithm as the *fadeIn* function.
fadeTo	*Fading*	Fades the opacity of all matching elements to a specified value.

Visual effects are obtained by modifying the values contained within certain CSS attributes: *display* for visibility, *height* for sliding, and *opacity* for fading.

Visibility functions come in two forms. A parameterless signature just shows, hides, or toggles elements immediately. You can employ a graceful animation that shows, hides, or toggles elements in a given timeframe and also fires an optional callback after completion. Here's an example:

```
$("btnOrdersInfo").click(
    function(e) {
        $("panelOrders").show(2000);
    }
);
```

In the code snippet, the panel with order information takes two seconds to appear (with free animation) and no function is run on completion. The duration of the animation can be set explicitly by passing the actual number of milliseconds or implicitly by passing any of the following predefined values: *normal*, *slow*, or *fast*.

Sliding and fading effects always require a speed argument—either a number of milliseconds or a predefined modality, as shown in the preceding example. The following code fades out the content of the order panel in one second, and then it loads fresh data synchronously from the server. When ready, it fades in the panel, and when it is done it changes the style of the panel.

```
$("btnOrdersInfo").click(
    function(e) {
        $("panelOrders").fadeOut(1000);
        populateOrderPanel();
        $("#panelOrders").fadeIn(2000,
            function() {
                $("#panelOrders").css(...);
            }
        );
    }
);
```

The heart of jQuery animations is the *animate* function. The function receives an array of property/value assignments where the property refers to a CSS attribute. The function simply animates the CSS property of each matching element from its current value to the specified value. Here's an example:

```
$("#Panel1").animate(
    { width: "70%",
      opacity: 0.4,
      borderWidth: "10px"
    },
    2000);
```

At the end of the animation, the *Panel1* element will have the specified width, opacity, and border width. The animation will take two seconds to complete. CSS properties must be specified using camelCase (that is, the first character is lowercase and first character of each following word is uppercase). For example, you should use *borderWidth* instead of *border-width*.

Note that you can also do relative animations, such as increasing (or decreasing) a property value by a percentage or by a fixed value, as shown here:

```
$("#Panel1").animate(
    { width: "-=70%",
      opacity: "+=0.4"
    },
    2000);
```

By default, all animations in jQuery are automatically queued and execute in an orderly manner, one after another. This is a necessary precondition to be able to chain multiple calls to animate and other animation functions. Let's consider the following example:

```
$("#div1").animate({ width: "90%" }, 5000 });
$("#div1").animate({ fontSize: '10em' }, 1000);
$("#div1").animate({ borderWidth: 5 }, 1000);
```

You have an animation made of three steps. They are automatically queued and execute sequentially. To gain some parallelism—if this is what you want—do as follows. Add a *queue: false* flag in the options of the *animate()* call you want to run immediately without queuing. Let's consider the following rewrite of the previous example:

```
$("#div1").animate({ width: "90%" }, {queue:false, duration:5000 });
$("#div1").animate({ fontSize: '10em' }, 1000);
$("#div1").animate({ borderWidth: 5 }, 1000);
```

The net effect is that the first two animations start together and the third won't begin until the font size has reached the expected value.

AJAX Functions

AJAX support in jQuery is centered around an abstraction of the browser's *XMLHttpRequest* object and counts on a bunch of helper functions. To compose and control all aspects of your Web request, you use the *ajax* function, as shown next:

```
$.ajax(
  {
    type: "POST",
    url: "getOrder.aspx",
    data: "id=1234&year=2007",
    success: function(response) {
      alert( response );
    }
  }
);
```

The *ajax* function gets a list of parameters, such as *type*, *url*, *data*, *dataType*, *cache*, *async*, and *success*. The *dataType* parameter indicates the type of the expected response, whereas *success* indicates the completion callback. The callback function receives the URL response as its sole argument.

In addition, a number of helpers exist to simplify common operations such as downloading a script. The following code shows how to load a script file. The script is automatically executed upon loading:

```
$.getScript("sample.js");
```

The load function is another very useful piece of code. It downloads markup and automatically injects it in the current DOM. The following code shows how to populate a menu programmatically:

```
// The content of the URL is attached to the specified section of the DOM
$("#menu").load("menu.aspx");
```

Finally, you have *get*, *post*, and *getJSON* functions to use GET and POST verbs and get some JSON content from a URL.

Caching

A client-side cache is essential to writing nontrivial JavaScript code to run within the browser. In this context, a cache doesn't refer to some sort of persistent storage; more simply, it's a data container where developers can store data that relates to a given DOM element. Here's an example:

```
var url = "...";
var response = $.get(url);
$("#grid").data("Markup", response);
```

The response of the URL is cached in a slot named *Markup* and associated with the local cache of the DOM element named *grid*. To read back the content of the store, you use the *data* function with just one argument—the name of the element:

```
alert($("#grid").data("Markup"));
```

Elements added to the cache can be removed by using the *removeData* function. The jQuery caching API is particularly helpful in the implementation of the Predictive Fetch AJAX pattern that we'll consider in Chapter 7, "Client-Side Data Binding." The UI leg of the jQuery library (more on this in a moment) also extensively uses the *data* function.

jQuery Plug-ins

A significant share of the jQuery capabilities we just examined has been developed as plug-ins on top of the root *jQuery* object. A plug-in is a jQuery mechanism for adding new functions to the library. A repository of community-developed plug-ins exists that contains a few hundred ready-to-use components. Check it out at *http://plugins.jquery.com*.

Using a plug-in is as easy as using a built-in jQuery function and, as mentioned, many of the features we considered (for example, animation) are built as plug-ins. Writing a plug-in involves nothing more than writing a bunch of public functions to extend the *jQuery* object. Here's an example:

```
jQuery.fn.traceWrappedSet = function() {
  var buffer = "";
  this.each(function() {
    buffer += this;
    buffer += "\n";
  });
  return buffer;
};
```

The function loops through the content of the wrapped set and traces out the type of the object selected. Clearly, this function returns a string, not a further chainable *jQuery* object. To use this new function, you do as follows:

```
$(document).ready(
    function() {
        var x = $("button").traceWrappedSet();
        alert(x);
    }
);
```

Admittedly, this example is not all that useful because it just outputs a vague string—*Object*—for each element in the wrapped set. However, making the trace function smarter—and subsequently more useful—is not a huge task and only requires looping over the prototype of each object or linking in the Microsoft AJAX library. The purpose of this section, though, is limited to showing *what* it takes to extend the jQuery library.

There are a few guidelines to adhere to so as not to break compatibility and to make it easier to integrate with other jQuery code.

First you need to distinguish between jQuery methods and jQuery functions. In jQuery, a method is a way to process the content of the wrapped set. A method should use *this.each* to iterate over the current wrapped set for promoting cleaner and more standard code. The method must return the *jQuery* object. If this is not the case (as in our example), it should be explicitly documented. Within the body of a method, *this* always references the current *jQuery* object.

A function is a piece of JavaScript code that performs an operation not specifically aimed at processing the content of a wrapped set.

Methods and functions both must end with a semicolon (;) so as not to break code during the process of minification. All new methods should be attached to the *jQuery.fn* object. All functions, on the other hand, should be directly attached to the *jQuery* object.

Inside of the plug-in code, you should always avoid using the *$* shorthand notation and use the *jQuery* object instead. This allows users to change the alias for *jQuery* in a single place. Finally, the convention is to name your plug-in file as *jquery.xxx.js*, where *xxx* is the name of your plug-in.

For more information and sample code, refer to *http://docs.jquery.com/Plugins/Authoring*.

The jQuery UI Framework

jQuery UI is the jQuery framework for the user interface. It features a set of visual controls as well as a wide range of plug-ins for increasing the interactivity of pages. The jQuery UI project is developed separately from the main core library. You can visit the project homepage at *http://ui.jquery.com* to get the source code and related demos.

The framework lists a number of core interaction plug-ins to add aspects to a set of matching elements. Aspects include special client-side capabilities such as draggability and resizability. The full list of interactions includes the following plug-ins: *draggable*, *droppable*, *resizable*, *selectable*, and *sortable*.

The *draggable* interaction makes elements in the set draggable by the mouse, whereas the *droppable* interaction transforms all elements in the wrapped set in drop targets. Similarly, *sortable* allows you to reorder a list of items via the mouse and *selectable* lets you select items in a list by clicking. Finally, the *resizable* interaction makes an element dynamically resizable.

Using such plug-ins couldn't be easier. All you have to do is define the wrapped set through selectors and then invoke the method, as shown here:

```
// The element can be resized dynamically
$("#grid").resizable();
```

If you apply the method to, say, a grid, you can resize only the surrounding table that defines the grid. It doesn't make columns resizable. However, by making smart use of the plug-in, you can code your way to getting a fully customizable grid.

All interactions have the same syntax made of four signatures. Here's the syntax for the *resizable* interaction:

```
resizable( options )
resizable( "disable" )
resizable( "enable" )
resizable( "destroy" )
```

The *options* argument consists of a set of assignments on a fixed set of properties that cover all UI plug-ins. For the *resizable* interaction, some interesting options are *handles* (where you drag to resize), *minWidth/minHeight* and *maxWidth/maxHeight* to delimit the range of resizability, and *aspectRatio* to specify whether the original ratio of the element must be preserved.

The other signatures simply refer to special actions such as enabling, disabling, or removing the interaction on the elements in the wrapped set.

In addition to interaction aspects, such as *draggable* and *resizable*, the jQuery UI has a number of widgets, including *Accordion*, *DatePicker*, *Dialog*, *Slider*, and *Tabs*. The *Accordion* widget represents a container of collapsible panels where only one can be visible at a time. You apply the method to a panel with child elements, as shown here:

```
<div id="Accordion1">
    <div>
        <h3>...</h3>
        <div>
            :
        </div>
    </div>
    :
</div>
```

Each item should contain two elements: *header* and *body*. To activate the accordion behavior, you use the following code:

```
$("#Accordion1").accordion();
```

Using jQuery UI is really easy. For example, to create a dialog box all you need to do is create a *<div>* to define the expected user interface. Next, you just invoke the *dialog* method, as shown here:

```
$("#DialogBox1").dialog();
```

All widgets depend on a few files. Typically, a widget depends on its own file plus some interaction plug-ins. For example, the *Dialog* widget depends on the *draggable* and *resizable* interactions because the resulting dialog box can be dragged around and resized at will. When using such a widget, you must reference all required script files in your pages.

You can check the *http://ui.jquery.com/download* Web site for the version of the library that is currently the most stable one available. When downloading, you can create your own package that contains only the components you need.

Summary

As emphatic as it might sound, knowing how to use JavaScript is a necessary skill today. However, you probably don't have to learn all the nitty-gritty details of the language to write good production code. This is because of the availability of powerful libraries such as jQuery.

jQuery delivers a number of benefits. In the first place, it makes JavaScript code easier and quicker to write. The library provides helper functions that dramatically increase your productivity while decreasing frustration. In addition, the resulting code is much easier to read (which greatly simplifies maintenance) and robust, because the higher level of abstraction hides a number of checks and error-handling procedures.

In a world of Web programming that is moving irreversibly toward client programming, jQuery is a broadly accepted and successful library. Centered around the idea of selectors and function chaining, the library allows you to write compact and cross-browser code. You can easily group HTML elements that match a condition and perform operations on them. Operations include DOM manipulation, styling, animation, plus advanced user interface operations.

Now that we know the tools to manipulate JavaScript more effectively, we can move ahead towards AJAX patterns. In the next chapter, we attack the patterns used to implement the most popular and requested features of Web applications—data binding and templating.

Chapter 6
AJAX Design Patterns

It is possible to fail in many ways, while to succeed is possible only in one way.

—Aristotle

AJAX is not a technology itself; it's all about how you, as an architect, use and combine a bunch of existing, and fairly stable and mature, Web technologies. AJAX tells you to employ *XMLHttpRequest* and the Document Object Model (DOM) in your site. AJAX suggests you opt for two-tier architecture with a JavaScript-based front end and a server-side façade of HTTP endpoints. However, AJAX doesn't really tell you how these technologies are used in the real world and how you should use them in your site. Quite the opposite, many times AJAX technical presentations are about what you *could* do rather than about what you *should* do and why.

As in general software design, if you're looking for guidance on the most applicable tested solutions to recurring problems, you need a set of simple design patterns. Because design patterns are essentially a package that includes a description of the problem, a list of participating actors, and a commonly accepted solution, it's not surprising that some of them are paradigm specific.

As we'll see in this chapter, some really general patterns—including Singleton, Factory, or perhaps Strategy—can be applied to AJAX applications as well as to any other type of application. In addition, the AJAX paradigm has its own set of design patterns inspired by the internal mechanics and peculiarities of AJAX applications.

Design Patterns and Code Development

The word *pattern* is one of those overloaded terms that morphed from its common usage to assume a very specific meaning in computer science. According to the dictionary, a pattern is a template or model that can be used to generate things—any number of things. In software, we use patterns in design solutions at two levels: implementation and architecture.

At the highest level, two main families of software patterns are recognized: design patterns and architectural patterns. You look at design patterns when you dive into the implementation and design of the code. You look at architectural patterns when you fly high looking for the overall design of the system. In AJAX, we are mostly interested in design patterns because there are not so many possible architectural patterns. There are two main architectural patterns, which we identified and discussed at length in Chapter 3, "AJAX Architectures": the AJAX Server Layer pattern and the Active Server Pages pattern.

Generalities About Design Patterns

A design pattern is a known and well-established core solution applicable to a family of concrete problems that might show up during implementation. A design pattern is a core solution and, as such, it might need adaptation to a specific context. This feature becomes a major strength when you consider that, due to their inherent flexibility, the same pattern can be applied many times in many slightly different scenarios.

Design patterns are not created in a lab; it's quite the opposite. They originate from the real world and from the direct experience of developers and architects. You can think of a design pattern as a package that includes the description of a problem, a list of actors participating in the problem, and a practical solution.

The primary reference for design patterns is the book *Design Patterns: Elements of Reusable Object-Oriented Software* by Erich Gamma, Richard Helm, Ralph Johnson, and John Vlissides (who are often referred to as "the GoF," or "Gang of Four").

Applying Design Patterns

You don't choose a design pattern; the most appropriate design pattern for the problem you're facing normally emerges out of your refactoring steps. We could say that the pattern is buried under your classes, but digging it out is entirely up to you.

The wrong way to use design patterns is by going through a list of patterns and matching them to the problem. Instead, it works the other way around. You have a problem and you have to match the problem to the pattern. How can you do that?

It's quite simple to explain, but it's not so easy to apply. Simply put, you have to understand the problem and generalize it.

If you can take the problem back to its roots, and get the gist of it, you'll probably find a tailor-made pattern just waiting for you. Why is this so? Well, if you really reached the root of the problem, chances are that someone else did the same in the past 15 years (the period during which design patterns became more widely used). So the solution is probably just there for you to read and apply.

As a general rule, keep in mind that design patterns are typically generalized solutions and should never be interpreted dogmatically. They won't save your project when it's in trouble, but they can definitely help you out.

The Real Value of Patterns

Many people would agree in principle that there's plenty of value in design patterns. Fewer people, though, would be able to indicate what the value is and where it can be found. Using design patterns, per se, doesn't make your solution more valuable. In the end, what really matters is whether or not your solution works and meets requirements.

Armed with requirements and design principles, you are up to the task of solving a problem. On your way to the solution, though, a systematic application of design principles to the problem sooner or later takes you into the immediate neighborhood of a known design pattern. That's a certainty because, ultimately, patterns are solutions that others have already found and catalogued.

At that point, you have a solution with some structural likeness to a known design pattern. It's up to you, then, to determine whether an explicit refactoring to more closely align with that pattern will bring some added value to the solution. Basically, you have to decide whether or not the known pattern you've found represents a further, and desirable, refinement of your current solution.

Don't worry, though, if your solution doesn't match a pattern. It means that you have a solution that works, and you can be happy with that.

In summary, patterns might be an *end* when you refactor according to them, and they might be a *means* when you face a problem that is clearly resolved by a particular pattern. Patterns are not an added value for your solution, but they are valuable for you as an architect or a developer looking for a solution.

> **Note** Much like cookbooks, you hardly read a pattern book from cover to cover. You hold on to it, keep it within reach, and then get it off the shelf when you need it. You probably won't read about the million different ways to prepare spaghetti. But if you are in the mood for, say, seafood spaghetti, you'll open the cookbook and flip through its pages with a clear idea of what you're looking for.

Patterns and Idioms

Software patterns indicate well-established solutions to recurring design problems. This means that developers end up coding their way to a given solution over and over again. And they might be repeatedly writing the same boilerplate code in a given programming language.

Sometimes specific features of a given programming language can help significantly in quickly and elegantly solving a recurring problem. That specific set of features is referred to as an *idiom*.

An idiom is a pattern hard-coded in a programming language or implemented out of the box in a framework or technology. Like a design pattern, an idiom represents a solution to a recurring problem. However, in the case of idioms, the solution to the problem doesn't come through design techniques but merely by using the features of the programming language. Whereas a design pattern focuses on the object-oriented paradigm, an idiom focuses on the technology of the programming language.

An idiom is a way to take advantage of the language capabilities and obtain a desired behavior from the code. In general, an idiom refers to a very specific, common, and eye-catching piece of code that accomplishes a given operation—sometimes as simple as adding to a counter or as complex as the implementation of a design pattern.

In C#, for example, the ++ operator can be considered a programming idiom for the recurring task of adding to a counter variable. The same can be said for the *as* keyword when it comes to casting to a type and defaulting to *null* in case of failure.

Events are the canonical example of a programming idiom. Behind events, you find the Observer pattern. The *foreach* construct, instead, is a hard-coded implementation of the Iterator pattern. In .NET 3.5, LINQ-to-SQL is a programming idiom for the Query Object pattern, whereas the *DataContractSerializer* class in the .NET Framework can be rightly considered an idiom for the Memento pattern. And the list goes on.

Patterns in AJAX Development

A Web-specific and quite special paradigm such as AJAX requires its own set of design patterns. These patterns are a variation of the classic categories of design software patterns you may know. All in all, I estimate that three general patterns apply to virtually any AJAX application and, together, capture the gist of AJAX.

As a Web architect with a full understanding of the AJAX paradigm, you're probably quite familiar with them already. If not, the following sections provide a good jumping-off point for fully comprehending the scope and power of AJAX.

Dynamic Data Download

AJAX is all about making asynchronous HTTP requests from within the displayed page. As a user, you can trigger some actions from within the current page and download extra data without necessarily navigating to a distinct page or URL.

You can download any kind of data over an HTTP connection, but to manage it successfully on the client you need data in a format that can be easily manipulated via JavaScript. As discussed in Chapter 3, this data can hardly be exposed as XML; most of the time, the JSON format is a better option.

The ability to dynamically download data can be further expanded to cover other interesting scenarios, such as dynamic download of script and auxiliary resources such as images, multimedia content, syndication, and live data.

Page DOM Manipulation

After data is downloaded in a client browser context, you have to process it, and this act will likely result in some display updates. The DOM makes it straightforward for your code to dynamically change the appearance and content of page elements. All you need to do is get a reference to the desired page element and simply change the appropriate property of that object. As a result, the browser immediately updates the displayed content without any page refresh.

The ability to manipulate the content and styles of page elements via the DOM is a feature second to none in AJAX. In my opinion, this ability is even more valuable than the canonical AJAX ability of placing out-of-band remote calls via *XMLHttpRequest*. If you can't update the page content, there's not much else you can do with any downloaded data.

User Actions

So, given AJAX you can download data at will and incorporate it in the currently displayed tree of content. All these things, though, are client-side actions triggered by the user's clicking in the user interface. How would you track user actions?

In a classic, non-AJAX application, a form submission is the only possible reaction to a user's action. Using a form submission as the sole response to user activity, though, is overall slow and limiting.

The application's response to a user action must be quick and aimed at holding the user's attention. In addition, because the action doesn't result in a full page refresh, it must result in some nice graphical effects that clarify the intended target of the action. As an example, sorting a table of data might be really quick to do, especially if the data is already cached locally. In this case, the pattern recommends that you make it graphically clear when the operation starts, how long it lasts, when it's finished, and what results it has produced.

In an AJAX application, you must take into account the state of critical portions of the user interface, in much the same way you do in a Microsoft Windows application. If the user is expected not to replicate a click, you should disable the button or, at the very minimum, display a warning message. Likewise, if the operation is expected to take a long time, you must inform the user and ideally do that only if it's taking more time than expected—whatever this means to you in the specific context. The wide application of this pattern definitely transforms a classic Web application into a real AJAX application with a level of interactivity and responsiveness comparable to desktop solutions.

As we'll see later in the chapter, this foundation pattern can be split into a number of more specific patterns that tell you how to combine the need for a superb and appealing experience with a limited number of roundtrips—which is really the new currency with which you measure the quality of AJAX applications.

Unique URL

Regardless of the technology used to create it, an AJAX application tends to replace URL-to-URL browser navigation with script-driven HTTP requests. Subsequently, the history of an AJAX application doesn't necessarily coincide with the list of its visited URLs.

More likely, an AJAX history is a list of action points scattered throughout one page or a few pages. In a nutshell, AJAX breaks the assumption that the previous state of a Web application coincides with the previously visited URL. This is a big change and can be seen as the offspring of the new paradigm that AJAX pushes for Web applications. The net effect is that all the user interaction with an AJAX page produces a single entry in the browser's history. Hence, when you click the Back button you are redirected to the previously visited distinct URL, which might be an entirely different page, even a page in a different application.

As of today, very few browsers provide an application programming interface (API) in their object model to add significant states of a page to the global browser history. Worse yet, many browsers lack the notion of a *save point*—that is, a significant state in the page lifetime that you want to store for returning to later. Browsers add only URLs to their history, and only URLs that you have reached through the browser itself. With AJAX pages, instead, you often reach URLs using a distinct HTTP engine based on the *XMLHttpRequest* object. All of this navigation would be lost if a recent browser isn't employed—a notable exception is the newest version of Internet Explorer (8.0)—or if the Web framework (for example, ASP.NET 3.5 SP1) isn't able to do some smart tricks.

The pattern you use to ensure that any relevant action is tracked properly and can be repeated is named *Unique URL*. The Unique URL pattern entails that you use, for each application state you want to track, a mangled URL that contains any relevant event-specific content following the hash (#) character. Here's an example:

```
http://www.contoso.com/default.aspx#s=1
```

The key fact to keep in mind here is that browsers consider any text that follows the hash (#) character to be an optional part of the URL. Therefore, the browser doesn't reload the page if a new URL is set that differs from the current one except for the hash. Whenever your application is in a state that needs be tracked, you set the location of the browser to the same base URL plus a different hash. Obviously, the hash will correspond to pieces of information that are useful for reconstructing the valid state of the application.

For example, in the sample URL just shown, the *#s=1* hash indicates information that the application can use to rebuild the corresponding state.

Interestingly, this basic AJAX pattern is natively implemented in some AJAX frameworks, such as the aforementioned ASP.NET 3.5 SP1. In this case, you can reasonably call it an idiom.

Patterns for JavaScript Development

No programming language is good at reinventing the wheel for every project. All applications share a common set of general behaviors. Subsequently, broadly accepted implementations of these behaviors exist and are frequently applied or adapted. These common solutions are design patterns. For many years, the amount of the JavaScript code required by Web pages and the complexity of that code was not significant enough to justify forming or using design patterns. With AJAX, this aspect changes radically.

Good libraries can simplify and smooth development. However, a library usually provides a set of features that *extend* the language capabilities by making it easier and faster to obtain a common feature. A library won't necessarily be of any help with the implementation of a recurrent behavior. A library is mostly a tool; sometimes you need to develop a strategy first. Enter patterns of JavaScript development.

The Singleton Pattern

The Singleton pattern is a classic pattern. Have you ever needed to use a global object (or a few global objects) to serve all requests to a given class? If you have, you have used the Singleton pattern.

Generalities of the Singleton Pattern

The Singleton pattern is described as a way to ensure that a class has only one instance for which a global point of access is required. Here's a C# example:

```
public class Helpers
{
    public static Helpers DefaultInstance = new Helpers();

    protected Helpers() {}

    public void DoWork(...)
    {
        :
    }

    public void DoMoreWork(...)
    {
        :
    }
}
```

In a consumer class, you take advantage of *Helpers* through the following syntax:

```
Helpers.DefaultInstance.DoWork();
```

What about JavaScript? The Singleton works perfectly in JavaScript, especially if you are using some layer of object orientation in your code.

The Singleton Pattern Used with the Microsoft AJAX Client Library

Suppose you create a JavaScript class with a set of public functions. With the Microsoft AJAX client library we discussed in Chapter 4, "A Better and Richer JavaScript," this is not really a hard thing to do. Here's an example:

```
Type.registerNamespace('Samples');

Samples.Helpers = function()
{
    Samples.Helpers.initializeBase(this);
}
```

```
Samples.Helpers.prototype = {
    DoWork : function(...)
    {
        ⋮
    },
    DoMoreWork : function(...)
    {
        ⋮
    }
}
Samples.Helpers.registerClass('Samples.Helpers');
```

To transform the preceding class into a Singleton pattern, you add an extra line to the script to create the default instance of the class:

```
Samples.Helpers._staticInstance = new Samples.Helpers();
```

Next, you define static entry points for the client code to call:

```
Samples.Helpers.DoWork = function(...)
{
    Samples.Helpers._staticInstance.DoWork(...);
}
Samples.Helpers.DoMoreWork = function(...)
{
    Samples.Helpers._staticInstance.DoMoreWork(...);
}
```

In your own implementation, you can exercise stricter control over the creation of the actual instance of the class. For example, you can use a static method—say, *getInstance*—instead of using the static field as in the example. In such a new *getInstance* method, you can add any logic for the factory.

The implementation of the Singleton pattern used in this example is the same as you find in the JavaScript proxy classes that the ASP.NET AJAX generates for any Web or WCF service registered via the *ScriptManager* control. (See Chapter 2, "The Easy Way to AJAX.")

The second implementation suggested is implemented by the *PageRequestManager* class in the Microsoft AJAX library—the client-side console that governs any partial rendering operation.

The Model-View-Controller Pattern

Separation of concerns (SoC) is important in the presentation layer for a number of reasons. First and foremost, SoC is a fundamental design principle that contributes to creating the right combination of coupling and cohesion for a component. Second, SoC makes it easier for the presentation layer to implement a navigational workflow to decide which view comes next. Does this apply to a presentation layer based on JavaScript? Sure it does, and why not?

Wherever you have complexity to handle in the presentation layer and with interaction between UI elements and the rest of the system, SoC is helpful. In particular, with regard to the user interface, the Model-View-Controller (MVC) pattern is an effective way to achieve separation of concerns and improved manageability and readability of the code, even with JavaScript code.

Introduced back in 1979 as a way to progress from monolithic and autonomous views, the MVC pattern went through a natural evolution and morphed into other patterns, such as Model2—a specific Web adaptation of MVC—and Model-View-Presenter (MVP).

In JavaScript, what really matters is that you end up writing code that is easy to read and maintain. In this context, all in all I consider the plain-old MVC pattern effective enough to go with as-is, putting aside more powerful patterns such as MVP that express most of their power when you have a multiplatform presentation. Let's revisit the basics of MVC and then see how to employ it in JavaScript.

Generalities of the MVC Pattern

The primary goal of MVC is to split the application into distinct pieces—the model, view, and controller. The *model* refers to the state of the application, wraps the application's functionalities, and notifies the view of state changes. The *view* refers to the generation of any graphical elements displayed to the user, and it captures and handles any user actions. The *controller* maps user actions to actions on the model and selects the next view. These three actors are often referred to as the *MVC triad*. Figure 6-1 shows the interaction between the members of the triad.

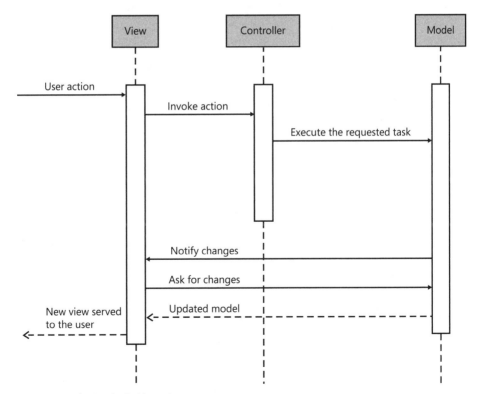

FIGURE 6-1 The MVC triad in action

A view is made of interactive elements such as input fields, buttons, and lists. The view waits for any user actions. When the user, say, clicks a button, the view simply forwards the call to the controller. How this happens has changed quite a bit over the years and is definitely an aspect that largely depends on platform, languages, and development tools. The controller performs the specified action and likely interacts with the model during execution. The model updates its state and notifies the view about the need to refresh. In some implementations of MVC, the controller tells the view to refresh. In one way or another, the view ends up refreshing its content after the controller has completed the requested operation.

For more information on the MVC pattern as well as other patterns for the presentation layer, you might want to check out Chapter 7 of the book *Microsoft .NET: Architecting Applications for the Enterprise* by Dino Esposito and Andrea Saltarello (Microsoft Press, 2008.)

MVC in JavaScript

To get a reasonable implementation of MVC, you need a bit of object orientation. The elements in the triad can be implemented as classes in a JavaScript library, such as the Microsoft AJAX library, Dojo, or perhaps PrototypeJS. Alternatively, the elements of the triad can be simpler closures that contain private and public methods and provide a given behavior.

The model is a JavaScript object that contains everything that describes the representation of the data the user interface is working with. If the user interface is about displaying a list of data items, the model will certainly contain an array with the data to display plus some methods to add, remove, and select elements from the in-memory list.

The view is an object where some of the methods are essentially dispatchers for controller actions. The view captures user-generated events and handles them by forwarding a call to a specific controller method. It's up to your MVC implementation to figure out how to map UI events to controller methods. For example, the mapping can be as simple as that shown in the following code:

```
Samples.Mvc.View.prototype = {
    init: function() {
        $get("Button1").onclick = function() {
            Samples.Mvc.Globals.getView()._controller.Button1_Click();
            Samples.Mvc.Globals.getView().refresh();
        };
    },
    :
    :
}
```

The view object features an initialization method in which all constituent elements of the view—typically, input fields—are mapped to built-in event handlers. These event handlers automatically invoke an appropriate method on the controller associated with the view. To keep things as smooth as possible, it's the MVC JavaScript library—not your page code—that takes care of the mapping.

The following listing shows a sample implementation of the MVC pattern in JavaScript. For simplicity, but without loss of generality, I'll assume that just one view exists for each Web page.

```
Type.registerNamespace('Samples.Mvc');


///
//   Globals
///

Samples.Mvc.Globals = function() {
    Samples.Mvc.Globals.initializeBase(this);
    this._view = null;
}

Samples.Mvc.Globals.prototype = {
    getView: function(elem) {
        // Retrieve the view for the specified DOM element
        :
        :
        return this._view;
    },
    registerView: function(view) {
        this._view = view;
    }
};

Samples.Mvc.Globals.registerClass('Samples.Mvc.Globals');
Samples.Mvc.Globals._staticInstance = new Samples.Mvc.Globals();

Samples.Mvc.Globals.getView = function() {
    return Samples.Mvc.Globals._staticInstance.getView();
}

Samples.Mvc.Globals.registerView = function(view) {
    Samples.Mvc.Globals._staticInstance.registerView(view);
}


///
//   The View
///

Samples.Mvc.View = function(objController, objModel) {
    Samples.Mvc.View.initializeBase(this);
    this._controller = objController;
    this._model = objModel;
    this.init();
}

Samples.Mvc.View.prototype = {
    init: function() {
        $get("Button1").onclick = function() {
            Samples.Mvc.Globals.getView(this)._controller.Button1_Click();
            Samples.Mvc.Globals.getView(this).refresh();
        };

        // Map other events here
        :
        :
    },
```

```
    refresh: function() {
        if (this._model.isDirty()) {
            $get("Label1").innerHTML = this._model.getTextForDisplay();

            // Update other parts of the UI here
            ⋮
        }
    }
}

Samples.Mvc.View.registerClass('Samples.Mvc.View');

///
//   The Model
///

Samples.Mvc.Model = function() {
    Samples.Mvc.Model.initializeBase(this);
    this._isDirty = false;
}

Samples.Mvc.Model.prototype = {
    getTextForDisplay: function() {
        this.setDirty(false);
        return new Date().toTimeString();
    },
    setDirty: function(state) {
        this._isDirty = state;
    },
    isDirty: function() {
        return this._isDirty;
    }
}

Samples.Mvc.Model.registerClass('Samples.Mvc.Model');

///
//   The Controller
///

Samples.Mvc.Controller = function(objModel) {
    Samples.Mvc.Controller.initializeBase(this);
    this._model = objModel;
}

Samples.Mvc.Controller.prototype = {
    Button1_Click: function() {
        this._model.setDirty(true);
    }
}

Samples.Mvc.Controller.registerClass('Samples.Mvc.Controller');
```

Upon instantiation, the view receives a reference to the model and controller. The view constructor initializes the view by registering built-in handlers for each UI event the view generates. For example, if the view contains a button and is interested in handling the *click* event on it, the view will register an *onclick* handler. This handler will simply invoke a method on the associated controller.

You still need to obtain a reference to the view from the button handler. For this reason, I created a global class that lists all views in the page and returns the view that a given input element belongs to. The view will register itself with the global object.

The model exposes a Boolean property to indicate whether its state has been modified since the last time the view has rendered. In addition, the model exposes members to make its content available to the view and the controller.

Finally, the controller lists methods to be bound to user interface events. These methods interact with the model to reflect the intention of user actions.

> **Note** A much simpler but equally effective MVC-like solution that you find in some pages entails simply grouping event handlers in controller classes. There's no explicit definition of *view* and *model* in this pattern, but the role of the controller is nearly the same as in classic MVC. The view is the entire DOM, and the model can be any data structure—an object as well as sparse scalar data.

The On-Demand JavaScript Pattern

Downloading JavaScript is essential for the behavior and functionality of any Web page and especially for AJAX pages. However, downloading JavaScript might have an impact on the perceived performance of the page. More often than not, the time it takes to download a single JavaScript file is minimal. However, when a Web page references many files, all of them need to be downloaded and processed before full interaction between the user and the interface is possible. This fact definitely suggests that the page is slow.

By placing all script references at the bottom of the page and, better yet, by using a tool to compose different scripts together, you can make the script download process more efficient from the user perspective. In particular, a solution that combines multiple JavaScript files into a single file reduces the number of browser requests, thus resulting in a faster download time for the user and less load on the Web server. The version of the *ScriptManager* control that comes with ASP.NET 3.5 SP1 supports exactly this feature through the new *CompositeScript* collection.

As an alternative to referencing script files statically, you can opt for dynamic download. The On-Demand JavaScript pattern can help with this.

Generalities of the On-Demand JavaScript Pattern

The pattern itself is simple and revolves around the problem of pulling JavaScript from the server after the page has been loaded. Downloading script is one common aspect of a more general pattern, known as Multistage Download, that focuses on downloading JavaScript files only and doing so using a strictly on-demand policy.

There are various ways to download JavaScript on demand. The first approach that springs to mind is using the AJAX *XMLHttpRequest* object to set up a synchronous or asynchronous download. Downloading a script, though, is not enough. The script must also be processed and initialized.

Another approach entails using the DOM and adding a new *<script>* tag on the fly. This approach saves developers from managing the download and initialization on their own. All that is required is adding the element to the DOM; the browser will do the rest.

The On-Demand pattern is useful in combination with other patterns that we'll cover in this chapter, such as the Predictive Fetch pattern, and in the next chapter, such as the HTML Template pattern.

Using *XMLHttpRequest* to Download Scripts on Demand

Through the *XMLHttpRequest* object, you open a socket to a given HTTP endpoint and download what the Web server returns for that endpoint. If it's JavaScript content, it must be processed through the *eval* function before it becomes usable. Any code not inside a function will be executed immediately.

Using the AJAX API in the jQuery library, here's the code you need to download on demand a JavaScript file as the user clicks a button:

```
<script type="text/javascript">
    $(document).ready(function() {
        $('#btnDownload').click(downloadPersonScript);
    });

    function downloadPersonScript() {
        url = "person.js";
        $.getScript(url, done)
    }

    function done() {
        var p = new Samples.Person("Dino", "Esposito");
        alert(p.ToString());
    }
</script>
```

You use the *$.getScript* method to reach a given URL and download its content. In particular, the *$.getScript* method expects to receive a JavaScript content type and fails otherwise. The *$.getScript* method passes any received content through *eval*.

More importantly, the *$.getScript* method works asynchronously. This is a key point to consider when it comes to dynamic download.

Unless you opt for using *XMLHttpRequest* in a synchronous manner, you need a callback function that fires when the download is complete and *eval* has been called. You can't simply check for the existence of the downloadable object, download it, and then start using it. Some synchronization is necessary. The following code won't work without synchronization:

```
if (!Samples.Person)
    downloadPersonScript();
var p = new Samples.Person("Dino", "Esposito");
```

Downloading scripts using *XMLHttpRequest* makes your code subject to the same common restrictions of the *XMLHttpRequest* object—in particular, you can download script only from the same origin URL of the requesting page.

Using the DOM to Download Scripts on Demand

As an alternative to using *XMLHttpRequest*, you can insert a made-to-measure new *<script>* element into the DOM, as shown here:

```
// Assume the <head> tag has a unique ID
var head = document.getElementById("myHead");

// Create a new <script> element and configure it
var script = document.createElement('script');
script.type = 'text/javascript';
script.src = "person.js";

// Add the newly created <script> element to the header
head.appendChild(script);
```

You can add the new *<script>* tag any place in the DOM, including to the *<head>* or *<body>* element. When you choose to add a new script via the DOM, you benefit from a number of free services offered by the browser's implementation of the DOM. In particular, the DOM itself will take care of initializing the script for you.

However, the differences between using the DOM and *XMLHttpRequest* don't end here. Let's take a closer look at other differences.

Along with the *<img>* tag, the *<script>* tag is the only HTML tag that can be set to any URL, regardless of the origin domain. Put another way, it's perfectly legitimate and legal to link script files from any domain you can reach via HTTP. If you opt for the DOM approach, you can then download script from anywhere in the Web; however, you're limited to the current Web server if you go with *XMLHttpRequest*.

If you use the DOM approach, the script remains in the DOM until the page is unloaded. Any script downloaded via *XMLHttpRequest* can't be further tracked as an object after it has been processed by the *eval* function. The fact that the script downloaded via DOM remains attached to the DOM itself might also be a problem if you run the download code periodically and each time add a new *<script>* tag to the DOM tree.

Generally, you could say that doing a download via DOM is more effective from a functional standpoint, but such effectiveness comes at the price of reduced flexibility. Going through the DOM limits you to dynamically downloading only JavaScript files. Going through *XMLHttpRequest* doesn't result in such a limitation. In fact, the URL can point to any other resource, such as plain data as well as JSON data. In particular, JSON can be a convenient way to download a self-contained object packed with data. This option can be pursued only if you opt for implementing the On-Demand pattern via the more flexible approach represented by *XMLHttpRequest* or any other functionally equivalent API provided by specialized libraries such as jQuery.

The Predictive Fetch Pattern

Let's take a look at a few fundamental patterns of AJAX applications that allow you to quickly and effectively achieve the primary goal of any AJAX application—providing a better user experience.

AJAX is mostly about making the user interface highly responsive. The application should respond to user actions quickly—ideally, instantaneously. Being more responsive doesn't necessarily mean that less data is being sent across the wire or that faster responses are generated on the server. AJAX is about getting a user any requested data quickly—regardless of how you obtain that and the complexity (in terms of time and space) that it takes.

The Predictive Fetch pattern helps you work out a solution to improve the user experience regardless of network and server conditions.

Generalities of the Predictive Fetch Pattern

Many actions that originate around a Web application require a response from the server and, subsequently, a roundtrip. How long will it take to complete a request? This value is known as the Time To Last Byte, or TTLB. Two main factors affect the TTLB value: latency related to data transfer, and server processing overhead.

Although you can try to smooth these two factors through specific network and code contrivance, using an appropriate pattern can drive you to a comprehensive solution that offers a better experience regardless of the network and code details.

Details of the Predictive Fetch Pattern

The two words that form the name of the pattern say it all. The idea behind the pattern is to predict the next user actions and preload some of the data that it will be necessary to show later.

Whether it's downloaded during idle time or simply asynchronously in the background, data is cached on the client using some JavaScript data structure. Next, when the user triggers the action for which that previously cached data is required, some client-side code retrieves it and uses it to refresh the user interface as appropriate.

In the end, the Predictive Fetch pattern is a sort of context-sensitive, client-side cache that requires a well-defined strategy about what to download and when to download it.

Motivations for Using the Predictive Fetch Pattern

In a Web application, the main hurdle on the way to full user satisfaction is the usually long waiting time the user experiences for results to be visible and consumable. Ideally, responses should be displayed in a range of time that is below the level of human consciousness, or at least very close to it. This means displaying results in just a few milliseconds. Is that really possible in a Web scenario?

Refreshing the user interface in 10 milliseconds or so is clearly possible in a Windows client, but it's difficult to make this happen in a classic Web application model. If a roundtrip is required, the user should typically be prepared to wait as long as a few seconds for the response to come back. This overhead is all part of the current game and can be overcome only by resorting to smart design tricks.

It's not just about user experience, however.

Another motivation for improving the actual response time is throughput. It's a simple equation, after all. If you can reduce the waiting time, you give users of your application more time to work with application, thus giving them one more chance to increase their productivity. Note, though, that in this context, productivity might be a relative concept. If the user expects to spend minutes on a page, can a savings of just a few seconds make a huge difference? Well, consider that the user's reduced level of frustration resulting from shorter waiting periods will put her in a positive mood. With AJAX, it always boils down to improving the user's experience by making the user feel like she's in control of the application.

Open Points Regarding the Predictive Fetch Pattern

From a functional standpoint, Predictive Fetch is not such a hard pattern to implement. It doesn't present high technical hurdles for you to clear. As we'll see in a moment, by using helpers from some JavaScript libraries, you can implement it quite quickly.

The important point to keep in mind about the Predictive Fetch pattern relates to devising an effective strategy for fetching data.

You can't prefetch just any data the user requests from any stage of the user interface. You must be careful to cover either the most likely actions or the most critical actions, regardless of their likelihood.

As you can see, the strategy you choose to employ is the most important aspect of the Predictive Fetch pattern, and it's not something that can be hard-coded in a recurring pattern solution. It's part of the architecture and belongs to the overall solution. For example, you must decide for which actions you want to preload data and then you have to guess the user's choice and download the right set of data, or at least the most likely set of data the user will need.

The main drawback of using the Predictive Fetch pattern is that it opens up the possibility of loading data that will never be requested by the user. This creates unnecessary traffic overhead and also can use some memory in the client PC unnecessarily.

Another point to consider is the resulting behavior of the application, which might appear to be sort of random, if not inconsistent, to the end user. Imagine two similar features in a page—one that supports predictive fetch and one that doesn't. Clearly, when the user selects the one that doesn't support predictive fetch, she will experience a much longer response time. When she selects the other function, the response time is immediate. This difference in performance can be confusing and possibly can contribute to creating a mysterious aura about your application, if not a really negative feeling.

Creating a Reference Implementation

Let's see how to implement predictive fetch using the jQuery library for client-side caching facilities.

A Sample Scenario for the Predictive Fetch Pattern

Figure 6-2 shows a sample Web page that allows the user to pick a customer name from a list and click it to see details about the customer, such as his address, country of residence, and contact name.

FIGURE 6-2 A sample page using the Predictive Fetch pattern

When the user selects a customer, he cannot be absolutely certain that he will also be able to examine the list of orders the customer has placed in a given period of time. However, as an architect who knows the arrangement of the pages in the site, you can anticipate that this is an action that's very likely to occur.

The page is designed in a way that requires two clicks to get to the orders. This is reasonable because, by design, viewing the orders is only a possible operation. Quite likely, the user will spend some time looking at the customer details and then turn his attention to the orders only later. A good strategy to implement, then, would be to bet on this behavior occurring and retrieve the orders immediately after displaying the customer details. In this way, it's likely that when the user focuses on the orders, all the information will already be on the client and only a click away from the user.

Managing Remote Calls

Retrieving the customer information is an operation that can be implemented in a variety of ways, including using partial rendering. The asynchronous retrieval of orders, instead, must be an out-of-band operation resolved via *XMLHttpRequest*. In this example, let's assume you use services for any remote connections:

```
<script type="text/javascript">
    function findCustomer() {
        var list = $get("<%= DropDownList1.ClientID %>");
        var customerID = list.options[list.selectedIndex].value;
        displayCustomer(customerID);
    }

    function displayCustomer(customerID) {
        // Get data through a roundtrip
        Samples.DataService.LookupCustomer(
                customerID,
                onSearchComplete,
                null,
                customerID);
    }

    function onSearchComplete(results, context, methodName) {
        // Display customer information
        $get("customerData").style.visibility = "visible";
        $get("companyID").innerHTML = results.ID;
        $get("companyName").innerHTML = results.CompanyName;
        $get("companyContact").innerHTML = results.ContactName;
        $get("companyCity").innerHTML = results.City;
        $get("companyCountry").innerHTML = results.Country;

        // Predict next step: download and display orders
        displayOrders(results.ID);
    }
        :
</script>
```

The *findCustomer* function is bound to the *click* event on a UI element and runs as the user chooses to retrieve customer information. The function reads the currently selected customer ID and invokes a remote service.

The data retrieval occurs asynchronously, and the *OnSearchComplete* callback is invoked when all details about the specified customer have been found and downloaded. As in the preceding code, the callback function populates the user interface with customer data and then triggers the download of orders:

```
function displayOrders(customerID) {
    // Prefetch (downloading HTML markup via the service)
    var orders = Samples.DataService.FindOrdersByCustomerAsMarkup(
        customerID,
```

```
            onPrefetchComplete,
            null,
            customerID);
}
function onPrefetchComplete(results, context, methodName) {
    // Display data
    $('#orderGrid').html(results);

    // Enable the "View Orders" button
    $('#btnViewOrders').attr('disabled', '');
}
```

Orders are downloaded in the background as the user consults the displayed information about the customer. The callback for the order retrieval operation updates the (hidden) portion of the user interface where orders will appear. Next, the callback function enables the button that provides access to that part of the user interface. When the user finally clicks on the View Orders button, the list of orders is displayed instantaneously.

Figure 6-3 shows the user interface immediately after downloading the customer details. The View Orders button is disabled, and the page is silently performing an asynchronous request for order information.

FIGURE 6-3 Prefetching order data for the displayed customer

When orders are ready for inspection, the View Orders button becomes clickable. At this point, though, the markup with the list of orders is already incorporated into the DOM.

The click causes the change of a CSS style, and the display is immediate, as shown in Figure 6-4.

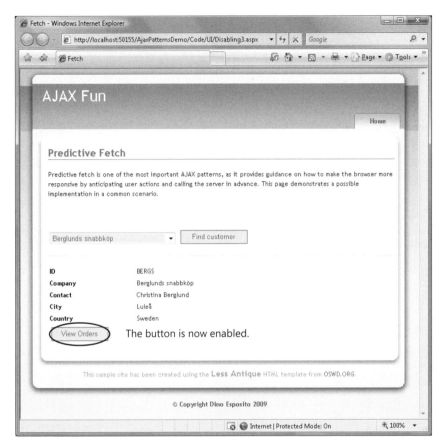

FIGURE 6-4 Screen shot showing the orders are ready for inspection

If the user is mainly interested in the orders that a given customer has placed during a particular period of time, in the case of severe latency he might have to wait a few seconds until the View Orders button becomes clickable. Clearly, this delay could be a source of problems.

However, rather than assuming the predictive fetch functionality isn't feasible, you should wonder whether such a design is optimal for the use case depicted in the page requirements. Such an implementation is best suited for a scenario where the user is primarily interested in customer details and might optionally show some interest in the orders. If the orders are the only information that matters, you're better off getting customer details and orders in the same roundtrip.

Caching Makes Applications Faster and Prettier

Imagine that a user, after viewing details about a given customer (say, customer A), moves to customer B. According to the sample implementation of the pattern just seen, the code will fire two pairs of requests—details and orders for customer A and customer B. So far, so good.

What if the user at some point goes back to customer A? Should you download details and orders again? And over and over again? Obviously not.

Client-side caching is an interesting enhancement that can save AJAX applications quite a few roundtrips in the context of each browser session. I'm not talking about persistent data storage obtained via cookies or other browser-specific capabilities. More simply, I'm talking about storing previously downloaded data (both customer details and orders) in an in-memory, client-side, JavaScript-based cache for as long as the current browser session lasts.

As you saw in Chapter 5, "JavaScript Libraries," the jQuery library—which, by the way, is a must-have in AJAX applications—provides an excellent client cache implementation through the *data* function. The *data* function represents the API to access an internal data container where developers can store data that relates to all DOM elements in the selected wrapped set. Here's how to rewrite the previous predictive fetch example to make use of a client caching mechanism:

```
<script type="text/javascript">
    function findCustomer() {
        var list = $get("<%= DropDownList1.ClientID %>");
        var customerID = list.options[list.selectedIndex].value;
        displayCustomer(customerID);
    }

    function displayCustomer(customerID) {
        // Check jQuery cache first
        var record = $('#customerData').data(customerID);
        if (typeof (record) !== 'undefined') {
            onSearchComplete(record, customerID, "");
        }
        else {
            // Get data through a roundtrip
            Samples.DataService.LookupCustomer(
                customerID,
                onSearchComplete,
                null,
                customerID);
        }
    }

    function onSearchComplete(results, context, methodName) {
        // Save to the jQuery cache
        $('#customerData').data(results.ID, results);

        // Display customer information
        $get("customerData").style.visibility = "visible";
        $get("companyID").innerHTML = results.ID;
        $get("companyName").innerHTML = results.CompanyName;
        $get("companyContact").innerHTML = results.ContactName;
        $get("companyCity").innerHTML = results.City;
        $get("companyCountry").innerHTML = results.Country;

        // Predict next step: download and display orders
        displayOrders(results.ID);
    }
    ⋮
</script>
```

In the *displayCustomer* function, you first check whether the customer record is held in the local cache. If so, you invoke the callback directly, passing the record in the cache as the data to process. The jQuery library associates a local data container with a DOM element. In this case, the DOM element of choice is named *customerData* and is the *<div>* that contains the HTML representation of the customer information.

```
<div class="actionPanel" id="customerData">
    <table>
        <tr>
            <td class="label"><b>ID</b></td>
            <td style="width:10px;" />
            <td><span id="companyID"></span></td>
        </tr>
        <tr>
            <td class="label"><b>Company</b></td>
            <td style="width:10px;" />
            <td><span id="companyName"></span></td>
        </tr>

            :
            :

        <tr>
            <td colspan="2"><input id="btnOrders" type="button" value="View Orders"
                disabled="disabled"
                onclick="viewOrders()" /></td>
        </tr>
    </table>
    <br />
    <span id="orderGrid"> </span>
</div>
```

The *onSearchComplete* function is responsible for adding fresh data to the cache. The jQuery's *data* function accepts two arguments: a key and the related value.

```
var key = results.ID;
var value = results;
$('#customerData').data(key, value);
```

Each data container, in fact, operates as a dictionary and requires a unique key to identify some content.

To cache orders, you use the same approach. In this case, though, there's an additional point to consider. Here's the revised code that downloads orders:

```
function displayOrders(customerID) {
    // Check jQuery cache first
    var record = $('#orderGrid').data(customerID);
    if (typeof (record) !== 'undefined') {
        onPrefetchComplete(record, customerID, "");
    }
    else {
        // Prefetch
        var orders = Samples.DataService.FindOrdersByCustomerAsMarkup(
                customerID,
```

```
                      onPrefetchComplete,
                      null,
                      customerID);
    }
}
```

You must pass the customer ID to the callback that processes retrieved orders for the callback to add it properly to the cache. You can use the *context* parameter of service proxies, as discussed in Chapter 3:

```
function onPrefetchComplete(results, context, methodName) {
    // Save to the jQuery cache
    var key = context;  // Represents the customer ID
    $('#orderGrid').data(key, results);

    // Display data
    $('#orderGrid').html(results);
    $('#btnOrders').attr('disabled', '');
}
```

In this example, I don't bother to remove data from the jQuery cache. This means that the size of the cache grows until you dismiss the browser window. Because the browser window consumes the memory of the local PC, this might not be an urgent problem to solve. However, nothing really prevents you from addressing this concern also in your solution. The jQuery cache API provides the *removeData* function to clear previously cached data items. The real point, though, is the strategy you use to decide which element you drop and when.

Summary of the Predictive Fetch Pattern

Predictive Fetch is a powerful pattern, but it requires you to make a number of architectural decisions. Architectural decisions are the most delicate part of the system. If a design decision is easy to make, it's not architectural. Period.

Ultimately, a predictive fetch is a guess. And, just like any guess, it can be right or wrong. The more you know the system, the more you can make accurate guesses where the chances of success are far beyond 50 percent.

Finally, note that although Predictive Fetch is presented as an AJAX pattern, it has some value also when applied to the server side in combination with an efficient caching technique or tool.

The Timeout Pattern

The beauty of AJAX is that you can serve your users Web applications that present live data, such as news and any other streamed content. Although mashup pages with live data are helpful for users—and are an essential part of the user experience—they definitely put a lot of pressure on the server that provides the service. This pressure isn't too bad if there's also a *live* user viewing and consuming that stream of data.

In particular with multitab browsers, it's easy for users to forget about a page opened in a hidden tab that regularly, and frequently, polls the server for fresh data. So it happens that users leave a workstation for hours while the application, unaware of the user's absence, keeps on polling.

A well-designed AJAX application will adopt some countermeasures to fight this bad user habit. The Timeout pattern is the most common (and effective) approach to use.

Generalities of the Timeout Pattern

The primary purpose of the Timeout pattern is determining whether the user is still active and working with the application and, if not, terminating the session. The expression "terminating the session" is a bit more vague than it might sound at first.

In particular, the expression doesn't necessarily refer to an ASP.NET session that is abruptly terminated by the runtime. It refers, instead, to any page-specific, costly practice that you want to terminate unless the user explicitly confirms an interest in it.

Details of the Timeout Pattern

As the name suggests, the purpose of the pattern is timing out a user who fails to prove she's still present and working with the application. By implementing the pattern, you claim your application's right to be lazy unless forced to work.

Implementing the pattern means monitoring the user's activity to the extent that it's possible. You will have the client-side code to determine whether the browser session is still active and suspend any server interaction if it isn't.

The pattern works well when a periodic refresh is needed, such as when the user is periodically downloading any sort of live data, including multimedia streaming, news, sports scores, stock quote updates, and so forth.

Motivations for Using the Timeout Pattern

Why would you use such a pattern? There's essentially one huge driving force: avoiding a massive waste of bandwidth and server resources. The fundamental principle is that no server work is done unless there's a live user to request that it be done.

Before AJAX, this condition was trivially true for each possible Web application. With AJAX, this is no longer the case. Within an AJAX application, requests can be triggered programmatically and, in the case of naïve pages, even against the user's will. Blocking abuse of server resources (and bandwidth) is precisely the intent of the Timeout pattern.

Terminating a Browser Session

In an AJAX application, the server-side session is much less useful than in a classic ASP.NET application. The state of an AJAX application is on the client and normally lasts as long as the browser's window is up and running.

You definitely don't want a client page to poll the server every 10 seconds for days because, say, the user is at home sick and forgot to shut down the machine on his last day in the office. This is definitely a scenario you could overlook in a classic Web scenario, but it's one you need to specifically address in an AJAX scenario.

You apply the same timeout mechanism you are familiar with for ASP.NET sessions and dispose of any state after a specified amount of time has elapsed without activity. The trick is, how do you detect client activity?

In classic ASP.NET, this question usually has an easy answer. Every request placed at the Web server for a specific application will keep the application live for another slice of the fixed timeout period.

What is the default action that restarts the timer on a client environment?

The simplest option entails you use a plain time-based approach. When the timer expires, you stop whatever operation in that context where the results are too expensive for you. For example, if that page is streaming some sporting events to a potentially huge audience, you might want to stop each connected browser every 45 minutes and ask the user—if any user is still there—to click a button to restart the streaming.

A more sophisticated approach entails that you set up a timer but then monitor input devices such as the keyboard and mouse. As your page receives keyboard and mouse events, the timer is restarted. When the timer naturally expires, the session is terminated.

A Timeout Pattern Reference Implementation

The Timeout pattern can have a number of different implementations, depending on the various features you want to enable and support. Let's look at a simple but significant example based on plain time-based session termination.

A Sample Scenario for the Timeout Pattern

You have a page that performs a periodic refresh of some sort. Let's consider, for simplicity, a digital clock that goes back to the server every few seconds to report the current time. Admittedly, this example is of no practical use, not even in a deliberately naïve application, but it perfectly serves the purpose of simulating a periodic user interface refresh without burdening the demonstration with unnecessary details.

Note If you need to display a digital clock in a Web page, you're much better off using a client timer to display the date and time on the local PC. You can obtain the local PC date and time through the *Date* object in JavaScript.

The digital clock is obtained using ASP.NET partial rendering and the newest *Timer* server control:

```
<asp:UpdatePanel runat="server" ID="UpdatePanel1">
    <ContentTemplate>
        <h4>
            <asp:Label runat="server" ID="Label1" />
        </h4>
    </ContentTemplate>
    <Triggers>
        <asp:AsyncPostBackTrigger ControlID="Timer1" EventName="Tick" />
    </Triggers>
</asp:UpdatePanel>

<asp:Timer ID="Timer1" runat="server" OnTick="Timer1_Tick" Interval="1500" />
```

The *Timer* control emits script code and configures the *setInterval* browser function. At every interval, the timer invokes a built-in JavaScript function that performs a postback on behalf of the *Timer1* server control. On the server, ASP.NET resolves the request by invoking the function associated with the *OnTick* handler:

```
protected void Timer1_Tick(object sender, EventArgs e)
{
    Label1.Text = DateTime.Now.ToLongTimeString();
}
```

Regardless of the relevance of the example, what you have here is a prototype of a periodic refresh scenario. You have a task that executes periodically and frequently from the client to request some work on the server. This task must go on only if there's a real user in front of the screen, or else the server's resources are simply wasted.

The simplest way to detect if a user is using the page is by setting up another timer and having it expire at the end of an interval large enough not to disturb a working user and small enough not to waste much bandwidth in the case of an absent user. This magic number, as you can see, is strictly dependent on the particular application. To make the example easily manageable and testable, let's set it to just a few seconds, as shown in the following code:

```
<script type="text/javascript">
    var timer = null;
    function pageLoad()
    {
        if (timer === null)
        {
            timer = new Samples.Components.Timer(5000, stopTask);
            timer.start();
        }
    }

    function pageUnload()
    {
        if (timer != null)
            timer.stop();
    }
```

```
function stopTask()
{
    // Stop the timer
    timer.stop();

    // Stop the periodic refresh
    stopPeriodicRefresh();

    // Ask the user to continue
    AskIfTheUserWantsToContinue();
}

function AskIfTheUserWantsToContinue()
{
    // Ask if the user wants to continue
    var answer = window.confirm("Is it OK to continue?");
    if (answer)
    {
        // Restart the periodic task
        startPeriodicRefresh();

        // Restart our own timeout engine
        if (timer !== null)
            timer.start();
        return;
    }
}

function stopPeriodicRefresh()
{
    // Anything that can stop the periodic task
    var clock = $find("<%= Timer1.ClientID  %>");
    clock._stopTimer();
}
function startPeriodicRefresh()
{
    // Anything that can start the periodic task
    var clock = $find("<%= Timer1.ClientID  %>");
    clock._startTimer();
}
</script>
```

Note that I'm using a custom timer class—the *Samples.Components.Timer* class. The class is just a wrapper around basic JavaScript timer functions such as *setTimeout* and *setInterval*. As a result, in the example the custom timer invokes the *stopTask* callback every five seconds. (Of course, this interval will be in minutes rather than seconds for a real application.)

Initially, when the timer expires, you stop the periodic refresh and display a message box to the user. Figure 6-5 shows an example.

If a user is really working at the PC, the dialog box will be handled in one way or another and result either in confirming the task or in an explicit termination. If the user left the workstation, the dialog box will stay up indefinitely; more importantly, the periodic refresh is delayed and all related bandwidth is saved.

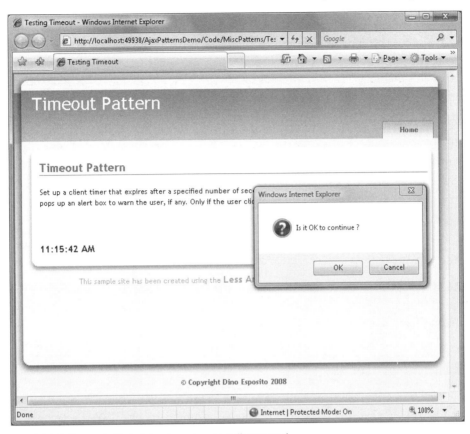

FIGURE 6-5 The periodic task has been temporarily stopped.

As mentioned, you can use a smarter approach to time out a user. Instead of blindly waiting for a given interval to expire, you can monitor keyboard activity and restart the timer each time the user types something. Here's how:

```
// Start the timer
var timer = setTimeout(callback, 5000);
⋮
// Registers a keyboard handler triggered whenever
// users type something into the specified input field
$get("TextBox1").onkeypress = adjustTimer;

function adjustTimer()
{
    // Clear the current timer and start another one
    clearTimeout(timer);

    // Renew the timer for another 5 seconds
    timer = setTimeout(callback, 5000);
};
```

The same trick can be applied to mouse events too.

Open Points Regarding the Timeout Pattern

The Timeout pattern implementation we've just discussed is ideal for situations where your primary concern is saving bandwidth and server resources. However, this is not the only possible scenario where the pattern is helpful. There are a number of possible options for an application to take once it has ascertained that the user is inactive.

For example, it might be wise to clear the content of a page that contains sensitive information. An inactive user might be a user who left the computer unattended or simply a user who minimized the browser window to do other things. If this scenario represents a security hazard, you might want to use the Timeout pattern to clear the content of the page by simply refreshing it and perhaps deleting any related cookies.

In some cases, before clearing the current content of the page you might want to save it on the server. Of course, you choose this sort of autosave option for pages where the user is expected to do quite a bit of work, such as filling out a long and complex form.

Another possible action related to clearing the page of an inactive user is letting the server application know about the inactivity. Depending on the application, the code on the server might decide to kill the server session, schedule its future actions differently, or both.

Related Patterns

A number of other AJAX patterns are related to the Timeout pattern and can be used in combination with it. The name of one of these patterns has been repeatedly mentioned in the preceding paragraphs—the Periodic Refresh pattern. Let's dig out a bit more detail.

The Periodic Refresh Pattern

Simply put, periodic refresh means sending an *XMLHttpRequest* request to some server endpoint periodically. The purpose of the pattern is to keep the user up to date with whatever type of information the server application is processing.

It's not always and not necessarily news or live updates to sports scores. The pattern also helps to track from the client the status of shared objects in a multiuser environment and the progress of some server tasks.

Without beating around the bush, let me say up front that periodic refresh can be quite an expensive operation. There are bandwidth costs and consumption of server resources. This option might not be a real source of troubles if the refresh occurs once an hour and for only a few users. However, for a period of a few seconds and for a large group of users, it's definitely problematic.

Not having the pattern in place is problematic too, as it significantly reduces the usability of the user interface and makes the overall user experience poorer.

As an architect, you own the design decision. A good approach that works most of the time is increasing the frequency of requests while diminishing the size of the content. One possible way to use it is to send just the portion of the information that has changed since the last refresh.

Another point to consider is the latency of server requests. If the impact of latency might be so high that a request takes more than the timer's period, you might want to do something to optimize the schedule. One idea is to issue a new request immediately after getting a response without waiting for the period to expire. Then, on the server, if necessary you defer the response until the application determines it is time to release the response.

The Heartbeat Pattern

In an AJAX application, it's quite common that the user is active and willingly working with the application but no requests reach the Web server for a while. On the other hand, the Web server has no way to figure out what's happening on the client. Subsequently, if it doesn't receive requests for a time, it just times out the server session. Therefore, when the user finally posts the completed form back to the server, she will get an unpleasant surprise.

To avoid that outcome, the client application should send a heartbeat message via *XMLHttpRequest* with appropriate frequency. A heartbeat message can have any form and content that is suitable in a particular scenario. For example, it can be an empty request that just proves the existence of life on the client and has the sole purpose of keeping the server session up and running. In this case, the interval must be any length that is less than the session timeout configured for the application.

In other cases, the server might need to track carefully which user is active and which user has abandoned the application. As you can see, in such a scenario the server imposes a stricter requirement and needs to know about users much more frequently than the 20 or 30 minutes of a typical server session timeout period. In the implementation of the Heartbeat pattern, you set the heartbeat interval to the few minutes you need and then have a server module track the last heartbeat received from each client. When no fresher heartbeat is received for the interval, the user is considered gone.

Not only is the frequency higher in the latter case, but also the content of the message might be significantly large. Higher frequency and larger content pose the same design issues we've just seen for the Periodic Refresh pattern.

The Event Scheduling Pattern

The more the logic gets sophisticated, the more you need to schedule actions to happen in the future. AJAX applications are no exception. In JavaScript code, you have just one tool to schedule events—timers. Timers are a powerful tool that allow you to repeat actions at fixed intervals or to schedule an action to happen only once, at a given time.

Timers require the use of callback functions, which is where you physically place the code you want to run at scheduled times. The browser's *setInterval* and *setTimeout* functions are essential in the implementation of this simple but extremely common AJAX pattern. The Event Scheduling pattern is hardly ever used alone; more often than not, you find it used in conjunction with Periodic Refresh and also with optimization patterns such as Submission Throttling, which I'll cover later in the chapter.

The Progress Indicator Pattern

When users of any computer application start a potentially lengthy operation, the user interface should be updated to reflect that some work is in progress and that results may not be available for a while. Implementing this pattern is relatively easy in Windows applications; however, you encounter structural difficulties if you try the same thing in a Web scenario.

In Web applications, displaying static text such as "Please, wait" just before the operation begins is easy. But what if you want to provide more informative feedback, such as the estimated time to completion or the percentage of work done?

In Web applications, lengthy tasks occur on the server, and there are no built-in facilities to push state information to the client browser. On the other hand, there's no easy way either for a client to grab status information and update a progress bar. So what's the point?

The Progress Indicator pattern offers guidance on how to structure the JavaScript client and the server application so that they can share information about server progress and report that information in a timely fashion to the user.

Generalities of the Progress Indicator Pattern

The purpose of the Progress Indicator pattern is to help developers provide feedback to users while users are waiting for server responses. The intended feedback here is not simply a "Please, wait" or "Loading..." message; the feedback should provide the real status of the server and the progress that has been made on the server.

Details of the Progress Indicator Pattern

A progress indicator is some piece of user interface that is displayed only for the time it takes to complete a lengthy remote operation. There are two basic ways to obtain the information to show.

One way is to estimate (or just guess) the time it should take and then relate that to the actual time that it's taking. To compute how long it took to get to the current point, you can obviously use a timer. With proper adjustments, you can show the user a gauge that moves constantly and that always reaches 100 percent when the operation is really completed.

The second approach entails designing the lengthy task to expose some progress information and using a second component to monitor any exposed information. The server operation can write to a known location its current status as it makes progress. At the same time, a second monitoring channel is enabled to make periodical reads from the same known location and report the current status to the client.

Associated with the monitoring channel will be a piece of user interface that incorporates server information in a layout that is visually pleasing to the user.

The ASP.NET *UpdateProgress* Control

It's important to clarify up front the fundamental difference that exists between an implementation of the Progress Indicator pattern and the built-in *UpdateProgress* server control you find in ASP.NET 3.5.

A powerful control with many handy properties, the *UpdateProgress* control can't do much more for you than display a static template, which at most is embellished with an animated GIF or a marquee. In other words, the *UpdateProgress* control alone is not good at obtaining and displaying context information about what's really going on with the server. No interaction is possible between the *UpdateProgress* control and the application code being executed.

In addition, the *UpdateProgress* control is tightly coupled with the partial rendering engine and the *UpdatePanel* control. For example, the *UpdateProgress* control doesn't work if you start the remote operation via an explicit *XMLHttpRequest* call either via custom script or the ASP.NET-generated JavaScript proxy for a Web or WCF service.

> **Note** You might think that *UpdateProgress* offers an excellent benefit in its ability to cancel ongoing calls. I'll return to this point later to discuss the details; for now, suffice it to say that all that the control can do is host a button with some JavaScript attached that, if clicked, closes the socket through which the client is receiving the response of the operation. No server functionality is ever exercised as a result of the cancel operation. Instead, the server processes its normal response regardless of the user's client-side cancellation request.

Open Points Regarding the Progress Indicator Pattern

To implement the Progress Indicator pattern effectively, you need to have available a monitor component and a "monitorable" task. The monitor component polls a shared piece of server memory and reads its content. The monitorable task consists of a normal piece of code that performs a given server-side task, plus an extra layer of code that publishes its state to a shared memory in agreement with the monitor.

The architectural decision, therefore, is about whether you prefer a simple empirical estimation of the remaining time or a precise report of what's going on. In the former case, you need to employ *magic* numbers for each monitorable action to establish the maximum expected length and update the feedback based on that.

To obtain a precise report, you need a client and server framework and you must force your monitorable task to expose a public API. Last, but certainly not least, in some cases this course of action might have an impact on the algorithm you employ for the task. For example, if you need to update 100 records on a database table and choose to do that via a single stored procedure call, you can hardly display the user feedback about the record being currently updated. To make the task monitorable, you must switch to a loop-based algorithm and call the stored procedure 100 times on a single record or fewer times on a small group of records.

Another open point relates to the precise moment when you should display the progress indicator. By default, the *UpdateProgress* control doesn't display its graphical template if the partial rendering operation completes in less than half a second. Let's say that one second is close to instantaneous for Web users. If the task will take more time than that, it's advisable to bring up some feedback.

Displaying the progress bar only after a fixed time is an instance of the Event Scheduling pattern and is resolved using a JavaScript timer.

A Progress Indicator Reference Implementation

Implementing the Progress Indicator pattern is a three-step operation. You define the API that reads and writes the status information from a persistent store, such as a database, disk file, or shared block of memory. Next, you provide an event sink for the client to connect via *XMLHttpRequest* to the server and read the current status. Finally, you set up a client JavaScript API that represents the monitoring service that periodically connects to the server to measure progress.

The pattern should be implemented to work regardless of the technique you use to start the partial page update—be it the *UpdatePanel* control, a page method, or a Web service method.

A Sample Scenario for the Progress Indicator Pattern

Figure 6-6 shows a sample page that uses an implementation of the pattern. When the user clicks to start the operation, two things happen. First, the task is effectively started on the server using, say, a page method. (See Chapter 2 for details.) Second, a monitor is activated to set up a periodic refresh of the user interface based on any content read from the server from a task-specific location.

In the sample application shown in Figure 6-6, the feedback displayed takes the form of a progress bar based on a percentage. In the figure, you also see a pseudo-gauge bar close to the "Please wait" message. That's not a real progress bar, though; it's merely an animated GIF that mimics the behavior of a progress bar.

Let's delve deeper into the steps that form such a solution.

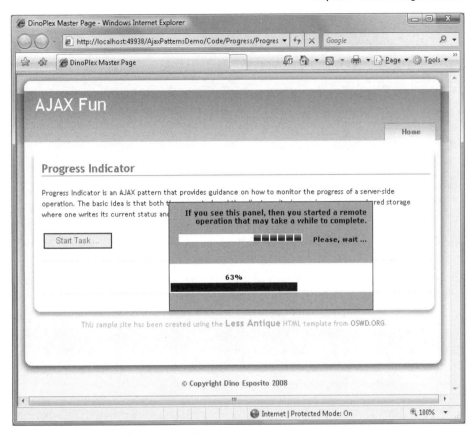

FIGURE 6-6 Monitoring the progress of a remote task

Definition of the Server API

You need a server-side, contract-based API to read and write status information from a
known container. In the following listing, you see the source code of a *ProgressMonitor* class
that implements a given interface:

```
namespace Samples.Server
{
    public interface IProgressMonitor
    {
        void SetStatus(int taskID, object message);
        string GetStatus(int taskID);
    }

    public class ProgressMonitor : IProgressMonitor
    {
        // Sets the current status of the task
        public void SetStatus(int taskID, object message)
        {
            HttpContext.Current.Cache.Insert(
                taskID.ToString(),
                message,
```

```
                    null,
                    DateTime.Now.AddMinutes(5),
                    Cache.NoSlidingExpiration);
        }

        // Reads the current status of the task
        public string GetStatus(int taskID)
        {
            object o = HttpContext.Current.Cache[taskID.ToString()];
            if (o == null)
                return String.Empty;

            return (string) o;
        }
    }
}
```

The interface features two methods—*GetStatus* and *SetStatus*—to read and write the status of the task, respectively. The choice of the data container is ultimately up to the class author. The *ProgressMonitor* class saves data to the ASP.NET *Cache*. The *SetStatus* method adds a new item and gives it an absolute expiration policy of five minutes. The value is arbitrary and can be adapted to meet the expectations of a particular application. You can also make it an external parameter and enhance the class to read the cached item duration from the configuration file. An explicit expiration date is helpful to avoid having the ASP.NET *Cache* fill up quickly with too many items with too short a lifetime. You use the task ID value as the key to add and retrieve status information from within the cache.

Note It's worth mentioning that from a performance standpoint it would be desirable to limit the pressure on the cache generated by frequent inserts and removals of short-lived items. A more scalable solution entails using a global hash table that is permanently stored in one fixed slot within the ASP.NET *Cache*.

Implementing the Task

The task to monitor must be refactored as a list of distinct steps. Between two successive steps you call the preceding *ProgressMonitor* class to save information about the current status of the task.

The task server API is there to serve any number of tasks that any clients might have started. Whether the data store for task information is a database or plain memory, you need a way to uniquely identify the task. An ID is an effective way. This information, though, must be generated somewhere and passed down to the task somehow.

Here's an example of how to structure a task to support monitoring:

```
private void Process(int taskID, /* params */ ...)
{
    ProgressMonitor progMonitor = new ProgressMonitor();
```

```
    // First step
    progMonitor.SetStatus(taskID, "Now performing first step...");
    DoFirstStep(...);

    // Second step
    progMonitor.SetStatus(taskID, "Now performing second step...");
    DoSecondStep(...);

    ⋮

    // Final step
    progMonitor.SetStatus(taskID, "Finalizing...");
    DoFinalStep(...);
}
```

The *SetStatus* method gets a string—it can actually be any .NET object—representing the
message to pass to the user interface. The monitoring component will read this message
from the shared memory location—the ASP.NET *Cache* in the example—and report it to the
client for actual display.

The task ID is generated as a random number on the client and passed as an additional
argument to the server method that implements the monitorable task. The following code
shows how to generate a random number in JavaScript that falls in a given range:

```
function getNumber(minNumber, maxNumber)
{
    var num = minNumber + Math.floor(Math.random() * maxNumber);
    return num;
}
```

On the server, the task ID is used as the key to set status information in whatever data
container you decide to use. The client uses the ID also to retrieve currently set information
about the progress of a given task.

Note Can the task ID be generated on the server? Of course, you can generate a random
number of a unique string (for example, a GUID) much more easily on the server than on the
client. On the client, in fact, you rely on JavaScript functions only to get a random number. If
you prefer a GUID, for example, you should consider making a roundtrip to the server, invoking
some service method that gets you a GUID, and then using it from the client to uniquely identify
the task. Alternatively, you could pregenerate some GUIDs and embed them in the page as
JavaScript data. For our purposes, a random JavaScript number large enough to include 10 digits
or more should be enough.

Definition of the Event Sink

In addition to the endpoint for starting the potentially lengthy operation, you also need
a second public API on the server that can be called from JavaScript to obtain status
information. As you know, there are two ways for an ASP.NET AJAX page to expose

client-callable endpoints: Web or WCF services and page methods. You can use any of these techniques to implement the monitoring service. (To implement the task, though, you can also opt for plain partial rendering.)

In terms of performance, calling a Web or WCF service or a page method is nearly the same. Writing a service gives you the benefit of a unique layer of code for all pages in the application. However, using a page method is easier in some regards because it doesn't require you to focus on extra details such as configuration and contracts.

Let's use a page method to enable the monitoring service. Whenever you opt to use a page method, though, you must have the *EnablePageMethods* attribute turned on in the *ScriptManager* control for the page.

As discussed in Chapter 2, a page method is specific to a page, meaning that if two pages need to monitor tasks, you need to replicate the monitoring code in each page. Although a service is probably the best option, a simple trick can save you from writing the same page method for each and every page that includes a potentially lengthy operation. It suffices that you inherited any such page from the same base class, like the one shown here:

```
public class UpdateProgressPage : System.Web.UI.Page
{
    static ProgressMonitor _progMonitor = new ProgressMonitor();

    [WebMethod]
    public static string GetCurrentStatus(int taskID)
    {
        return _progMonitor.GetStatus(taskID);
    }
}
```

Note that the name of the public method—*GetCurrentStatus*—is arbitrary, but once you have chosen it then it must be considered fixed because you have to hard-code it in a JavaScript client file. The *GetCurrentStatus* method essentially polls the shared data container where the task stores its status, and it reports any content back to the client. The overall pattern is depicted in Figure 6-7.

The server task is triggered via *XMLHttpRequest* and, therefore, requires some client code. If you trigger the task via partial rendering, the JavaScript code might not be written by you, but it still exists and runs. The monitoring service, instead, is triggered and controlled by some custom JavaScript code. That's why you need a client API for the Progress Indicator pattern.

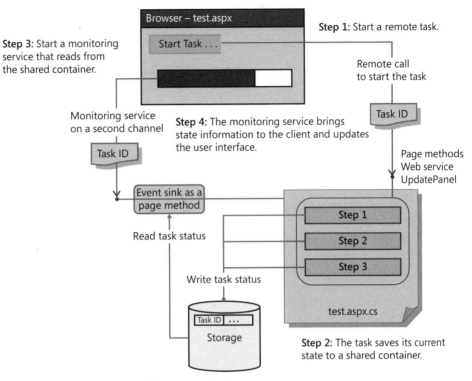

FIGURE 6-7 A graphical view of the Progress Indicator pattern

Definition of the Client API

In Figure 6-6, you see a Start Task button that upon being clicked starts the remote task to be monitored. Let's see the JavaScript code attached to that button. This code, in fact, is responsible for initiating the implementation of the Progress Indicator pattern.

```
<script type="text/javascript">
    var progressManager = null;

    // Called when the page is fully loaded. Use it to complete the initialization.
    function pageLoad()
    {
        progressManager = new Samples.Progress();
    }

    // Called when the user clicks to start the operation.
    function startTask()
    {
        // Start the remote task (using a page method named "ExecuteTask "in this case).
        var taskID = progressManager.getTaskID();
        PageMethods.ExecuteTask(taskID, taskCompleted, taskFailed);
```

```
            // Turn on the progress monitor
            updateUI(true);
            progressManager.startMonitor(taskID, 2000, updateProgress,
              updateProgressCompleted);
        }

        // Callback that signals that the remote method execution terminated.
        function taskCompleted(results, context, methodName)
        {
            // Stop progress and reset UI
            progressManager.stopMonitor();
            updateUI(false);

            // Update page DOM with task results
            $get("<%= Label1.ClientID %>").innerHTML = results;
        }
        :
        :
```
</script>
```

Associated with the *click* event of the button in Figure 6-6, the *startTask* method does three main things. First, it gets a random number to use as the unique task ID. Second, it starts the server-side task to monitor via a progress bar. Third, it activates the monitoring service to poll the status and update the user interface.

As you can see in the preceding listing, the server-side task is implemented as a page method—the *ExecuteTask* method—and invoked via the *PageMethods* proxy. This is arbitrary and certainly doesn't limit your programming power. You can start a remote task using Web or WCF services or even using partial rendering.

The client API for the monitoring service is all in the *Samples.Progress* JavaScript class written using the Microsoft AJAX Client JavaScript library. Instantiated upon page loading, the class has three essential public methods: *getTaskID*, *startMonitor*, and *stopMonitor*. As mentioned, *getTaskID* returns a randomly generated number used to uniquely identify the task. If you don't trust the JavaScript *Math* object, you can get a GUID from a Web service or pregenerate some GUIDs on the server and embed them in the page. You can use the *Page. ClientScriptRegisterArrayDeclaration* method to easily embed a JavaScript array in a Web page.

The *startMonitor* method takes the ID of the task to monitor and the desired interval in milliseconds. In addition, the method accepts a couple of callbacks—one to update the user interface with status information, and one to reset the user interface at the end of the operation. Here's the source code of the *Samples.Progress* class:

```
Type.registerNamespace('Samples');

// Constructor
Samples.Progress = function Samples$Progress()
{
    Samples.Progress.initializeBase(this);
    this._timerID = null;
    this._taskID = null;
```
```

```
        this._progressCallback = null;
        this._msInterval = null;
        this._callback = null;
}


// Start the timer to periodically check the status of the ongoing task
function Samples$Progress$startMonitor(taskID,
        msInterval, progressCallback, progressCompletedCallback)
{
    if (arguments.length !== 4) throw Error.parameterCount();

    // Update internal members
    _taskID = taskID;
    _msInterval = msInterval;
    _progressCallback = progressCallback;
    _progressCompletedCallback = progressCompletedCallback;
    this._startTimer();
}


// Stop the timer
function Samples$Progress$stopMonitor()
{
    window.clearTimeout(_timerID);
    if (_progressCompletedCallback !== null)
        _progressCompletedCallback();
}


// Get task ID
function Samples$Progress$getTaskID(taskID)
{
    return Samples.Random.getNumber(0, 10000000);
}


// Start the timer to control progress
function Samples$Progress$_startTimer()
{
    this._callback = Function.createDelegate(this, this._checkProgress);
    _timerID = window.setTimeout(this._callback, _msInterval);
}


// Modify the request to add the task ID to a hidden field (for UpdatePanel pages)
function Samples$Progress$modifyRequestForTaskId(request, taskID, hiddenField)
{
    var body = request.get_body();
    var token = "&" + hiddenField + "=";
    body = body.replace(token, token + taskID);
    request.set_body(body);
    return request;
}


// Timer function(s)
function Samples$Progress$_checkProgress()
{
    PageMethods.GetCurrentStatus(_taskID,
        this._onFeedbackReceived, this._onFeedbackFailed, this);
}
```

```
function Samples$Progress$_onFeedbackReceived(results, context)
{
    context._startTimer();
    if (_progressCallback !== null)
        _progressCallback(results);
}


function Samples$Progress$_onFeedbackFailed(results)
{
    // No major catastrophe...the user interface simply won't be updated.
}
// Class prototype
Samples.Progress.prototype =
{
    getTaskID:               Samples$Progress$getTaskID,
    startMonitor:            Samples$Progress$startMonitor,
    stopMonitor:             Samples$Progress$stopMonitor,
    modifyRequestForTaskId:  Samples$Progress$modifyRequestForTaskId,
    _startTimer:             Samples$Progress$_startTimer,
    _checkProgress:          Samples$Progress$_checkProgress,
    _onFeedbackReceived:     Samples$Progress$_onFeedbackReceived,
    _onFeedbackFailed:       Samples$Progress$_onFeedbackFailed
}

// Register the new class
Samples.Progress.registerClass('Samples.Progress');
```

The *Samples.Progress* class is built around the timer that polls the server at regular intervals.
Implemented through the window's *setTimeout* function, the timer calls back an internal
method when the interval has elapsed. This method does one key thing: it calls the event sink
on the server that retrieves the current status of the task.

```
function Samples$Progress$_checkProgress()
{
    PageMethods.GetCurrentStatus(_taskID,
            this._onFeedbackReceived, this._onFeedbackFailed, this);
}
```

As mentioned, the event sink is a publicly exposed method that the JavaScript client can
invoke. In this implementation, I assume it's a page method named *GetCurrentStatus*. The
call to the event sink is a classic ASP.NET AJAX remote method invocation. Hence, it requires
a couple of callbacks for success and failure and can optionally carry a context object. No
special action is required in case of failure; it just won't update the user interface. Instead,
whenever significant status information is downloaded to the client, you need to update the
user interface and restart the timer for the next update:

```
function Samples$Progress$_onFeedbackReceived(results, context)
{
    context._startTimer();

    if (_progressCallback !== null)
        _progressCallback(results);
}
```

The success callback receives the *Samples.Progress* object through the context parameter and restarts the timer. After that, it just invokes the page-defined callback and updates the progress bar. In the ASP.NET page, you start the monitoring service when the user clicks to begin the operation and stop the service from within any callback (success or failure) that runs after the operation has completed.

Updating the User Interface

So much for the infrastructure, but how would you update the user interface? A key element is the callback function you pass to *startMonitor* to refresh the user interface with the current status. What this function does depends on the markup in the page that is used to show the progress.

If all that you have is a *<span>* tag to display a message, the following is a good example of a callback:

```
function updateProgress(msg)
{
    $get("Label1").innerHTML = msg;
}
```

The callback function receives any value that the task publishes as its current status through the server progress API. It can be any .NET object, provided that the content is serializable. Let's suppose the task status is a number that indicates the percentage of progress made. Suppose you signal progress using the following code:

```
progMonitor.SetStatus(taskID, "5");
```

The *updateProgress* callback function will just receive a value of "5" and is entirely responsible for updating the user interface interpreting that value. If you want to display a classic progress meter, you have to code it here. Here's an example of how you can do it:

```
function updateProgress(perc)
{
    var table = "<table width=100%><tr><td>{2}%</td></tr>" +
                "<tr><td bgcolor=blue width='{0}%'> </td>" +
                "<td width='{1}%'></td></tr></table>";

    table = String.format(table, perc, 100-perc, perc);
    $get("Label1").innerHTML = table;
}
```

To display a progress bar, you build a dynamic *<table>* tag and split one of its rows into two cells. The leftmost cell takes a share of the row equivalent to the work done and is rendered with a different color. The dynamically built markup is then attached to the DOM wherever you like. If you want it centered in the page, you can style it properly using CSS. Figure 6-8 shows the result with an indication of the ongoing polling.

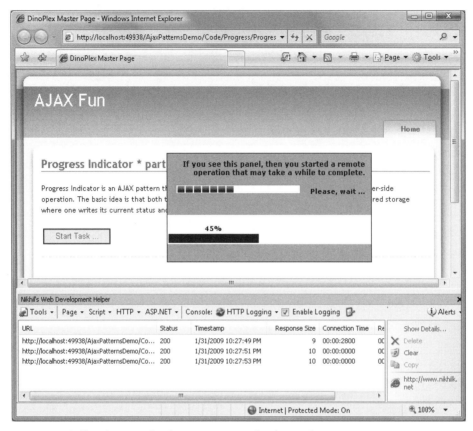

FIGURE 6-8 Polling the server for the current status of a given task

The Web Development Helper tool at the bottom of the browser window logs all requests from the browser. (Get it for free at *http://www.nikhilk.net*.) As you can see, the monitoring service places calls for feedback every two seconds. (See the Timestamp column.) The response of each request consists of a number that indicates the percentage of work done. This number is passed to the *updateProgress* function and is used in the building of a dynamic HTML table.

Canceling an Ongoing Remote Task

After the task has been triggered, the client no longer has control over it. You need a homemade client and server framework like the one we just discussed to know about its ongoing status. The client page regains control over the overall operation only after the response generated by the task has been downloaded to the client.

The solution presented shows a way to "read" the status of the task on the fly, but it lacks a mechanism to "pass" data to the task dynamically, as the task proceeds. In the preceding implementation, the framework is not bi-directional. What would be the advantage of a bi-directional monitor framework? Primarily, such a framework would give you a chance to abort an ongoing task from the AJAX client.

The Too-Easy Way of Canceling Tasks

ASP.NET AJAX supplies some machinery out of the box that makes canceling a remote operation a really easy job. This machinery has some limitations and can't be considered a full-fledged solution. In the first place, the task must be accomplished as a partial rendering operation. Second, no extra work should be required on the server to compensate for abruptly stopping the task.

Figure 6-9 shows a sample page that pops up a progress template with a Cancel button. By clicking the button, you cancel the ongoing operation. But is this really what happens?

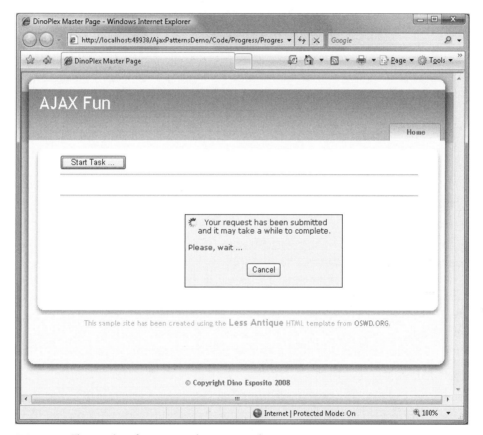

FIGURE 6-9 The user interface to cancel a remote task

The progress template contains a client button bound to a piece of JavaScript code. The following code is attached to the *click* event of the button:

```
function abortTask()
{
    var manager = Sys.WebForms.PageRequestManager.getInstance();
    if (manager.get_isInAsyncPostBack())
        manager.abortPostBack();
}
```

As its first step, the function retrieves the page request manager. In the Microsoft AJAX client library, the *PageRequestManager* object is the nerve center of partial rendering. Upon page initialization, the page request manager registers a handler for the form's *submit* event. In this way, the request manager is involved each time the page is going to post back. The request manager makes a copy of the request's body as prepared by the browser and runs it through the current HTTP executor—by default, the popular *XMLHttpRequest* object.

The page request manager sets up the eventing model of partial rendering and tracks the ongoing operation. If there's any pending operation, the Boolean property named *isInAsyncPostBack* returns *true*. When the user clicks the Cancel button shown in Figure 6-9, the page request manager kicks in and aborts the current request through its *abortPostBack* method.

To understand exactly why this approach won't take you that far, let's briefly take a look at the source code of the *abortPostBack* method within the *PageRequestManager* class in the Microsoft AJAX client library:

```
function Sys$WebForms$PageRequestManager$abortPostBack()
{
    if (!this._processingRequest && this._request)
    {
        this._request.get_executor().abort();
        this._request = null;
    }
}
```

If there's a pending request, the manager instructs the executor of the request to abort. The executor is a JavaScript class that inherits from *Sys.Net.WebRequestExecutor* and takes care of sending the request and receiving the response. In the Microsoft client AJAX library, there's only one executor class—the *Sys.Net.XMLHttpExecutor* class. The class therefore uses the *XMLHttpRequest* object to execute a request. In brief, when the preceding code calls up the abort method, it basically tells the *XMLHttpRequest* object to abort. Put another way, it simply orders the object to close the socket through which the executor will receive any response data.

Can you see where this leads to? Let's suppose that the remote task performs a disruptive action on the server. For example, let's say that the user is given a chance to delete a few records from a database table with a button click. Canceling the operation through a Cancel button, as shown earlier, doesn't really stop the server operation. It simply closes the socket through which you can receive a confirmation message. The *abortPostBack* method on the *PageRequestManager* object is merely a client-side method that has no effect on what's going on in the server.

Designing an Interruptible Server Task

In addition to be monitorable, an interruptible task will periodically check if any feedback came from the client that requests it to quit. Some enhancements are required to the previously discussed framework to make the server code receive and process dynamic client feedback such as a click on the Cancel button.

The progress server API is now based on the following contract:

```
public interface IProgressMonitor
{
    void SetStatus(int taskID, object message);
    string GetStatus(int taskID);
    bool ShouldTerminate(int taskID);
    void RequestTermination(int taskID);
}
```

Compared to the contract discussed in the preceding section there are two new methods: *ShouldTerminate* and *RequestTermination*. The former returns a Boolean value indicating whether or not the ongoing task should be terminated. The *RequestTermination* method represents the entry point in the progress server API for clients willing to stop a task. When invoked, the method creates a task-related entry in the data container (for example, the ASP.NET *Cache*) that *ShouldTerminate* checks to determine whether interruption was requested.

```
public bool ShouldTerminate(int taskID)
{
    string taskResponseID = GetSlotForResponse(taskID);
    object o = HttpContext.Current.Cache[taskResponseID];
    if (o == null)
        return false;
    return true;
}

// Sets the task for termination
public void RequestTermination(int taskID)
{
    string taskResponseID = GetSlotForResponse(taskID);
    HttpContext.Current.Cache.Insert(
        taskResponseID,
        (object) false,
        null,
        DateTime.Now.AddMinutes(CONFIG_MAX_TIME_MINUTES),
        Cache.NoSlidingExpiration);
    return;
}

private string GetSlotForResponse(int taskID)
{
    return String.Format("{0}-Quit", taskID);
}
```

To support dynamic interruption, the task will periodically invoke *ShouldTerminate* right before updating the status. In this way, it will be informed on a timely basis of any client requests to quit. Here's the typical structure of a monitorable and interruptible task:

```
public static string ExecuteTask(int tasked, /* params */ ...)
{
    InMemoryProgressMonitor progMonitor = new InMemoryProgressMonitor();
```

```
// Preliminary check
if (progMonitor.ShouldTerminate(taskID))
{
    // Compensate if needed
    :
    return "Task aborted--0% done";
}

// First step: 5%
progMonitor.SetStatus(taskID, "5");
DoFirstStep(...);
if (progMonitor.ShouldTerminate(taskID))
{
    // Compensate if needed
    :
    return "Task aborted--5% done";
}

:

// Another step: 69%
progMonitor.SetStatus(taskID, "69");
DoSecondStep(...);
if (progMonitor.ShouldTerminate(taskID))
{
    // Compensate if needed
    :
    return "Task aborted--69% done";
}

:

// Final step
progMonitor.SetStatus(taskID, "100");
DoFinalStep(...);
if (progMonitor.ShouldTerminate(taskID))
{
    // Compensate if needed
    :
    return "Task aborted--100% done";
}

// Response
return "Task completed at: " + DateTime.Now.ToString();
}
```

The method is articulated in individual steps. Around each step, the method first reads any communication from the client that has arrived in the meantime and then, if allowed to continue, it writes the current status. If requested to stop, the method attempts to roll back or compensate what has been done so far and then returns. Figure 6-10 shows a possible user interface after the user has interrupted an ongoing server task.

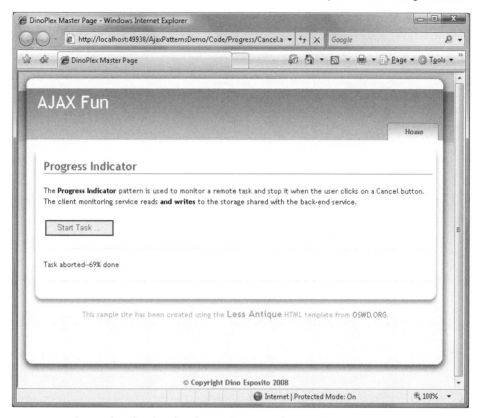

FIGURE 6-10 Screen shot showing that the user interrupted an ongoing server task.

Interrupting a Task from the Client

To abruptly terminate a remote task from the client, you add a Cancel button to the user interface. This time, though, you make the *click* handler point to your own abort method in the client progress API:

```
<script type="text/javascript">
var progressManager = null;
var taskID = null;

function pageLoad()
{
   progressManager = new Samples.Progress();
}

:

function abortTask()
{
    // The task ID is set when the task is started
    progressManager.abortTask(taskID);
}
</script>
```

Let's take a look at the modified client progress API. To stop an ongoing task or, more precisely, to place a request to quit a task, you invoke a new server method exposed by the progress monitor server API as part of the application's server-side logic:

```
// Cancel the operation
function Samples$Progress$abortTask()
{
    PageMethods.TerminateTask(_taskID,
        null,
        null,
        null);
}
```

The *TerminateTask* method now pairs *GetCurrentStatus* in the base page class that incorporates the API for the monitoring component:

```
public class UpdateProgressPage : System.Web.UI.Page
{
    static ProgressMonitor _progMonitor = new ProgressMonitor();

    [WebMethod]
    public static string GetCurrentStatus(int taskID)
    {
        return _progMonitor.GetStatus(taskID);
    }

    [WebMethod]
    public static void TerminateTask(int taskID)
    {
        _progMonitor.RequestTermination(taskID);
    }
}
```

Implemented in this way, task cancelation is far more effective as you produce effects on the server code. The bi-directional progress monitor framework is a duplex channel that a server task and its JavaScript client can use to exchange data in the form of messages.

What About Rollbacks?

The framework built to monitor and stop running an ASP.NET AJAX task doesn't really stop anything—it only notifies the task that the user requested it to quit. If properly designed, the task promptly stops and returns. What about the work it has done already?

In general, when a task is interrupted, it should undo any changes it has made and return. How can you get this behavior?

There's not much that progress monitor framework can do on its end. All the work is delegated to the actual implementation of the task. If any behavior within the remote task can be wrapped in the outermost transaction, you can roll it back after the task has been interrupted. You can easily achieve the same result if you use a workflow. In this case, you wrap the task in a *TransactionScope* activity, use a *Code* activity to set the current status, and check about any termination request. If the task has to terminate, you throw an exception and automatically cause the transaction to roll back.

Unfortunately, not all operations can be easily rolled back automatically. This is true for database updates, but what about changes made to, say, a Microsoft Office document? In general, you can implement the task within a *TransactionScope* block and safely and effectively use any objects that implement the *ITransaction* interface. If you do so, all of these objects will roll back or commit accordingly. And each of these objects will know how to undo its changes. In the worst case, at the very minimum you inform the user that the task has been notified of the user's request for termination.

Other Patterns

The patterns we just covered represent building blocks of most AJAX applications. As mentioned, patterns should not be used dogmatically, nor should they be pursued at all cost. Patterns just help, and that's good enough for patterns to exist and thrive.

Among other things, designing an AJAX application means understanding the range of new options you have for accomplishing the application's task. On the other hand, wasn't AJAX declared to be all about enhancing the user's experience since the beginning? Do you recall the sentence from Chapter 1, "Under the Umbrella of AJAX," that described how the acronym *AJAX* was introduced back in 2005? It sounded was something like, "*Begin to imagine a wider, richer range of possibilities.*"

Well, AJAX patterns make up the compass to orientate you in a new Web world. A good place to read about the state-of-the-art developments related to AJAX patterns is *http://www.ajaxpatterns.org*. If you feel unsecure about how to go forward with a given feature, maybe there's an AJAX pattern to start you off or steer you back onto the right track.

Let's explore a few more patterns of AJAX applications.

The Micro-Link Pattern

If I have to summarize in a single sentence the entire content and impact of AJAX in the world of the Web, I'd say AJAX is about showing new content on the existing page without reloading the whole page. The Micro-Link pattern is just the formal definition of this characteristic.

Page Links and Micro-Links

The Micro-Link pattern is at the core of AJAX because it's about showing new and updated content quickly and smoothly. In a way, a micro-link is an evolution, if not an abstraction, of the classic page hyperlink. Most of the time, a hyperlink involves a roundtrip to the server to download new content via a full page refresh.

As an example, consider a weather Web site. It initially shows a list of cities and offers to dig out more information for each city. You select the city and you are shown the current conditions. The page, however, also includes links to, say, a 10-day forecast for the area, reported airport delays, the satellite map, and maybe a video with the forecast.

All this content likely can't fit into one page. On the other hand, classic links that take you to a different page, or to a different view of the same page, would force a page refresh. A micro-link, therefore, is used. It's a lighter hyperlink that either displays content that is already downloaded but currently hidden or downloads content from the server using an *XMLHttpRequest* call.

As a result, the user clicks on a button or scrolls over some text and gets the additional content displayed in the way that you, as the page author, chose—as a popup, by dynamic DOM manipulation, as a modal dialog box, as a ToolTip, and so forth.

The impact on the page flow is minimal, content appears more quickly, and the browser works less. In addition, only information that is relevant at a given time is presented, perhaps topped with some animation to further enhance it. The state of the page is maintained (on the client side), thus generating an overall working model similar to a desktop scenario.

Micro-Links in Action

More often than not, a micro-link entails downloading some content on demand from the server through an *XMLHttpRequest* call and inserting it on the page. Micro-links are ideal to use to help the user drill down into some content, by expanding out deeper levels of information.

The key decision to be made is whether the content has to be downloaded on demand, fetched in advance, or even incorporated in the initial page content but kept hidden until the user clicks. If you opt for on-demand download, local caching is another aspect to take into account.

Micro-links don't necessarily have to be clickable anchor tags. The trigger of a micro-link can be nearly any event you can capture around the page, including clicking, tapping the keyboard, making mouse movements, and switching input focus ("blur").

What kind of action can a micro-link consist of, anyway? Whatever action you want to associate with a micro-link, it has to be implemented with some JavaScript code. The code can simply turn on or off the CSS *visibility* or *display* attribute of some elements. Likewise, the code can download data or HTML from a remote server and attach it to the DOM. Finally, the code can just create new markup on the fly using the DOM API.

The new content can be appended to the current page, or it can replace some existing content. No options are precluded; it all depends on page requirements. As an example, consider that by using micro-links a site that mainly serves the purpose of showing information can completely remove the need for page reloads.

Micro-Links in jQuery

In the jQuery library (which is discussed in Chapter 5), you find some helpers to more easily implement the Micro-Link pattern. The *load* method, in particular, gets some HTML from a remote resource and injects it into the DOM. Here's how:

```
// The content of the URL is attached to the specified section of the DOM
$("#menu").load("menu.aspx");
```

As you can see, when attached to a DOM event handler, such a method does most of the micro-link work for you. More generally, the implementation of the Micro-Link pattern consists of a remote call plus some DOM manipulation. This is just what the *load* method does with a single instruction.

If you plan to use the jQuery's *load* method, though, you might want to consider making it point to a custom HTTP handler. In this way, you save a bit of work in the ASP.NET runtime pipeline and can more easily shape up the response.

The complete syntax of the jQuery *load* method is shown here:

```
load( url, [data], [callback] )
```

The *url* parameter clearly indicates the source of data to download. The *data* parameter is an optional collection of name/value pairs for the server to process. Finally, the *callback* parameter is an optional callback function that will be invoked after the download is completed either successfully or not.

The *load* function performs a GET request unless the data argument is specified; if that's the case, it switches to a POST request.

The Cross-Domain Proxy Pattern

If you ask around about what the main reason is for introducing AJAX features into a Web application, you'll likely find that *user experience* is the most popular answer. And what about the second most popular answer? This is likely to be *mashup*.

A *mashup* is a Web page that generates its content by combining data from a variety of Internet sources. You know the Web is rich and large and much of its content is freely available. You also know that when the content is not free, it can likely be licensed by entering into an agreement with the owner. So why should you re-create content if existing content is already available? A mashup is a new type of Web page that aggregates existing content from various legal sources.

The Same Origin Policy Problem

The external content you want to access lives outside of your site domain. To access it, you need to perform an HTTP call. It can be a plain HTTP GET or POST, or it can go through the public interface of an exposed Web service.

There's no limitation at all in placing HTTP in any Web server calls from within a full-trust application such as the ASP.NET runtime or the client browser. But when the caller is script code, restrictions apply. In a nutshell, browsers apply the Same Origin Policy (SOP), meaning that any script loaded from one "origin" can't access a resource on a different "origin." In this regard, an *origin* refers to a domain, name, protocol, and port. SOP is a defensive measure that involves not trusting content loaded from any Web sites as a means of preventing cross-site scripting (XSS) attacks.

SOP doesn't apply to some tags, such as *<script>* and *<img>* tags. This means that you can download images and scripts from any site, but your local or downloaded script is not allowed to place an *XMLHttpRequest* call to a different server than from where the script came.

> **Note** Although using SOP makes complete sense as a defensive measure to avoid XSS attacks, it seems to blindly cut off safer activities you can perform via *XMLHttpRequest*. This point is being debated and will likely be settled soon.
>
> The direction that browsers are taking seems to be that of enabling only *XMLHttpRequest* calls to reach cross-domain resources if the remote server opts in using specialized XML-based policy files. Internet Explorer 8, for example, provides an ad hoc object named *XDomainRequest* to exchange data across domains. Because the *XDomainRequest* object does not refer to any standard, Microsoft kept it separate from *XMLHttpRequest*, which is, conversely, steadily on its way to becoming a Word Wide Web Consortium (WC3) ratified standard. *XDomainRequest* has been created by Microsoft and is currently supported only in Internet Explorer 8.

Web Remoting via JavaScript

Although waiting for more powerful (and hopefully standard and cross-browser) tools to place cross-domain calls via JavaScript, there's just one way to code mashups in an AJAX application. The client script calls into a proxy hosted in the same Web server as the current page. This step will work around the SOP limitation.

The proxy is any code behind a SOP-compatible HTTP endpoint. It's likely made of managed code running within the ASP.NET worker process. The proxy, then, will perform a regular call to the service of choice using plain HTTP verbs or more sophisticated protocols such as SOAP. The response is received on the server, formatted as required, and then sent back to the browser, as shown in Figure 6-11.

For example, suppose the implementation of the Micro-Link pattern enables your users to drill down into a feature to get more information. And suppose also that this extra information must come from a mashup. In this case, you can use jQuery's *load* method to point to a custom ASHX HTTP handler in your site, which in turn will connect to the desired source to get requested data. The custom HTTP handler you pass to the *load* method is, in fact, your cross-domain proxy.

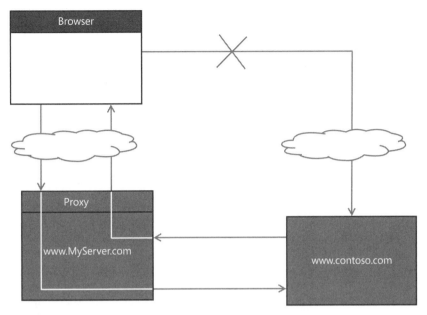

FIGURE 6-11 A graphical view of the Cross-Domain Proxy pattern

Handling Errors

A page that relies on the content provided by some external provider must be ready to handle any failed access. The problem could be caused by some network failure or result from your improper handling of received data.

This possibility is more likely than you might think, and it also depends on the agreement you have with the service provider. For example, some sites enable you to grab content, but they reserve the right to disconnect you in case of increased traffic. When you arrange a mashup, make sure you have a well-defined recovery plan. In many cases, you still need to display data to your users. That's why it's so important to have a plan B you can switch to in case of trouble.

Among the options to consider if you can't get fresh data from the provider, I'd list showing cached results or an alternate service. If neither of these solutions works, you still have the option of admitting the failure and displaying a graceful message to your users.

> **Note** Last but not least, whenever you build a mashup you should determine whether the content is free and under what conditions it is free to use. It's not unusual that Web sites that own information of public interest make it available for free only for personal and noncommercial use. In this case, of course, there's no guarantee that you'll be always able to access that information via a Web service or HTTP. If traffic increases, and cuts are needed, noncommercial users are the first to be cut off. If you intend to make commercial use of external content, you might want to consider a service-level agreement with the organization providing the content.

The Submission Throttling Pattern

Web pages work by submitting data to the Web server. In the classic Web model, the browser is the only actor that is able to communicate with the Web server. The browser, though, is driven by the user. In addition to typing a new URL in the address bar, the user can click in the displayed page to navigate somewhere or she can submit the content of a filled-in form. In a non-AJAX scenario, the submission of the form can only be explicit and happen when the user clicks on an HTML button of type *submit*.

In AJAX, there are more options and submission of any content doesn't have to be explicit. Let's review some of the approaches, starting with an AJAX revisitation of the explicit submission model.

The Explicit Submission Pattern

This pattern is familiar to millions of users of Web applications. As a user, you do some work with the page and then, when you're ready, you click some button to send content to the server. In AJAX, you can explicitly submit content using any button (not necessarily an HTML *submit* button) and even by using any event as the trigger.

More importantly, because in AJAX you have much more power on the client, you can even consider submitting any content to the server in chunks and in multiple steps instead of a single shot. If you opt for sending it all at one time, you're performing an explicit submission; otherwise, you're throttling your submission, mostly for performance reasons.

In the end, it's key to note that when using AJAX, explicit submission via a fixed type of button is no longer the sole option. Pick any of the available options, but be aware of the alternatives.

Piecemeal Submission

The primary alternative to classic explicit submission is an implementation of the Submission Throttling pattern. Simply put, the pattern suggests you cache the content to submit in a browser buffer and submit it piecemeal over multiple steps. What's the benefit of this approach?

Some AJAX applications are characterized by a high number of requests. The canonical example is the server-based autocompletion engine. As the user types into a text box, a request is made to the server for suggestions. You can only imagine the number of requests that hit the Web server at peak times! Bandwidth and server considerations make unfiltered content submission impractical.

To reach a reasonable compromise between the responsiveness of the application and the Web server workload, you might want to take control of the submission process and never let the user explicitly submit a form. To understand throttling, let's examine how a typical autocompletion feature is actually implemented. The discussion is based on the source code of Microsoft's *AutoComplete* extender in the AJAX Control Toolkit.

The autocomplete extender seems to place a request for suggestions as the user types content into the input box. So you would expect a handler for the *keypress* event that makes the call to the specified Web or WCF service. If you dig out the code, however, this is not what you find. Here's an excerpt of what you find instead:

```
// Handler for the text box keydown event
_onKeyDown: function(ev)
{
    // A key has been pressed, so we reset the timer
    this._timer.set_enabled(false);

    // Is it a special key?
    if (k === Sys.UI.Key.esc) {
        :
    }
    else if (k === Sys.UI.Key.up) {
        :
    }
    else if (k === Sys.UI.Key.down) {
        :
    }
    else if (k === Sys.UI.Key.enter) {
        :
    }
    else if (k === Sys.UI.Key.tab) {
        :
    }
    else {
        this._timer.set_enabled(true);
        // Start the timer to retrieve results since now it's an actual key
    }
}
```

First, the extender uses an internal timer configured to an interval of one second (by default). The timer is started when a text box gets the focus. As soon as a key is pressed down, the timer is stopped and an analysis of the key begins. If the key is one with a special meaning (such as Enter, ESC, arrows or Tab) the extender proceeds with its own code. If the key pressed indicates content to be entered in the text box buffer, the timer is started.

The timer is stopped and restarted every time an actual key is typed. If you stop typing for one second (or whatever interval you configure), on the tick of the timer, the actual content of the input field is submitted to receive suggestions. Not a big change for users, but great news for the server.

Timers to Simulate Multithreading

As you might already know, there are no multithreading capabilities in JavaScript. This simply means that the language doesn't offer any construct through which you can describe a chunk of code that runs in "parallel" with another one. Any piece of JavaScript code runs in a single execution thread. The interpreter takes any code we provide and executes it as fast as possible, but sequentially. Period.

Timers, though, are an inherently asynchronous tool. By creating a timer in JavaScript, you're telling the interpreter to run that code as soon as possible, but not necessarily right away. If the code you associate with the timer callback is simple enough and the interval is appropriate, the interpreter will be able to schedule it properly and advance multiple tasks simultaneously.

In other words, JavaScript doesn't publicly expose thread constructs to the script developer. However, it makes timers available, and timers are an effective way to schedule tasks so that multiple tasks can progress concurrently.

Timers are an essential element in the implementation of a submission-throttling solution.

The Live Form Pattern

The fundamental need related to submission throttling is to send requests to the server in a controlled way, at fixed intervals, instead of uploading them as the need arises. In an AJAX world, a request can take various forms. It can be a call to a Web service as well as a plain GET call made via *XMLHttpRequest*. It can also be a POST request made to upload information to the server.

In the autocompletion example, submission throttling is used to reduce the number of requests that hit the Web server. As a result, some of the events that would cause a request to fire are swallowed by the client code and only a subset is actually served. If a user types multiple characters in a text box in less than one second (or whatever interval is configured), only one request is placed instead of many.

Throttling is also useful for form submission processes. In this case, the pattern takes a different name—Live Form. The idea is that you don't wait for the user to complete his work and explicitly submit the form; instead, you anticipate the user's actions by sending partially filled form content to the server for immediate validation and feedback.

A common implementation consists of placing an *XMLHttpRequest* call every time the user tabs out of a field. The request goes asynchronously and modifies the form and user interface as a result. Another approach might consist of a scheduled upload that occurs every few seconds.

When you choose to throttle the data submission, you also need to decide how the server can figure out if it's time to begin processing uploaded data. As far as forms are concerned, I like a mix of Live Form and Explicit Submission. That is, you implement Live Form and have the content uploaded and validated asynchronously. When some valid content is available on the server, you enable the Submit button for users to click explicitly. When the server receives input via the Submit button, it can start processing the request.

Should you upload the current content of the form when the user clicks the button to explicitly submit? Or should you rely on the fact that valid data is already on the server? Well, both options are valid in theory. In practice, it depends on the particular form and your needs. If you detect that further changes have been made to the client that makes the client content different from the server content, a full explicit data submission is required.

Summary

AJAX applications are peculiar because they are Web applications designed and implemented in a way that is significantly different from the canonical request/response pattern of classic Web processes. In AJAX, patterns also have the value of showing developers and architects what can be done in addition to submitting the content of a form over a browser-led HTTP communication.

Although today we still tend to refer to AJAX as something external to the known world of Web and something to explain and understand via explicit patterns, in the near future it will be incorporated into the same notion of the Web. AJAX is not a temporary trend; AJAX is the new partner that will revitalize the Web.

Patterns help you to find effective solutions. In AJAX, however, they also help to spot problems and potential caveats. Many of the AJAX patterns you find documented are trivial to understand. In this chapter, I selected patterns that, in my opinion, are the foundation of the new AJAX mindset.

Chapter 7
Client-Side Data Binding

Do not fear to be eccentric in opinion; every opinion now accepted was once eccentric.

—*Bertrand Russell*

No doubt that if you bought this book you have a strong interest in AJAX. As repeatedly mentioned in earlier chapters, though, along with its many shiny lights AJAX also has a dark side. AJAX is quick and easy to implement for simple individual features of a page; you'll find that it's much less trivial as you scale it to the size of an entire application.

More often than not, Web applications are the front end of one or more enterprise systems. Data from these enterprise systems is variegated and must be aggregated, perhaps even formatted, before display. Sure, you might say, "Isn't this that cool thing called *mashup*?" Yes, sort of.

Mashup isn't necessarily a complicated thing. It's all about capturing data and assembling it into a presentation format. In classic ASP.NET, you have ad hoc server controls that expose HTML templates and data source properties. Undoubtedly, this has been the coolest feature of the ASP.NET platform since it came out a few years ago. A data source property refers to a collection of objects; a template is a piece of HTML with placeholders for data. Creating a server-side mashup is a task you accomplish in three relatively simple steps: you define the templates; you get the data; you connect data to the templates. This is the gist of data binding and, more importantly, the essence of data-driven Web applications—the most popular (if not the only) type of Web application.

The power of classic ASP.NET data binding lies in the fact that you do everything on the server using a true programming language and rely on powerful tools, such as facilities in the Microsoft .NET Framework and data-bound server controls. Furthermore, these server controls often offer important extra features such as paging and sorting.

With classic ASP.NET, data binding isn't really an issue. It's as powerful and flexible as you might reasonably need. But it takes a full page reload for each interaction.

With AJAX, you realize that many tasks that were traditionally performed on the server can now take place on the client. This results in fewer roundtrips to the server, saves valuable bandwidth and, last but not least, offers users an overall better experience. However, employing AJAX means offloading most of the data binding work to the client, where only JavaScript can be used. And this is really a tricky point.

The programming environment you find within a client browser has little in common with the programming power the .NET Framework offers on the server. Client-side data binding is still possible and viable, but it's a much less obvious option than one might think at first.

In this chapter, I'll review a couple of general approaches to client-side data binding that are developed around a pair of popular AJAX design patterns. Then I'll review the tools that the next ASP.NET platform will offer out of the box.

An Architectural Tour of ASP.NET Data Binding

In general, data binding is the process that retrieves data from a given source (whether it's a database query, an XML file, or in-memory data) and dynamically associates this data with properties on user interface elements.

In ASP.NET, user interface elements are essentially server controls that have been specifically designed to support data binding—that is, *data-bound controls*. Data-bound controls are not another family of controls; they're simply server controls that feature a few well-known data-related properties and feed them using a well-known set of collection objects.

Up until now, in ASP.NET data binding has been a server-side process. The data binding process in general, though, doesn't necessarily have to be only a server-side process. Let's examine the characteristics of server-side ASP.NET data binding so that we can identify key actions and components to replicate those same characteristics in a client-side scenario.

The whole idea of Web data binding is held up by two pillars: the HTML template and the data source.

Defining the HTML Template

The purpose of the vast majority of software applications is to present some content to users through their user interface. The purpose of a Web application is to present some content to users through HTML.

How would you generate the HTML?

There are two main approaches. One entails using automated markup factories that take some data in as input and massage that into a fixed-schema user interface. The other stems from the idea of using templates and a declarative syntax to express bindings between markup elements and data fields. In the latter case, the final shape of the user interface is not known in advance and is largely subject to developer customization.

Automated HTML Factories

If you made it this far, I think it's safe to assume you're familiar with the *DataGrid* control. The *DataGrid* control is a good example of an automated HTML factory.

Like other ASP.NET server controls, the *DataGrid* control generates HTML markup. However, the resulting HTML is the result of an assembling process whose rules are hard-coded. When you use a *DataGrid* control, you pass data and some optional settings to the component. In return, you always get an HTML table.

The schema of the output you get is fixed and can't be changed to something significantly different. You can customize the style of cells and rows. You can change the number of cells in a given row and group the values of multiple cells in a single one. You can add or remove a header or footer. But that's about all you can do.

For *DataGrid* controls, you can't apply a custom template for each data item; you can't even apply the same custom template to all data items. The only possible template for bound data is the one that is hard-coded in the component.

In general terms, an automated HTML factory is a component that generates markup algorithmically using a hard-coded workflow. Here's an example of how it could work:

```
// This factory generates an HTML table
string GenerateMarkup(List<Customer> data)
{
    StringBuilder buffer = new StringBuilder("<table>");
    foreach(Customer c in data)
    {
        buffer.Append("<tr>");

        buffer.AppendFormat("<td title=\"{0}\">{1}</td><td>{2}</td><td>{3}</td>",
                            c.CustomerID, c.CompanyName, c.Country, c.ContactName);
        buffer.Append("</tr>");
    }

    // Finalize
    buffer.Append("</table>");
    return buffer.ToString();
}
```

The structure of the resulting markup is set in stone in the code of the factory. The only changes allowed are those explicitly provided for by the programming interface of the factory.

Template-Based HTML Factories

Another popular server control in ASP.NET is the *Repeater* control. At its core, the *Repeater* control simply loops through a given data collection and applies a user-defined HTML template to each bound data item.

To this category of HTML factories belong controls that implement an extremely simple rendering algorithm with no hard-coded workflow logic except the basic loop over bound data. In the ASP.NET toolbox of controls, you find the *ListView* and *DataList* controls in addition to the aforementioned *Repeater* control.

The functioning of a template-based HTML factory is illustrated in the following pseudo-code:

```
// This factory generates a completely custom HTML structure
string GenerateMarkup(List<Customer> data,
                      string headerTemplate,
                      string itemTemplate,
                      string footerTemplate)
{
    StringBuilder buffer = new StringBuilder();

    // Apply the header template
    if (!String.IsNullOrEmpty(headerTemplate))
    {
        string header = GenerateHeader(headerTemplate);
        buffer.Append(header);
    }

    // Apply the item template
    if (!String.IsNullOrEmpty(itemTemplate))
    {
        foreach(Customer c in data)
        {
            string item = GenerateItem(itemTemplate, c);
            buffer.Append(item);
        }
    }

    // Apply the footer template
    if (!String.IsNullOrEmpty(footerTemplate))
    {
        string footer = GenerateFooter(footerTemplate);
        buffer.Append(footer);
    }

    // Finalize
    return buffer.ToString();
}
```

Any user interface based on a list of data items will reasonably have an optional header and footer, plus a template for the data item. (It might even have more items, such as separators, but this is enough to demonstrate the concept.) The algorithm simply applies the header template, loops through the item list, and finally applies the footer.

The final format of the HTML results from the markup used for the header, footer, and items. It's another way of building an HTML table or producing a horizontal, breadcrumb-like list of items.

I haven't said much about HTML templates or answered questions about how you might define them. Well, the answer is, "It depends." In particular, it depends on the tools you're using. In ASP.NET, an HTML template is a plain piece of markup intertwined with <% ... %> code blocks.

Code blocks basically contain data binding expressions that are evaluated at compile time and translated into executable statements. At runtime, then, statements produce literals integrated with markup.

In general, an HTML template contains placeholders for external bindable data. The syntax for defining these data placeholders is determined by the framework.

The *ITemplate* Interface

In ASP.NET, an HTML template is exposed by data-bound controls as a property of type *ITemplate*. Here's the definition of the interface:

```
public interface ITemplate
{
    void InstantiateIn(Control container);
}
```

As a developer, you don't work with this interface directly most of the time. Often, all you do is define a chunk of HTML with some code blocks. This content is then parsed and compiled into a class that implements the *ITemplate* interface. Hence, an HTML template is ultimately an object that implements the *ITemplate* interface.

The *InstantiateIn* method is responsible for manipulating the structure of the provided container to incorporate data-bound content. Looking at the pseudo-code just shown, you can compare the *ITemplate* object to the method *GenerateItem* because it generates the user interface markup in accordance with an HTML-explicit schema. Generally, though, in ASP.NET the *ITemplate* interface is the mechanism through which data-driven parts of the HTML user interface are generated.

The following code snippet shows HTML templates in an ASP.NET *Repeater* control. The final output is a list of bulleted points showing the last and first names of Northwind employees.

```
<asp:repeater runat="server" ID="Repeater1">

   <HeaderTemplate>
     <b>Employees</b>
     <hr />
     <ul>
   </HeaderTemplate>

   <ItemTemplate>
     <li>
         <b><%# Eval("lastname") %>, </b>
         <%# Eval("firstname") %>
     </li>
   </ItemTemplate>

   <FooterTemplate>
     </ul>
   </FooterTemplate>

</asp:repeater>
```

You define the appearance by defining the header, footer, and item templates. Templates are defined as plain markup. ASP.NET compiles each template element to an *ITemplate* object whose code is similar to the following listing. The listing shows that the code behind HTML templates returns a list of bulleted points:

```
public class BulletedPointHeaderTemplate : ITemplate
{
    public void InstantiateIn(Control container)
    {
        // Add markup literals to the page tree
        container.Controls.Add(new LiteralControl("<b> Employees</b> <hr /> <ul>"));
    }
}

public class BulletedPointFooterTemplate : ITemplate
{
    public void InstantiateIn(Control container)
    {
        // Add markup literals to the page tree
        container.Controls.Add(new LiteralControl("</ul>"));
    }
}

public class BulletedPointItemTemplate : ITemplate
{
    public void InstantiateIn(Control container)
    {
        // Add markup literals to the page tree
        container.Controls.Add(new LiteralControl("<b>"));

        // Add a data-bindable element
        Label lblLastName = new Label();
        lblLastName.DataBinding += new EventHandler(this.BindLastName);
        container.Controls.Add(lblLastName);

        // Add markup literals to the page tree
        container.Controls.Add(new LiteralControl("</b>, "));

        // Add a data-bindable element
        Label lblFirstName = new Label();
        lblFirstName.DataBinding += new EventHandler(this.BindFirstName);
        container.Controls.Add(lblFirstName);
    }

    // Handler of the DataBinding event for the Label element
    // that renders the lastname column in the template.
    private void BindLastName(Object sender, EventArgs e)
    {
        Label l = (Label) sender;
        IDataItemContainer container = (IDataItemContainer) l.NamingContainer;
        l.Text = DataBinder.GetPropertyValue(container.DataItem, "lastname").ToString();
    }
```

```
    // Handler of the DataBinding event for the Label element
    // that renders the firstname column in the template.
    private void BindFirstName(Object sender, EventArgs e)
    {
        Label l = (Label) sender;
        IDataItemContainer container = (IDataItemContainer) l.NamingContainer;
        l.Text = DataBinder.GetPropertyValue(container.DataItem, "firstname").ToString();
    }
}
```

There are many possible ways to create a template. First and foremost, you can create it explicitly using plain markup. In addition, you can also create it as a code-only class. In this case, you set the template properties as shown here:

```
Repeater1.HeaderTemplate = new BulletedPointHeaderTemplate();
Repeater1.FooterTemplate = new BulletedPointFooterTemplate();
Repeater1.ItemTemplate = new BulletedPointItemTemplate();
```

Finally, you can populate an HTML template with the content of an ASCX user control, as shown here:

```
Repeater1.HeaderTemplate = Page.LoadTemplate("bulletedpointheader.ascx");
Repeater1.FooterTemplate = Page.LoadTemplate("bulletedpointfooter.ascx");
Repeater1.ItemTemplate = Page.LoadTemplate("bulletedpointitem.ascx");
```

The ASP.NET's *ITemplate* mechanism is unique, powerful, and flexible. At a higher level of abstraction, though, you can recognize two overall approaches to producing HTML. You can define the user interface via chunks of HTML literals intertwined with declarative pieces of data. You use a tailor-made and arbitrary syntax to specify bindings. Alternatively, you pass the bindable date to a class method and do everything via code.

To top off the discussion, let's briefly compare the two approaches.

Template-Based Approach vs. Automated Approach

A template-based approach to generating the user interface Web application is clearly an approach that's easier to follow and implement. As a developer, you specify explicitly the HTML markup you desire, which also enables you to use designer tools. Maintenance is greatly facilitated.

An approach based on code gives you total control over the rendering algorithm, but once it's developed this approach can't be changed without recompiling. An automated generator doesn't depend on any external syntax to insert placeholders; at the same time, however, it provides you with a fixed way to place and expand bindings.

In classic ASP.NET, you typically use a template-based approach and resort to automated HTML factories when you need to implement a particular rendering algorithm. In this case, you usually develop a custom data-bound control.

In classic ASP.NET, though, you do your job entirely on the server, where you have available to you powerful designer tools such as the Microsoft Visual Studio 2008 Web Forms designer, first-class languages such as C#, and the power of the full .NET Framework.

Defining HTML templates to be used from within the client browser in a JavaScript environment is a bit more complicated. Likewise, creating automated HTML factories in JavaScript might not be a walk in the park. Nonetheless, effective AJAX solutions require powerful data binding, and they require it to happen entirely on the client side.

Defining the Data Source

Many .NET classes can be used as data sources—and not just those that have to do with database content such as ADO.NET data containers. In ASP.NET, any object that exposes the *IEnumerable* interface is a valid bindable data source. Many bindable objects, though, actually implement more advanced versions of *IEnumerable*, such as *ICollection* and *IList*.

Feasible Data Sources in ASP.NET

The *IEnumerable* interface defines the minimal application programming interface (API) to enumerate the contents of the data source:

```
public interface IEnumerable
{
    IEnumerator GetEnumerator();
}
```

Richer interfaces such as *ICollection* and *IList* add other members, including *Count*, *CopyTo*, *Add*, and *Remove*. In particular, you can bind a Web control to the following classes:

- ADO.NET container classes such as *DataSet*, *DataTable*, and *DataView*
- Data readers
- Custom collections, dictionaries, and arrays

To be honest, I should note that the *DataSet* and *DataTable* classes don't actually implement *IEnumerable* or any other interfaces that inherit from it. However, both classes do store collections of data internally. These collections are accessed using the methods of an intermediate interface—*IListSource*—which performs the trick of making *DataSet* and *DataTable* classes look like they implement a collection.

Today, as it will be in the near future, the most common approach is binding controls to collections of custom objects. Custom objects, then, will be more and more a representation of entities from the problem's domain created using ad hoc frameworks such as LINQ-to-SQL and Entity Framework.

Data Binding Properties

All data-bound controls implement the *DataSource* and *DataSourceID* properties, plus a few other properties that serve the purposes of certain data-bound controls.

The *DataSource* property lets you specify the data source object the control is linked to. Note that this link is logical and does not result in any overhead or underlying operation until you explicitly bind the data to the control.

You activate data binding on a control by calling the *DataBind* method. When the method executes, the control actually loads data from the associated data source, evaluates the data-bound properties (if any), and generates the markup to reflect changes. Here's the declaration of the *DataSource* property:

```
public virtual object DataSource {get; set;}
```

The *DataSource* property is declared to be of type *object*, and it can ultimately accept objects that implement either *IEnumerable* (including data readers) or *IListSource*. By the way, only *DataSet* and *DataTable* implement the *IListSource* interface.

The *DataSource* property of a data-bound control is generally set programmatically. However, nothing prevents you from adopting a kind of declarative approach as follows:

```
<asp:DropDownList runat="server" id="theList"
    DataSource="<%# GetData() %>"
    :
    :
/>
```

In this example, *GetData* is a public or protected member of the code-behind page class that returns a bindable object.

The *DataSourceID* property gets or sets the ID of the data source component from which the data-bound control retrieves its data. This property is the point of contact between data-bound controls and a family of data source controls that includes, among others, *SqlDataSource* and *ObjectDataSource*. Here's the declaration of the *DataSourceID* property:

```
public virtual string DataSourceID {get; set;}
```

By setting *DataSourceID*, you tell the control to turn to the associated data source control for any needs related to data—retrieval, paging, sorting, counting, or updating.

As mentioned, both *DataSource* and *DataSourceID* are available on all data-bound controls. However, the two properties are mutually exclusive. If both are set, you get an invalid operation exception at runtime. Note, though, that you also get an exception if *DataSourceID* is set to a string that doesn't correspond to an existing data source control.

> **Note** A few other data binding properties are supported in ASP.NET. They are *DataMember*, *DataTextField*, *DataValueField*, and *DataKeyField*.
>
> *DataMember* gets or sets the name of the data collection to extract when data binding to a data source. *DataMember* has no relevance if you bind to data using *DataSourceID* with standard data source components. The *DataTextField* property specifies which property of a data-bound item should be used to define the display text of the nth element in a list control. Similar to *DataTextField*, the *DataValueField* property specifies which property of a data-bound item should be used to identify the nth element in a list control.
>
> Finally, the *DataKeyField* property gets or sets the name of key field in the specified data source. The property lets data-bound controls uniquely identify a particular object in the bound list.

Data Binding at the Time of AJAX

ASP.NET server-side data binding is a mature and consolidated technology backed by a number of rich controls for creating grids, lists, and trees to represent hierarchical data. All the work is done by server controls, and customization is allowed through HTML templates. Data is specified using a collection of entity objects or ADO.NET containers.

How can we port this whole solution to the client side?

In this section, I'll briefly outline the key facts of client-side data binding and then explore them in depth in the remainder of the chapter.

Tools for Effective Client-Side Data Binding

In a Web scenario, any data to display comes from the server. And the server manages data in formats that depend on the server platform. In an ASP.NET context, within the Web server, data is represented as a collection of .NET objects. On the client, however, data must be represented in a format that JavaScript can manipulate.

The first point to deal with is the marshaling of data across the wire and from a .NET representation to a JavaScript-compliant representation. In Chapter 3, "AJAX Architectures," we identified the ideal marshaling format in JSON, the JavaScript Object Notation format. ASP.NET AJAX provides a built-in layer of code to automatically expose server data returned by Windows Communication Foundation (WCF) services as JavaScript objects. Internally, the transformation is accomplished using JSON as the intermediate format, as shown in Figure 7-1.

After you have data on the client in a format that you can handle, you need to decide how to format it into displayable HTML.

Unfortunately, there are no controls on the client comparable to ASP.NET's *DataGrid* control or any other ASP.NET controls. The browser doesn't feature any component that, bound to data, can generate markup, as in classic server-side ASP.NET. Subsequently, you need a client-side engine that performs data binding, preferably with some template support. Currently, ASP.NET AJAX is not much help here.

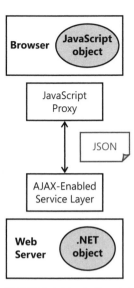

FIGURE 7-1 Marshaling data from the server side to the client side

How can you build such a client-side engine for data binding?

Out of the box, the browser has only two low-level tools for turning data into HTML. One is the *innerHTML* property. Exposed by all elements in the Document Object Model (DOM), this property replaces the content of the element with the provided HTML string. A similar functionality is also offered by the somewhat slower DOM API. The standard DOM API works by creating and editing a tree of objects that represent HTML elements and related attributes.

In the end, a client-side engine for data binding must first be able to generate HTML based on an array of JavaScript objects. The final layout can be determined algorithmically, or it can result from HTML templates. The production of the HTML is not a process completely separated from displaying the content. If you opt for generating HTML as a string, you can display it only via the *innerHTML* property—the faster option. Otherwise, you can opt for designing the desired HTML layout by composing a tree of HTML elements via the DOM API. In this latter case, you make a tradeoff between flexibility and speed of rendering.

Note I guess that after reading these words some readers might reasonably wonder whether things really can be more flexible than creating a string. My point here is contrasting two approaches for generating HTML—building an HTML string via code, or specifying an HTML template and having some library do the rest. Building an HTML string via code is, these days, a task that is greatly simplified by a client-side *StringBuilder* object that the Microsoft AJAX library has made available. In this way, you write HTML the way you want as you write code for it.

Again, is there a way to gain more flexibility? Flexibility is a concept with many attributes and variables, and although we may agree on a general definition, it may mean slightly different things to different people. In this context, I believe that the key question to answer is, how easy will be modifying the HTML you produce via code? Sometimes a simple modification to an HTML template can do the trick much quicker and in a less error-prone way. On the other hand, if changes require you to add a lot of logic to the rendering process, the flexibility of code is largely unparalleled.

Partial Rendering Is Still an Option

In Chapter 2, "The Easy Way to AJAX," we explored ASP.NET partial rendering and labeled it as the easy way to AJAX. The key fact about partial rendering is that it provides an excellent compromise between the need to implement asynchronous data loading and display and the desire to use the same, familiar ASP.NET application model.

Data binding is certainly a hot topic these days for Web applications. It represents one of the most difficult tasks to implement in an AJAX way, if only because there is no (current) framework support. Applied to data binding, partial rendering is still a viable option for the time being.

The main problem we face today is the lack of proper tools on the client to turn data into HTML quickly and effectively. Options do exist, but the likelihood is high that you'll find holes in any options when you try to apply them to your particular context. Later in this chapter, we'll examine a preview of ASP.NET AJAX 4.0, which is scheduled to be released later in 2009. ASP.NET AJAX 4.0 is a promising attempt from Microsoft to supply a powerful and effective platform for client-side, data-driven applications.

Limited to data binding, the *UpdatePanel* control and the entire partial rendering paradigm is an option to consider. I recommend taking a careful look at it, especially if you need a rich data display that includes sorting, paging, and filtering capabilities. Obtaining that through partial rendering takes only a moment. Getting the same functionality via a pure AJAX approach definitely takes more time and might be a more error-prone approach.

On the other hand, as you might recall from Chapter 2, the *UpdatePanel* control works on top of a full postback that includes the transportation of full view state and the execution of almost the entire page life cycle. However, rendering happens on the server, where you have a lot of powerful tools to control the HTML being produced.

In partial rendering, the response is much smaller than in classic ASP.NET, but the whole request isn't really faster. In practice, though, this might not be a problem. What Web application do you want? What's most important for you? Is it pure performance? Or is it the quality of the user experience? If it's the latter, partial rendering might still work for you.

A pure AJAX approach almost always performs better than an approach based on partial rendering. When the rendering happens on the client and the server sends back only data, the response is usually tiny—several times smaller than a classic ASP.NET response. However, this simple fact alone doesn't make it a full-fledged solution. To be really effective and also to substantially reduce the number of roundtrips, it has to be combined with an effective HTML generation engine and client-side caching.

As of today, no tools exist that are quick to use, effective, mature, and consolidated. Someone will certainly develop such tools one day, and probably in the not-too-distant future. Until then, partial rendering will remain an option for data binding, and any other pure AJAX approach will require lots of work on your part or it will require you to use third-party products.

The Browser-Side Template Pattern

Let's see what you can do yourself to implement a client-side data binding solution. Aside from partial rendering, you can take one of two routes. You can have the Web server send only data to the client and have the client prepare HTML either algorithmically or based on templates. This approach is referred to as the Browser-Side Template (BST) pattern.

The second option entails the server generating and returning HTML. This approach is known as the HTML Message (HM) pattern. With this approach, the request is less efficient than with BST, but it's much faster and smaller than with partial rendering. And it doesn't require a powerful JavaScript framework.

Let's attack browser-side template first.

Generalities of the BST Pattern

HTML is a text format; so ultimately creating an HTML display is a matter of creating a big string of text. You can loop over the bound data and algorithmically produce a big HTML string using concatenation and other string manipulation tools. This approach works. Period. But is it a solution that's efficient and easy to maintain?

The BST pattern is centered on rules to produce a string of HTML markup as the final output while having a collection of objects with a few public properties as the input. The idea behind the pattern is that you use HTML templates to define how you would like the final HTML to appear. And then you employ a relatively simple (and separated) engine to bind data to the template.

The BST Pattern Explained

In the design of a client-side engine for data binding, you need to strive for separation between the user interface and presentation logic. The user interface is the HTML you produce; the presentation logic is the logic you use to combine data and HTML elements.

The user interface is expressed using HTML templates—namely, hidden chunks of HTML that contain placeholders for actual data. At rendering time, such templates become the input of a tailor-made JavaScript framework that parses the HTML and expands placeholders based on bound data.

The resulting HTML is then displayed using the *innerHTML* property. Alternatively, the JavaScript client engine might parse the HTML templates to a DOM tree. However, in this case the burden of the JavaScript would be significant and probably so high as to invalidate the decision to use HTML templates.

What's an HTML Template Exactly?

I've used the expression "HTML template" many times already, but I haven't yet shown you an example of what it could look like. Here's an example:

```
<tr style="background-color: #F0FAFF;">
    <td align="left"> #Symbol </td>
    <td align="right"> #Quote </td>
    <td align="right"> #Change </td>
</tr>
```

The template contains standard HTML elements and placeholders defined using a framework-specific declarative syntax. In the example, *#Quote* and other similar strings represent placeholders for bound data. Marking placeholders with a leading # symbol is an arbitrary choice made by the author of the JavaScript framework. In other words, you can use any syntax you like as long as the JavaScript binding engine can recognize it. (The code later in the chapter will distinguish between the property to be substituted and the background color.)

You might think of placeholders as context variables to be substituted in at rendering time. Clearly, such a template gives it more flexibility than a static HTML page.

As you can see, the preceding HTML template is a partial chunk of HTML. Taken alone, an HTML template doesn't represent a displayable piece of HTML. This poses another problem. How do you place a template in a Web page without disturbing the browser? As you know, each browser could react differently to incomplete or invalid markup. In some cases, there's a risk that the HTML template leaks in the displayed document without it having been massaged first.

There are many ways to hide HTML fragments in a Web page. You can use, for instance, customized HTML tags. You can use XML data islands. Or you can use plain HTML tags that are hidden from view using CSS styles. Here's an example that combines XML data islands and CSS styles:

```
<xml id="item" style="display:none">
    <tr style="background-color:#F0FAFF;">
        <td align="left"> #Symbol </td>
        <td align="right"> #Quote </td>
        <td align="right"> #Change </td>
    </tr>
</xml>
```

The combination of a browser-supported tag and the no-display CSS style ensures that the markup is correctly loaded in the DOM but is not displayed until some code runs to turn it on.

Mixing Data and Templates

For data binding to happen, you need a JavaScript component that loads the content of the template and parses it. In doing so, the component will recognize and expand placeholders to include bound data.

The JavaScript component is not a generic HTML builder. Instead, it must be targeted to a particular HTML layout—either a grid, a list, or perhaps a hierarchical tree. In a sense, the JavaScript component is a sort of client-side control that incorporates a rendering algorithm and makes it customizable through templates and public members.

In general, you can have many such components—one for each data-bound layout you intend to use and support. Each layout can, in turn, support one or multiple HTML templates. For example, to obtain a simple list of data items, you might want to define three templates: header, footer, and item. The item template is the only one that will reasonably support binding. The JavaScript HTML list builder will first render the header. Next, it will look through the bound data collection and render an instance of the item template for each bound data item. Finally, it will render the footer.

This is the simplest possible approach to building HTML on the client because it barely implements the minimal set of features one would expect from a browser-side template and binding engine. As we'll see in a moment, in the real world you need a more sophisticated HTML builder that accepts a few function delegates to style any piece of bound data before it's appended to the HTML buffer. Put another way, you need a JavaScript component with a programming model that looks similar to that of an ASP.NET data-bound control. Whereas a *DataGrid* control fires an *ItemDataBound* event, the JavaScript HTML builder will execute a JavaScript callback to customize the rendering process to a large extent.

Dual-Side Templating

The Dual-Side Templating pattern is a variation of BST that attempts to combine server and client code to optimize the rendering process and make it the smoothest whenever and wherever possible. Suppose you need to display a grid of data and want it to automatically refresh at a given interval. The periodic refresh can be achieved via AJAX by placing a remote call to some service, grabbing data, and displaying that data through client-side data binding and HTML templates. But what about the initial display of data?

You have a few options.

First, you can fire a call to the service and grab data as soon as the page is loaded from the Web server. After it's on the client, the data is processed by the HTML builder and packaged into markup using embedded HTML templates. You reuse the same scheme you would use for periodic updates. The model doesn't change, but you fire an extra request to the service and delay the first display of the page.

A second option to consider is one that addresses the latter point—it delays the first display of the page. You grab any data to be bound on the server and serve it to the client using a pre-initialized JavaScript variable. Upon loading the data, you have some ad hoc code to read data from the variable and build the markup accordingly. Again, you have just one rendering model and save an extra roundtrip. On the flip side, you have some extra code to embed (and run) in the page startup.

A third option to consider entails the server just serving up the initial display of the grid as plain HTML. At the same time, ad hoc HTML templates and JavaScript will be embedded in the page as usual. When needed, an asynchronous request is placed, data is downloaded and packaged into markup, and finally data is displayed, replacing the initial grid.

Ultimately, dual-side templating is an optimization of BST and the key difference is in the content of the page placeholder that receives and hosts data. The placeholder is empty in classic BST. The placeholder is either filled programmatically on the client or populated on the server in dual-side templating. As a general recommendation, if you're considering using BST, you should also consider using dual-side templating.

Creating a BST Reference Implementation

A key achievement of the BST pattern is separating the code that produces the view of data from the data displayed in the view. This concept can be summarized for ASP.NET developers by saying that you need the JavaScript counterpart of data-bound server controls. In JavaScript, this means having a set of specific HTML builders exposing their own programming model.

Let's go through an example of how to design and implement an HTML builder that renders a template-based grid of data.

BST: The Big Picture

In Figure 7-2, you see the full diagram of the steps involved in a BST solution. The page contains the hidden HTML templates to be used, and it also defines a placeholder for the area where the downloaded data should be displayed.

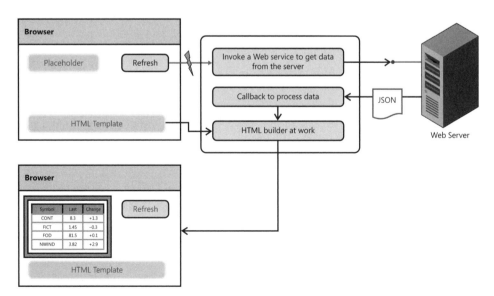

FIGURE 7-2 Browser-side templates in action

The user triggers a remote call that downloads some data to the client. The data is managed by a JavaScript callback, which takes care of instantiating a new breed of component—the HTML builder.

The HTML builder receives a reference to one or more HTML templates in the page DOM and the downloaded data, and it returns an HTML string. Finally, the callback injects the string in the page DOM. Figure 7-3 is a preview of the sample page we'll start building in a moment.

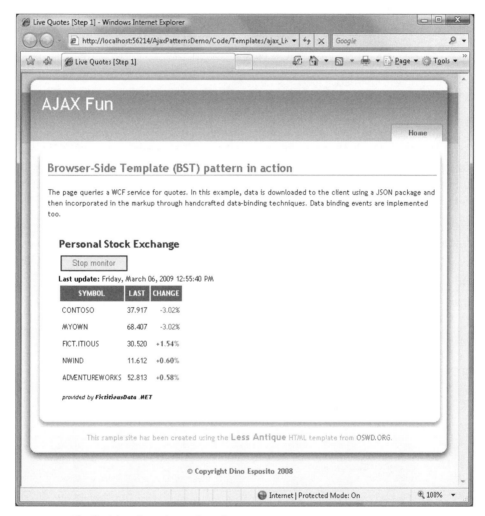

FIGURE 7-3 The final data-bound page in action

This said, let's have a look at some code.

Preparing the Page

The heart of BST is a JavaScript class that implements the rendering engine. In the sample implementation I'm presenting here, this class is named *HtmlListBuilder*. The class accepts up to three HTML templates—for the header, footer, and data-bound items. You can reference these templates directly from the DOM or specify them as plain string literals. Here's an excerpt of the initialization code for each page with data binding capabilities:

```
// This variable represents an HTML builder component
var builder = null;

// Using the Microsoft AJAX client library
function pageLoad()
{
    if (builder === null)
    {
        builder = new Samples.HtmlListBuilder();
        builder.loadHeader($get("header"));
        builder.loadFooter($get("footer"));
        builder.loadItemTemplate($get("item"));
    }
}
```

You can embed HTML templates directly in the page in invisible *<div>* tags. This works as long as the markup in the block is well formed. However, this is not always possible. As you'll see in a moment, when building a table you can't just express header, footer, and item templates as three independent and well-formed HTML fragments.

> **Note** Here we are making an important (and implicit) assumption: each necessary template must be expressed individually. Another option would be to use just one complete HTML template that uses some ad hoc syntax to indicate which parts are to be repeated for each data item and which ones are either static or data-bound but repeated only once. In many cases, using just one complete template works, and this is the approach taken by ASP.NET AJAX 4.0. The approach in this demo is more akin to what happens in ASP.NET server controls, where you have a distinct HTML template property for each portion of the final user interface you want to customize.

A better option is to embed templates as XML data islands, as shown here:

```
<xml id="header" style="display:none;">
    <table cellpadding="4" cellspacing="2">
        <tr style="background-color:#6B696B;color:White;">
            <th>SYMBOL</th>
            <th>LAST</th>
            <th>CHANGE</th>
        </tr>
</xml>

<xml id="footer" style="display:none;">
    </table>
</xml>

<xml id="item" style="display:none;">
    <tr">
        <td align="left"> #Symbol </td>
        <td align="right"> #Quote </td>
        <td align="right"> #Change </td>
    </tr>
</xml>
```

As you can see, the template is a chunk of HTML that refers to binding fields using a custom notation. In this case, I'm using the *#PropertyName* expression to indicate the placeholder for a bound value. In particular, the expression refers to the value of the property *PropertyName* on the currently bound data item. The syntax you use to identify the bound value is totally arbitrary; any expression that you know how to parse within the HTML builder might work. When data is finally available, you invoke the *bind* method on the HTML builder and obtain the generated HTML as a string.

The following code shows how to make a call to a WCF service that returns a collection of objects. Each object represents the current quote and last change of a stock symbol.

```
// Invoked after a user clicks some UI button
function getLiveQuotes()
{
    // Invoke a WCF service that gets updated stock quotes. Note that
    // you are actually calling a service defined in your domain. If needed
    // the service will implement the Cross-Domain Proxy pattern and forward your
    // call to a remote service.
    Samples.WebServices.LiveQuoteService.Update(onDataAvailable);
}

// Callback invoked when the results of the service call have been downloaded
function onDataAvailable(results)
{
    // The variable results contain the JavaScript version of the
    // service response. This is expected to be a collection of JavaScript objects.

    // Have the HTML builder generate the HTML markup
    var html = builder.bind(results);

    // Display the markup within the browser
    $get("grid").innerHTML = html;
}
```

Clearly, in this example the element named *grid* is the placeholder in the page that expects to receive the final output.

The HTML Builder

The component responsible for combining HTML templates and external data is the *Samples. HtmlListBuilder* object. An instance of this JavaScript object is created upon page loading and properly initialized by loading HTML templates:

```
builder = new Samples.HtmlListBuilder();
builder.loadHeader($get("header"));
builder.loadFooter($get("footer"));
builder.loadItemTemplate($get("item"));
```

An HTML builder is essentially a factory for HTML markup and implements a fixed rendering algorithm. As mentioned, the algorithm for the *HtmlListBuilder* component consists of looping through the bound data and applying a template for each item. Before and after the item template, the builder applies a static (that is, not data-bound) template for the header and footer.

The component can be written in plain JavaScript or by using any JavaScript library with a flavor of object orientation. In this case, I'll use the Microsoft AJAX client library. The following code shows the constructor of the component:

```
Type.registerNamespace('Samples');

// Class constructor
// This code gets called when you instantiate this class
Samples.HtmlListBuilder = function Samples$HtmlListBuilder()
{
    // Calls the base constructor, if any
    Samples.HtmlListBuilder.initializeBase(this);

    // Initializes the private members
    this._header = "";
    this._footer = "";
    this._itemTemplate = "";
}

Samples.HtmlListBuilder = function Samples$HtmlListBuilder(header, footer)
{
    // Calls the base constructor, if any
    Samples.HtmlListBuilder.initializeBase(this);

    // Initializes the private members
    this._header = header;
    this._footer = footer;
    this._itemTemplate = "";
}
```

When you instantiate the builder, you can optionally provide header, footer, and item templates via the constructor. In this case, templates must be passed in as plain HTML strings.

If you don't specify templates through the constructor, you'll use ad hoc members to set them. In particular, the builder features three properties—one for each supported template.

```
// PROPERTY header: string
function Samples$MarkupBuilder$get_header()
{
    if (arguments.length !== 0)
        throw Error.parameterCount();

    return this._header;
}

function Samples$MarkupBuilder$set_header(value)
{
    // Note Function._validateParams is defined by the AJAX Framework...
    var e = Function._validateParams(arguments, [{name: 'value', type: String}]);
    if (e)
        throw e;

    this._header = value;
}
```

```
// PROPERTY footer: string
function Samples$MarkupBuilder$get_footer()
{
    if (arguments.length !== 0)
        throw Error.parameterCount();

    return this._footer;
}

function Samples$MarkupBuilder$set_footer(value)
{
    var e = Function._validateParams(arguments, [{name: 'value', type: String}]);
    if (e)
      throw e;
    this._footer = value;
}

// PROPERTY itemTemplate: string
function Samples$MarkupBuilder$get_itemTemplate()
{
    if (arguments.length !== 0)
        throw Error.parameterCount();

    return this._itemTemplate;
}

function Samples$MarkupBuilder$set_itemTemplate(value)
{
    var e = Function._validateParams(arguments, [{name: 'value', type: String}]);
    if (e)
        throw e;

    this._itemTemplate = value;
}
```

In the Microsoft AJAX client library, you define properties using a pair of functions: one for accessing the value, and one for assigning the value. Moreover, the library provides some helpers to validate parameters, such as the *validateParams* method, which takes the list of arguments used in the function call and validates it against the provided list of expected arguments.

The *header*, *footer*, and *itemTemplate* properties don't contain any special logic. All that properties do internally is check input and manage an associated private member. HTML template properties can also be set programmatically using the content of the DOM subtree. Here's the list of methods you can use:

```
// METHOD:: loadHeader()
function Samples$MarkupBuilder$loadHeader(domElement)
{
    var temp = domElement.innerHTML;
    this._header = temp;
}
```

```
// METHOD:: loadFooter()
function Samples$MarkupBuilder$loadFooter(domElement)
{
    var temp = domElement.innerHTML;
    this._footer = temp;
}


// METHOD:: loadItemTemplate()
function Samples$MarkupBuilder$loadItemTemplate(domElement)
{
    var temp = domElement.innerHTML;
    this._itemTemplate = temp;
}
```

The *loadHeader, loadFooter,* and *loadItemTemplate* methods take a DOM reference and extract the HTML out of it to save back into the property.

Finally, the generation of HTML takes place in the *bind* method. This is where the rendering algorithm is implemented:

```
function Samples$MarkupBuilder$bind(data, callback)
{
    var temp = this._generate(data, callback);
    return temp;
}

function Samples$MarkupBuilder$_generate(data, itemCallback)
{
    var pattern = /#\w+/g;  // regular expression
    var _builder = new Sys.StringBuilder(this._header);

    for(i=0; i<data.length; i++)
    {
        var dataItem = data[i];
        var template = this._itemTemplate;
        var matches = template.match(pattern);

        for (j=0; j<matches.length; j++)
        {
            var text = matches[j];
            var memberName = text.slice(1);

            // Invoke a callback to further modify the data to be bound
            var memberData = dataItem[memberName];
            var temp = memberData;
            if (itemCallback !== undefined)
            {
                temp = itemCallback(memberName, dataItem);
            }

            template = template.replace(matches[j], temp);
        }

        _builder.append(template);
    }
```

```
    _builder.append(this._footer);

    // Return the markup
    var markup = _builder.toString();
    return markup;
}
```

The *bind* method takes two arguments. One is the JavaScript array representing the data to bind. The other is the JavaScript callback to be invoked during the rendering to personalize individual items based on run-time conditions and data values. I'll return to discussing the role of the callback in a moment.

The *bind* method essentially accumulates HTML text in a buffer. The buffer is represented by a *Sys.StringBuilder* JavaScript object. As a first step, the header template is loaded into the buffer. Next, a loop is started over the bound collection of data. The item template string is parsed to isolate all substrings that match the syntax you used for data bindings. In the sample code, bindings take the form of *#PropertyName*.

The following regular expression recognizes all occurrences of words prefixed by the # symbol:

```
var pattern = /#\w+/g;
```

The *match* method on the JavaScript *string* object takes the expression and returns an array of matching substrings. For each match, you first cut off the leading # character and then replace the property name with the actual value for that property in the current data item.

At the end of the loop, the footer template is appended to the buffer and the entire buffer is then returned to the caller.

> **Note** The list rendering pattern discussed here is common and can be applied to nearly all possible markup layouts you can think of. Obviously, you might want to create more specific rendering algorithms, such as one for rendering a grid or a tree. The need for a more specific rendering algorithm might also arise from the need to use more specific callbacks to customize particular portions of the user interface.

Customized Item Rendering

Is there anything in this code that we can improve? The code presented in this chapter barely implements the minimal set of features that one would expect from a browser-side template and binding engine. Let's have another look at Figure 7-3, which presents current quotes and changes for some stock prices. Wouldn't it be nice if you could render in red the stocks that have fallen and render in green stocks that have risen?

In a classic server-side data binding model, you likely use a *DataGrid* or *GridView* control to produce the HTML. For a *GridView*, for instance, you can handle the *RowDataBound* event of the *GridView* control and directly modify the style of the cells involved:

```
void GridView1_RowDataBound(object sender, GridViewRowEventArgs e)
{
    // Let's assume cell #2 contains the current change and the
    // change is a string that already includes a leading + for
    // rising stocks and a leading - for falling stocks.

    if (e.Row.Cells[2].Text.StartsWith("+"))
        e.Row.Cells[2].ForeColor = Color.Green;
    else if (e.Row.Cells[2].Text.StartsWith("-"))
        e.Row.Cells[2].ForeColor = Color.Red;
}
```

As you can see, this is neat and effective. Unfortunately, this is a server-side solution.

In a client-side solution, you need a more sophisticated HTML builder that accepts one or more JavaScript callbacks. JavaScript callbacks will be used essentially to inject some custom code and massage any piece of bound data before it's appended to the buffer. Such JavaScript callbacks can be given any programming interface that works for you.

In the following example, you see a slightly modified version of the code shown earlier. The code invokes a remote service and grabs data asynchronously. Data is then passed to the HTML builder along with a JavaScript callback. As a result, the generated markup includes the standard HTML layout hard-coded in the builder, plus any page-specific customization applied by the callback.

```
// Invoked after a user clicks on some UI button
function getLiveQuotes()
{
    // Grab data from a remote source
    Samples.WebServices.LiveQuoteService.Update(onDataAvailable);
}

// Callback invoked when the results of the service call have been downloaded
function onDataAvailable(results, applyFormatting)
{
    // Have the HTML builder generate the HTML markup using the
    // callback to further style the output
    var html = builder.bind(results, applyFormatting);

    // Display the markup within the browser
    $get("grid").innerHTML = html;
}

// Callback function to personalize the markup
function applyFormatting(memberName, dataItem)
{
    var propValue = dataItem[memberName];
    if (memberName === "Change" && propValue.charAt(0) === "+")
```

```
    {
        return "<span style='color:green;'>" + propValue + "</span>";
    }

    if (memberName == "Change" && propValue.charAt(0) === "-")
    {
        return "<span style='color:red;'>" + propValue + "</span>";
    }

    return propValue;
}
```

As mentioned, the prototype of the callbacks, as well as the injection points, are entirely up to you. In this case, the rendering callback is invoked for each bound data item and for each binding element found in the item template. As an example, for the following HTML template, the callback is invoked three times for each element in the collection to personalize the markup for the *Symbol*, *Quote*, and *Change* properties:

```
<xml id="item" style="display:none;">
    <tr >
        <td align="left"> #Symbol </td>
        <td align="right"> #Quote </td>
        <td align="right"> #Change </td>
    </tr>
</xml>
```

In the example, the callback is expected to receive the data item itself plus the name of the property for which it's invoked. The idea is to style the content of the *Change* property in a way that reflects the course of the stock—green for a stock rising in price, and red for a stock that is falling in price.

```
function applyFormatting(memberName, dataItem)
{
    // Return the modified markup to append to the buffer
}
```

The callback returns a string containing the modified markup to be appended to the builder's buffer.

Customized Markup Rendering

The approach discussed can be further extended and applied virtually to any piece of the markup the builder is generating. Put another way, wherever you have a *#Word* expression in the HTML templates, you can have a piece of JavaScript to dynamically expand it to a data-bound or static chunk of HTML. Let's consider the following template:

```
<xml id="item" style="display:none;">
    <tr>
        <td align="left"> #Symbol </td>
        <td #Style1 align="right"> #Quote </td>
        <td align="right"> #Change </td>
    </tr>
</xml>
```

As you can see, the second *<td>* element contains a *#Style1* expression. Because the expression matches the *#Word* pattern, it will be caught by the regular expression manager. As a result, the rendering callback is invoked with the following arguments:

```
applyFormatting("Style1", dataItem)
```

Any string the function returns is substituted for the *#Style1* expression in the template. Here's a possible example:

```
function applyFormatting(memberName, dataItem)
{
    if (memberName === "Style1")
    {
        if (dataItem["Change"].charAt(0) === "+")
            return "style='background-color:yellow;'";
        else
            return "";
    }
    :
    :
}
```

If the data item currently being bound represents a rising stock, the background color of the cell that contains the *#Style1* expression is styled as yellow. (See shaded numbers in the Last column in Figure 7-4.) Note that legitimate constructs using the "#" notation, such as CSS color values, are also provided to the *applyFormatting* method. However, once there, the color values are ignored (they don't match a named property in the data item).

By injecting JavaScript callbacks in the rendering process that generates the markup for the incoming data, you gain a lot of flexibility and can achieve nearly any combination of styles, data, and markup you might dream of.

Note The HTML templates you use for data binding might contain elements with a unique ID. These elements can be further referenced and scripted but not until the HTML template is processed by the browser. After the *innerHTML* property of a page element has been updated to include an element with a given ID, you can start scripting that element. The following code shows exactly how to do that:

```
function onDataAvailable(results)
{
    // Bind data
    var temp = builder.bind(results, applyFormatting);

    // Update the UI
    $get("grid").innerHTML = temp;

    // Now you can script elements (such as "lblProvider") in the HTML templates
    $get("lblProvider").innerHTML = results[0].ProviderName;
}
```

An HTML template defined as pure HTML and stored in a hidden *<div>* tag is still part of the DOM, so you're not strictly required to wait until the template is bound and displayed within its page container. However, the empirical rule of waiting for the template to display before you script template elements keeps you on the safe side in case the technology used for HTML templates is not entirely based on plain HTML.

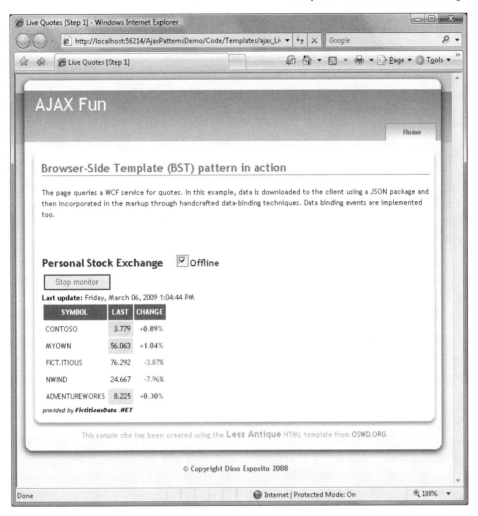

FIGURE 7-4 Customized rendering for data-bound pages

Making Your Solution Juicier with jQuery Effects

The jQuery library contains a number of visual facilities and effects that you can employ during data binding. For example, you can hide or overlay the template for the time it takes for fresh data to be downloaded. When data is received, you can update the template in the background and fade it in slowly.

The following code shows a jQuery-enabled version of the callback that displays data-bound templates after a remote call to a service is made:

```
function onDataAvailable(results)
{
   // Bind data and update the UI
   var markup = builder.bind(results, applyFormatting);
```

```
// A bit of jQuery animation
$("#grid").fadeOut(1000, function() {

        // Update the DOM with the data-bound template
        $("#grid").html(markup);

        // Display the grid with a fade-in effect
        $("#grid").fadeIn(1000);
});

// Display service description
updateServiceDescription(results[0].ProviderName);
}
```

The *fadeOut* method hides the content of the specified DOM element (the grid) in one second. At the end of the fade-out algorithm, the specified callback runs to update the *innerHTML* property of the grid and fade it in slowly in one second.

The HTML Message Pattern

The BST pattern forces you to generate any HTML you need in the browser using the JavaScript language. In general, this is a good thing because it allows you to isolate all (or, at least, most) of the presentation logic in the one tier. In addition, by using templates and JavaScript callbacks you can keep up with the inherently dynamic nature of HTML and manage to accommodate characteristics of the data and the user's expectations.

Templates help you a lot in wedding code flexibility with ease of maintenance. A general-purpose class such as the *HtmlListBuilder* presented here completes the offering and closes the circle. You can't reasonably rely on plain JavaScript statements to generate HTML and mix generation with sprinkles of presentation logic. Code will soon get too complex, hard to read, and inevitably error-prone. Helper classes, which are better if developed with the help of a rich framework such as the Microsoft AJAX client library, come to the rescue.

Although the BST approach seems to perfectly embody the philosophy of AJAX, you should also wonder whether it's the only approach possible to building data-driven applications that don't cause full postbacks and page reloads.

Let's consider an alternative to the browser-side templating model. In particular, I'll present here the HTML Message (HM) pattern, which is a smarter implementation of the partial-rendering feature of ASP.NET AJAX.

Generalities of the HM Pattern

According to the HM pattern, the server-side code is responsible for generating blocks of HTML markup to be displayed in the browser. A user action that requires, say, a grid refresh generates an HTTP request that the ASP.NET application resolves by responding with an HTML fragment.

How is this approach different from classic ASP.NET or ASP.NET partial rendering? Isn't partial rendering just returning a piece of HTML? What's the point of using the HM pattern?

The HM Pattern Explained

In HM, you still need to write a good deal of JavaScript in client pages. So typically you place a call to a remote Web or WCF service (or even a plain ASP.NET page method) using JavaScript. This step marks a huge difference from classic ASP.NET. So what, then, is the difference between HM and BST?

Unlike BST, an HM solution is based on the idea that you receive ready-made, data-bound markup from the server instead of plain data. In this way, the logic required on the browser side is extremely thin and simple. All that is required, in fact, is merely the display.

A possible implementation of the pattern entails that you make a call to a remote URL to receive an HTML snippet ready for display. The remote URL can either be a Web or WCF service or an ad hoc HTTP handler. The client asks the server for some data, and the server returns data plus layout and style information. The request is still asynchronous and AJAX-based; the size of the response should generally be small and subsequently limited to relatively short snippets to preclude lengthy update delays or partial UI flashing. Figure 7-5 shows the mechanics of the HM pattern.

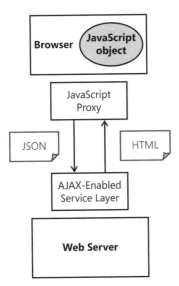

FIGURE 7-5 The mechanics of the HM pattern

On the client, the HTML snippet is appended to the DOM by using the *innerHTML* property of the designated container. In an HM scenario, the service or the HTTP handler that returns HTML snippets is clearly application-specific, because the HTML response is closely tied to the application's display style and expectations.

Motivation for Using the HM Pattern

At first glance, you might reasonably wonder what the point of using the HM pattern is. The pattern is concerned with making a request and getting HTML fragments back. As you know, HTML fragments typically contain both markup and data. But in an AJAX world, we tend to prefer to minimize content transfer by moving around only data and leaving any layout and formatting of information to the client.

If you delve deeper, you can find other reasons for not using the HM pattern. Here's a brief list of shortcomings. Be cautious with HTML responses because such responses might not only affect bandwidth but also create an undesired coupling between the server-side services and pages. If this happens, at a minimum, you might find it hard to develop the middle and presentation tiers simultaneously. Furthermore, any change you decide to make to the structure of the user interface most likely will have an impact on the server-side HTML factory and will therefore increase coupling there. Finally, a naïve implementation of the server-side code might lead to coupling the HTML factory with business logic. However, when you opt for this pattern, it's always a good idea to work to keep the HTTP endpoint and the HTML factory at a low level of coupling. By doing this, changes to the HTML factory don't affect the outermost HTTP endpoint—be it a WCF service or an ASP.NET HTTP handler.

Note that in this section, which is trying to explain the motivation for using the HM pattern, I still have yet to provide a single valid reason to justify the use of the pattern. This weird approach is deliberate.

The HM pattern is the offspring of the classic request-for-markup Web model. The difference is that you now use *XMLHttpRequest* to carry the request instead of the request being browser-led. When is HM recommended?

If you're porting an existing large application to AJAX, it's not unusual that you work with conventional ASP.NET pages where all the HTML generation happens on the server side. In cases where you have a large quantity of legacy code, you might find it quicker to implement HTML responses to preserve existing code as much as possible. (Keep in mind that an HM solution is still more efficient than partial rendering, though not as fast to implement.)

Another scenario in which you might want to consider using HM is when your presentation code and markup are particularly complex and you prefer to build it on the server, where you can rely on more powerful programming languages and tools. Finally, another valid situation to use it in is when your team has a clear server-side programming bias and doesn't feel particularly comfortable using JavaScript.

BST vs. HTML Message

The HM pattern moves the entire burden of UI generation to the server and, in particular, to the endpoint you call from the client. On one hand, the HM pattern allows you to use managed code to implement any complex logic required to generate the markup. On the server, you can read configuration files, connect to remote services, and access databases of HTML templates with a freedom and programming power that is impossible to obtain within the client browser using BST.

At the same time, with HM you write the code that generates the markup without having much help from visual tools such as designers. This means that any required changes to the markup have to be addressed with C# code and there's no clear separation between layout, data, and code-behind files vs. layout/markup files.

A possible workaround consists of defining some internal ASP.NET pages that the service queries for markup in a server-to-server scenario. These pages work as templates; they can be created with Visual Studio 2008 and simply deployed in the same Microsoft Internet Information Services (IIS) application that hosts the AJAX service layer. These pages will be invoked programmatically, and the markup they return is then forwarded to the client.

In addition, the HTML Message pattern tends to generate more traffic than plain calls going to a service that returns raw data. I should note, though, that the HTML Message pattern results in less traffic than partial rendering. The more you add styles and HTML sugar, the more the size of the packet you return grows. In light of this, you can decouple HTML styling from HTML layout and embed in the markup only references to client-side CSS classes for styling. If you reduce the HTML markup to just layout and data, the percentage of extra stuff that is transferred beyond raw data might be significantly smaller.

However, BST is not free of risks as far as excess data is concerned. If the data objects you serialize to JSON contain much more data than needed, you still risk consuming more bandwidth than strictly necessary. A badly optimized BST solution might be the weaker solution when compared with a hyper-optimized HM solution.

HM is ideal for specific and relatively simple actions the user can accomplish from a page, such as asking to see the balance of an account. In this case, you can develop a simple HTTP factory, put it behind an HTTP endpoint, and get markup to show directly. But this approach must be carefully evaluated for data binding and more sophisticated things.

Developing an HM Reference Implementation

Let's see what it takes to build a sample application based on the HTML Message AJAX design pattern. We'll just rework the previous example and invoke a service asynchronously to get a list of stock quotes rendered as a nice-looking HTML grid.

HM: The Big Picture

In an HM implementation, all the work occurs on the server. From a client perspective, the AJAX call is a call that brings ready-made HTML to the client that will then be displayed. (See Figure 7-6.)

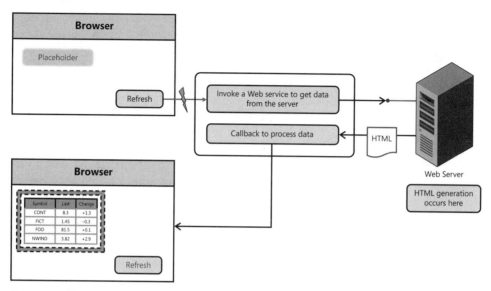

FIGURE 7-6 The HM pattern in action

The following code shows all that you need to have and run on the client:

```
function getLiveQuotes()
{
    // Invoke a proxy for a WCF service designed to return HTML responses.
    // Input data is read from a configuration file.
    Samples.FinanceInfoService.GetQuotesFromConfigAsHtml(onDataAvailable);
}

function onDataAvailable(results)
{
    // Update the UI
    $get("grid").innerHTML = results;
}
```

From the client, you invoke a service and receive a string as the response. The string is made of HTML that the AJAX callback just attaches to the *innerHTML* property of the placeholder element.

> **Note** The Dual-Side Template pattern also can be combined with the HTML Message pattern, which results in pages that first display HTML content generated on the server and then periodically, or upon the user's request, connect and get fresh updates.

The Remote Service

While discussing the BST example, we didn't pay much attention to the structure of the sample service returning data. All in all, that was a not as relevant an aspect in the context of a BST scenario as it will be for an HM scenario. Things are a bit different if you consider an HM solution. So let's briefly examine what we expect from the data provider service.

The following bit of code shows the contract of the stock quote service we used in the BST and HM examples:

```
[ServiceContract(Namespace="Samples.Services", Name="FinanceInfoService")]
public interface IFinanceInfoService
{
    [OperationContract]
    StockInfo[] GetQuotes(string symbols);

    [OperationContract(Name="GetQuotesFromConfig")]
    StockInfo[] GetQuotes();

    [OperationContract(Name = "GetQuoteseAsHtml")]
    string GetQuotesAsHtml(string symbols);

    [OperationContract(Name = "GetQuotesFromConfigAsHtml")]
    string GetQuotesAsHtml();
}
```

The service is built around a couple of internal components—the finder and renderer. The finder connects to a given public finance service and obtains live data. The finder component is characterized by an interface, and the actual finder class to use is read from the configuration file. As you can easily imagine, this is an aspect of the implementation that lends itself very well to the use of dependency injection or some similar patterns, such as Plugin or Service Locator.

Any data that is obtained through a finder class is then composed into an HTML snippet using a renderer component. The renderer component exposes an interface and can be replaced also by simply changing a setting in the configuration file. The default HTML renderer builds a table with some hard-coded styles.

The following code snippet shows the interfaces of the finder and rendered classes:

```
public interface IFinanceInfoFinder
{
    string ProviderName { get; }
    StockInfo[] FindQuoteInfo(string symbols);
}

public interface IFinanceInfoRenderer
{
    string GenerateHtml(StockInfo[] stocks);
}
```

The interfaces guarantee smooth interoperability as the data obtained by the finder flows directly into the methods of the renderer.

Here's the implementation of service methods:

```
public StockInfo[] GetQuotes(string symbols)
{
    // Get the finder component to use (using a locator/factory pattern)
    IFinanceInfoFinder finder = ResolveFinder();
    if (finder == null)
        throw new NullReferenceException("Invalid Finder component.");

    // Find and return quote information
    return finder.FindQuoteInfo(symbols);
}

public StockInfo[] GetQuotes()
{
    // Get the list of symbols from an entry in the configuration file
    string symbols = ResolveSymbolsFromConfig();

    // Return information
    return GetQuotes(symbols);
}

public string GetQuotesAsHtml(string symbols)
{
    // Get stock information
    StockInfo[] stocks = GetQuotes(symbols);

    // Get the Renderer component to use
    IFinanceInfoRenderer renderer = ResolveRenderer();
    if (renderer == null)
        throw new NullReferenceException("Invalid Renderer component.");

    // Generate HTML and return
    return renderer.GenerateHtml(stocks);
}

public string GetQuotesAsHtml()
{
    // Get the list of symbols from an entry in the configuration file
    string symbols = ResolveSymbolsFromConfig();

    // Return information
    return GetQuotesAsHtml(symbols);
}
```

An essential implementation of the finder component is coded in a base class from which actual finder classes will inherit:

```
public class BaseFinanceInfoFinder : IFinanceInfoFinder
{
    public BaseFinanceInfoFinder()
    {
    }
```

```
    public virtual string ProviderName
    {
        get { return "BaseInfoFinder"; }
    }

    StockInfo[] IFinanceInfoFinder.FindQuoteInfo(string symbols)
    {
        return this.FindQuoteInfo(symbols);
    }

    protected virtual StockInfo[] FindQuoteInfo(string symbols)
    {
        return null;
    }
}
```

Each finder class will override the *ProviderName* property and the *FindQuoteInfo* method to set up a Cross-Domain Proxy pattern, connect to any configured service, and grab data.

Markup Rendering

In the sample implementation, the *GenerateHtml* method of the renderer builds a table based on some predefined and hard-coded settings. In general, it can use any other style information that might be passed around from the client. However, the stock quote service is designed to pick up any renderer "service" that is configured as the official HTML generator. Any interaction between the stock quote service and the renderer occurs through the *IFinanceInfoRenderer* interface.

To actually generate HTML, you can take any possible approach. You can use in-memory versions of data-bound server controls, you can extract HTML templates from user controls, or finally, you can build HTML by hand, as shown here:

```
public class DefaultFinanceInfoRenderer : BaseFinanceInfoRenderer
{
    public DefaultFinanceInfoRenderer()
    {
    }

    protected override string GenerateHtml(StockInfo[] stocks)
    {
        string[] headers = { "SYMBOL", "LAST", "CHANGE", "TIME" };
        string[] columns = { "Symbol", "Quote", "Change", "Time" };

        StringBuilder builder = new StringBuilder();

        // Construct HTML
        builder.AppendFormat("<table cellpadding='{0}'
                                     cellspacing='{1}'
                                     border='{2}'
                                     rules='{3}'
                                     frame='{4}'
                                     style='{5}'>",
            4, 0, 1, "rows", "hsides", "background-image:url(./images/bkgnd.gif);");
```

```
builder.AppendFormat("<tr style='background-color:{0};color:{1};'>",
                     "#6B696B", "white");

// Define header
for (int i = 0; i < headers.Length; i++)
{
    builder.AppendFormat("<th>{0}</th>", headers[i]);
}
builder.Append("</tr><tr>");

// Define body
for (int i = 0; i < stocks.Length; i++)
{
    StockInfo stock = stocks[i];
    for (int j = 0; j < columns.Length; j++)
    {
        string value = (string) Utils.GetPropertyValue(stock, columns[j]);
        builder.AppendFormat("<td style='color:{0}' align='{1}'>{2}</td>",
            (value.StartsWith("+") ? "green"
                                 : (value.StartsWith("-") ? "red" : "")),
            (j == 0 ? "left" : "right"),
            value);
    }

    builder.Append("</tr><tr>");
}

// Define footer
builder.AppendFormat("<td style='background-color:#eeeeee;'
                         align='right'
                         colspan='{0}'><small><i>
                         provided by <b>{1}</b></i></small></td>",
    columns.Length,
    stocks[0].ProviderName);
builder.Append("</tr></table>");

return builder.ToString();
    }
}
```

As you can see, the HTML renderer contains a mix of markup, data, layout, and, in some cases, even logic. If you have reasons to opt for an HTML Message approach, it's your responsibility to pay a lot of attention to how you design the server-side code to maintain coupling at an acceptable level.

The *DynamicPopulate* Extender

In the AJAX Control Toolkit (which you can see at *http://www.codeplex.com/AjaxControlToolkit*), you can find an ad hoc component—the *DynamicPopulate* extender—that works well with an HTML Message service. Bound to a client trigger control (say, a button), the extender invokes a service method and attaches the results to the *innerHTML* property of a friend DOM element.

Obviously, the *DynamicPopulate* extender requires an HTML Message service in the server layer. Here's some code that demonstrates the use of the extender:

```
<act:DynamicPopulateExtender runat="server"
    ID="DynamicPopulateExtender1"
    BehaviorID="DynamicPopulateExtender1"
    ClearContentsDuringUpdate="false"
    TargetControlID="grid"
    UpdatingCssClass="updating"
    ServicePath="LiveQuotes.svc"
    ServiceMethod="GetQuotesFromConfigAsHtmlEx"
/>
```

The *DynamicPopulate* extender imposes an additional requirement on the service. The method you reference from the *ServiceMethod* attribute is required to have the following prototype:

```
string MethodName(string contextKey);
```

The *contextKey* parameter can contain any data serialized in any format that the service method knows how to process.

One of the issues you might run into when using the extender is that it doesn't prevent the default event when the user clicks on a button. So if the button is an ASP.NET button, the postback still occurs, which invalidates the service call. Here's a more common way of using the *DynamicPopulate* extender:

```
<asp:Button runat="server" id="btnRefresh" text="Live Quotes"
    onclientclick="invoke();return false;" />
```

The JavaScript *invoke* function does the following:

```
function invoke()
{
    // Retrieve the extender through the MS AJAX library hierarchy
    var extender = $find("DynamicPopulateExtender1");

    // Invoke the extender
    var contextKey = "";    // or any other string the method will understand
    extender.populate(contextKey);
}
```

Based on this code, the UI is updated by merging the HTML response with the element specified through the *TargetControlID* property of the extender.

A Quick Demo in ASP.NET MVC

Overall, the HM pattern can be seen as a specialized version of the partial-rendering approach that doesn't include view state and gives you total control over the response for the client. Good support for HM, which is also better than MS AJAX-based partial rendering, is offered through the newest Microsoft platform for ASP.NET development—the ASP.NET Model-View-Controller (MVC) pattern framework. Let's briefly go through an example.

In ASP.NET MVC, any response for the client is generated by the controller component. Any client action that results in a server request must be directed at a controller method. The name of the controller and its method are coded into the URL in a pure REST fashion. The controller method normally invokes a *View* object to generate the full view for the browser. However, the controller method can just return an HTML snippet generated internally.

The framework makes available the AJAX *ActionLink* component for when you want to quickly incorporate HTML into the client page in response to a user action. If the invoked controller action returns HTML markup, this content can be automatically inserted into the inner space of the specified DOM element. To get this, you just specify the element to update in the *AjaxOptions* settings:

```
<%= Ajax.ActionLink("Details",
        "/MyController/GetCustomerDetails",
        new AjaxOptions { LoadingElementId="lblWait", UpdateTargetId="pnlDetails" })%>
```

The *ActionLink* component generates a hyperlink, and the first parameter indicates the text of the hyperlink. The second argument is the URL that contains information about the controller and the method to involve in the processing of the request. In this case, it will be the *MyController* class and the *GetCustomerDetails* method.

Any HTML this method returns is attached to the body of the *pnlDetails* DOM element. The *lblWait* DOM element is displayed for the time it takes to download the response and is hidden immediately after. Here's a sample controller method:

```
public string GetCustomerDetails(string id)
{
    // Return HTML
      ⋮
}
```

It's also recommended that any element you use as the loading element be initially hidden from view using CSS.

A Look at ASP.NET AJAX 4.0

The reason why I'm covering ASP.NET AJAX 4.0 here in a data binding chapter is that the upcoming release of ASP.NET AJAX provides strong and largely enhanced support for data-driven applications. In particular, ASP.NET AJAX 4.0 will provide support for declarative HTML templates, a declarative data binding syntax, and facilities to call ADO.NET Data Services from a JavaScript client.

ASP.NET AJAX Templates

Earlier in the chapter, I discussed why having HTML templates simplifies the process of creating a dynamic data-driven user interface in the browser. Your client code calls a remote service, gets JavaScript data, and then binds bits and pieces of that data into ad hoc placeholders defined in the templates. In the end, ASP.NET AJAX 4.0 provides some built-in scaffolding for implementing the BST pattern.

ASP.NET AJAX templates can be used in ASP.NET pages as well as in plain HTML pages as long as a few JavaScript files are linked—in particular, *MicrosoftAjaxTemplates.js*.

Structure of a Template

In ASP.NET AJAX, an HTML template is essentially a *<div>* tag that contains fixed and repeatable parts. A fixed part is a fragment of HTML that is emitted only once—such as a header or footer. A repeatable part is an HTML fragment that is linked to data and repeated for each bound element.

An HTML template is initially hidden from view, and the framework takes care of turning on the visibility attribute of interested parts as appropriate. A common way to control visibility is by defining in the page a *sys-template* CSS style, as shown here:

```
<style type="text/css">
    .sys-template { display:none; visibility:hidden; }
</style>
```

The *sys-template* style is the discriminating element that determines whether a fragment of HTML will be emitted once or repeated. Let's consider the following template:

```
<div>
  <table id="grid" class="sys-template">
    <tr>
        <th>SYMBOL</th>
        <th>LAST</th>
        <th>CHANGE</th>
    </tr>
    <tr>
        <td align="left">{{ Symbol }}</td>
        <td align="right">{{ Quote }}</td>
        <td align="right">{{ Change }}</td>
    </tr>
  </table>
</div>
```

As you can see, the entire table uses the *sys-template* style. This means that a table will be created for each bound element. To emit a table row for each bound item without repeating the header row, you need a different approach, as shown here:

```
<div>
  <table>
    <tr>
        <th>SYMBOL</th>
        <th>LAST</th>
        <th>CHANGE</th>
    </tr>
```

```
        <tbody id="grid" class="sys-template">
          <tr>
            <td align="left">{{ Symbol }}</td>
            <td align="right">{{ Quote }}</td>
            <td align="right">{{ Change }}</td>
          </tr>
        </tbody>
      </table>
    </div>
```

The table now contains a *<tbody>* element styled as a *sys-template*. That part will be repeated for each bound item. To identify a repeatable part, you use a unique ID. In this case, the ID is *grid*.

The syntax used to insert data-bound expressions consists of wrapping property names in a pair of double curly brackets *{{ ... }}*. For example, the *{{ Symbol }}* expression indicates a placeholder for the value of *Symbol* property on the bound data item object.

To render a template, you can embed the following code in your page and control every aspect of data binding, from data download to rendering:

```
// Target element is where you attach and display the templated markup
var target = $get("productList");
target.innerHTML = "";
for (var i = 0, i < dataSource.length; i++)
{
    // Element productListTemplate is the element with the sys-template style
    productListTemplate.createInstance(target, dataSource[i]);
}
```

ASP.NET AJAX 4.0 compiles the template into an internal object that exposes the *createInstance* method. The method takes a reference to the target DOM element where the HTML must be displayed. In addition, the method requires the data object to bind.

A much better option is using a data display component, such as the *Sys.UI.DataView* component. The *DataView* component automates many tasks.

The *Sys.UI.DataView* Component

Associated with a bindable HTML template, the *DataView* component is a relatively easy way to create data-driven user interfaces. In the test page, you place an HTML template and link to an external service, be it a WCF service or anything else, including an ADO.NET data service.

In addition, you must create an instance of the *DataView* component. You can do that in either of two ways: by using JavaScript in a script block or via markup. Let's examine the JavaScript approach first.

The following JavaScript function is invoked after a user event such as a button click or a timer tick. In this case, I'm assuming the code will be called after a timer tick and the global *DataView* instance is disposed of and then re-created.

```
var dv = null;
    :
function getLiveQuotes()
{
    // UI value to pass to the service
    var isOffline = $get("<%= chkOffline.UniqueID %>").checked;

    // Create the DataView and pass arguments for the associated data source
    if (dv !== null)
        dv.dispose();

    dv = $create(
            Sys.UI.DataView,
            {
                serviceUri: "/LiveQuotes.svc",
                parameters: {isOffline:isOffline},
                query: "GetQuotesFromConfig"
            },
            {},
            {},
            $get("grid"));
}
```

You use the *$create* shortcut from the Microsoft AJAX client library to instantiate the component. The *$create* facility takes the type of the object to create and the initial configuration. The final argument indicates the DOM element that the component should be attached to.

The net effect of the preceding code is invoking the *Livequotes.svc* WCF service to call the *GetQuotesFromConfig* method. The method call is passed a value for the *isOffline* formal argument. The value comes from the JavaScript *isOffline* variable.

To initialize the *DataView* component via markup, you first add a few *xmlns* attributes to the *<body>* tag of the page:

```
<body
  xmlns:sys="javascript:Sys"
  xmlns:dataview="javascript:Sys.UI.DataView"
  sys:activate="*">
```

The attributes register a namespace and map a tag prefix to the *DataView* class. The *sys:activate* attribute specifies the IDs of elements that will be used to display data in the template. By using an asterisk (*), you indicate that all elements are candidates.

You use a *sys:attach* attribute to cause ASP.NET AJAX to create an instance of the *DataView*. The following example shows how to instantiate a *DataView* control by using a *sys:attach* attribute:

```
<div sys:attach="dataview"
     dataview:serviceuri="livequotes.svc" >
  <ul>
    :
  </ul>
</div>
```

The value you pass to *sys:attach* will match the prefix registered for *Sys.UI.DataView* in the *<body>* tag. To set properties on the *DataView* instance, you use attributes scoped with the component's namespace.

Injecting Logic into the Template

What if you want to inject some logic into the template so that certain parts are based on run-time conditions and the content of bound items? You can do that in two ways. First, you can handle the *itemCreated* event on the *DataView* component in much the same way you did in server-side ASP.NET programming with data-bound controls.

Alternatively, you can add inline code in the template using the declarative syntax that Microsoft provides. The syntax is based on JavaScript fragments wrapped by HTML comments:

```
<table>
    <tr>
        <th>SYMBOL</th>
        <th>LAST</th>
        <th>CHANGE</th>
    </tr>
    <tbody id="grid" class="sys-template">
      <tr>
        <td align="left">{{ Symbol }}</td>
        <td align="right">{{ Quote }}</td>
        <td align="right">

        <!--*
             var prefix = Change.substr(0, 1);
             if (prefix === "+")
             {
          *-->
            <span style="color:green">
        <!--* } else {*-->
            <span style="color:red">
        <!--* } *-->
           {{ Change }}
            </span>
        </td>
      </tr>
    </tbody>
</table>
```

When it comes to rendering the third cell of each row, ASP.NET AJAX 4.0 runs some code that checks the first character of the *Change* property on the bound data item. If this character is a plus sign (+), it means the current stock is rising in price. Subsequently, the text is wrapped by a green *<span>* tag; otherwise, a red *<span>* tag is used.

Figure 7-7 shows that ASP.NET AJAX 4.0 allows you to obtain the same graphical results we obtained with the manual implementation of patterns but without writing complex pieces of JavaScript code.

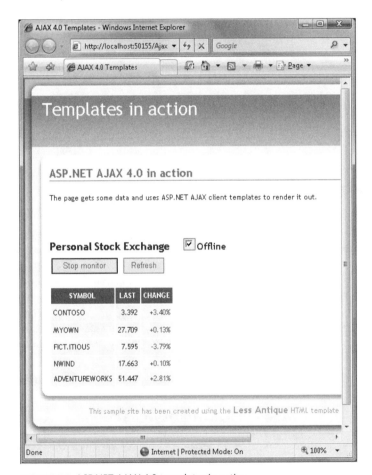

FIGURE 7-7 ASP.NET AJAX 4.0 templates in action

The *Sys.Data.DataSource* Component

The *DataView* component works in conjunction with a data source. The data source can be anything that is, or returns, a collection of data. When you create a *DataView*, you can specify the URL to a service. The service URL, as well as details on how to call it, are grouped into a data source component—an instance of the *Sys.Data.DataSource* class. The creation of the data source is implicit when you specify a service URL.

The *DataView* also features a read/write property named *data* through which you can execute binding using explicit data. In this case, the bound data can be any JavaScript array object as well as a property of any object returned from a service. The data property is useful when you want to set up a master/detail scenario.

```
<body xmlns:sys="javascript:Sys"
      xmlns:dataview="javascript:Sys.UI.DataView"
      sys:activate="*">

  <div id="grid" class="sys-template">
    <table sys:attach="dataview" dataview:data="{{ myData }}">
      <thead>
          <tr><td>Name</td><td>Description</td></tr>
      </thead>

        ⋮

    </table>
  </div>
</body>
```

In the listing, the variable passed to *data*—that is, the *myData* variable—is any JavaScript variable that contains an array of data objects.

Note ASP.NET AJAX 4.0 features many more capabilities, including UI commands and live data binding. In particular, live data binding is responsible for updating the user interface of a *DataView* component so that it reflects changes in the data as they occur.

Live data binding is a form of two-way data binding. In this case, if the user modifies a bound value, the underlying data item is updated. Likewise, if the underlying data item is modified from another source, the displayed UI element is updated. At the same time, you can define interactive elements in the template that fire a client command as the user clicks or enters keystrokes. These commands are aimed at executing further commands that might involve server operations such as Select, Delete, Edit, or Update.

ASP.NET Library for ADO.NET Data Services

In ASP.NET AJAX 4.0, you also find a set of wrapper classes for consuming ADO.NET Data Services from a JavaScript client. An analogous set of classes has existed for Silverlight since the release of Silverlight 2.0.

Generalities of the ADO.NET Data Services Framework

ADO.NET Data Services is a new framework introduced with the .NET Framework 3.5 Service Pack 1 (SP1) that allows you to access data services over the Web. An ADO.NET data service makes data available through a service interface so that you can query, filter, and update data using URIs and HTTP verbs in a RESTful fashion.

Through the ADO.NET Data Services framework, you can expose a data source as a REST service. The data source is typically an object model created using LINQ-to-SQL or the Entity Framework. Some sample URIs are shown here:

```
/Customers('ALFKI')/ContactName
/Customers?$orderby=Country
/Customers('ALFKI')/Orders?$filter=ShippedDate ge '2007-01-01'
```

The first URI returns the contact name of the specified customer; the second URI returns all customers in the data source ordered by country. The final URI returns all orders for the specified customer where the ship date is 2007 or later.

To access an ADO.NET data service from JavaScript, you need a proxy class. ASP.NET AJAX provides facilities for you to place calls to a data service.

Using a Proxy for ADO.NET Data Services

The *Sys.Data.AdoNetServiceProxy* class simplifies the interaction between an ASP.NET AJAX page and ADO.NET Data Services. You create an instance of the proxy, as shown here:

```
var service = new Sys.Data.AdoNetServiceProxy("/northwind.svc");
```

After you hold an instance of the proxy, you call the method *query* to retrieve data. Here's how to retrieve all the content of the Customers data store. (The Customers data store might or might not be a database table.)

```
exampleService.query("/Customers$orderby=Country", onSuccess, onFailure);
```

The *AdoNetServiceProxy* class uses the information you provide to build the actual URL for the service. The query you specify is appended to the URL of the service. When the real URL is ready, the proxy class takes care of executing the request asynchronously. You can indicate a callback for when the call is successful, and you can also indicate one for when the call fails.

The *AdoNetServiceProxy* class provides methods to perform Create, Read, Update, Delete (CRUD) operations from the client via the data service. In addition to executing individual INSERT, DELETE, and UPDATE operations immediately, you can also combine multiple actions. You use the *createActionSequence* method when you want to execute multiple data modification actions as a batch.

Finally, the proxy also supports deferred loading, meaning that not all relationships in the model entities are expanded upon loading. If deferred loading is enabled, the proxy takes care of loading extra data on demand.

Displaying Content from an ADO.NET Data Service

The content returned by an ADO.NET data service can be bound to the user interface using an ad hoc data source component. To facilitate this, ASP.NET AJAX 4.0 supplies the *Sys.Data.AdoNetDataSource* class.

The *DataView* component works well in conjunction with the *AdoNetDataSource* object. The following code shows how to use the *AdoNetDataSource* control with the *DataView*. Here's an example:

```
<div>
  <ul class="sys-template"
      sys:attach="dataview"
      dataview:datasource="{{ new Sys.Data.AdoNetDataSource() }}"
      dataview:serviceuri="/northwind.svc"
      dataview:query="Customers?$filter=ShippedDate ge '2007-01-01'">
    <li>
      {{ CompanyName }}
    </li>
  </ul>
</div>
```

Summary

To build a data-driven presentation, you have two options. First, you download data asynchronously to the client and then parse it to create some application-specific HTML presentation. Second, you generate the user interface on the server and then serve it up to the client. In the latter case, the presentation is extremely thin and simple.

Two popular AJAX patterns have been developed to illustrate these scenarios: the Browser-Side Template pattern and the HTML Message pattern. The BST pattern is generally faster and moves less data over the wire. On the other hand, BST requires more programming work and ideally some tools and frameworks that as yet only partially exist. ASP.NET AJAX 4.0 seems to be leaning in this direction with its *DataView* component and declarative syntax for client data binding.

As far as AJAX and the browser are concerned, JavaScript is the only possible way of coding any behavior. If you're not happy with JavaScript, you might want to look at Silverlight—which is exactly the topic I'll cover in the next chapter.

Chapter 8
Rich Internet Applications

Train up a fig tree in the way it should go, and when you are old sit under the shade of it.

—Charles Dickens

What really makes an Internet application rich? Is it the ability to deep-zoom into displayed images? Or is it the ability to display a compelling user interface within the browser while connecting to server-side services and to download and process data?

Like many of you, I love watching videos while comfortably sitting in my living room or while I'm waiting for the next flight in an airport. I'm happy that the quality of this media can be so high and that I can fully enjoy it. But frankly, I would define the term *Rich Internet Application* (RIA) another way.

I consider an RIA to be an application that works over the Web in a canonical Web site. In addition, this application must be able to offer an appealing user interface and connect asynchronously to services. An RIA must have programming power on the client and possibly an effective programming model. Finally, an RIA must be a secure application.

Although my criteria for an application to qualify as an RIA seem to be met by nearly any Web site that makes intensive use of AJAX features, an RIA is different from a Web application. More precisely, an RIA is more than just a Web application. This is so for one reason in particular: you need an ad hoc platform and run-time environment to build and execute an RIA.

Microsoft Silverlight is the latest (and most compelling) of these platforms.

Looking for a Richer Web

I'm not too far from the truth when I say that the browser has been the most important application of the 1990s. By leveraging the Transmission Control Protocol/Internet Protocol (TCP/IP) infrastructure and some new languages (both markup and scripting), the browser changed our lives and introduced us to the world of the Internet.

The Web as we know it today was officially born in 1993 and came of age only a few years later. Since then, though, it started a quest for a sort of Web Holy Grail. And the quest is probably destined to last for at least some of the foreseeable future. It's a quest to have binary code running within the browser—in a secure manner and with maximum interoperability.

The Dream of Binary Code Running over the Web

The dream of using the Web to deploy rich and trusty applications to virtually any user visiting a site is probably as old as the Web itself. And this dream has never been completely fulfilled. Today, with Silverlight version 2.0 (and probably even more with Silverlight 3.0), we've never been so close to making that old dream come true.

The Initial ActiveX Attempt

You might recall that Microsoft joined the Internet party relatively late, back in 1997. However, the company was pretty quick to learn the basics and soon started to lead the development efforts.

We owe Dynamic HTML to Microsoft, and Dynamic HTML later made it to the HTML 4.0 World Wide Web Consortium (W3C) standard. We owe *XMLHttpRequest* to Microsoft, and you know the key role played by this component in AJAX.

I'm fairly sure that had Microsoft failed to create that component some other company would have done it instead. So my purpose here is not to reinvigorate a pointless argument about the role of Microsoft in the growth of the Web. My point is to show that Microsoft made a couple of great contributions to Web development in its early days.

When a software boom is consolidating, many companies and many people have a lot of ideas, but not all of these ideas will prove successful or work. In the early days of Web development, along with *XMLHttpRequest* and Dynamic HTML, Microsoft also came out with ActiveX.

The idea of ActiveX was to enable browsers to execute binary code for building rich solutions instead of being limited to HTML and JavaScript. Although ActiveX components are still supported and used, it certainly has not been a big success. Frankly, we could even call it a failure—or, more precisely, the right thing done in the wrong way.

The Thorns of Security and Interoperability

At the beginning of the Web, security was not a concern. In fact, it was quite the opposite. The Web was born from the notion that information should be freely shared. The theme of Web security gained importance only when the Web became attractive to and rewarding for hackers and fraudsters.

ActiveX was not designed with a strong security model. There was security in ActiveX, but not a really effective model. Simply put, an ActiveX component is expected to tell the host environment how safe it is to run and script it. This is sort of the same as asking the chef whether his or her recommendation is really a good choice. Can you guess the answer?

At some point, to prevent problems browsers started defaulting to more restrictive security settings, with the result that users had to change settings manually to run some applications based on ActiveX.

That's generally why ActiveX failed.

In addition to security, another particularly large and sharp thorn affected ActiveX—interoperability. The Web is all about reach. Browsers and servers running on heterogeneous platforms can connect and work together. With ActiveX, the client was limited to the Microsoft Windows platforms, and often also limited to the Internet Explorer browser. These limitations were definitely too severe to gain wide acceptance for the technology.

The Flash Attempt

To some extent, though, ActiveX was headed in the right direction. HTML and JavaScript alone are not sufficient to build rich user interfaces and applications hosted within a browser. In the late 1990s, Adobe Flash emerged as a more reliable way to run more powerful code within the browser, but entirely on the client side.

Flash employed a restrictive security model by essentially stopping running code from performing potentially dangerous operations. Flash didn't open the entire client platform to programming; instead, it offered a common set of functionalities on virtually any software platform. It was secure. It was fully interoperable. And it let users write much richer and more powerful applications than by using pure HTML and JavaScript.

For a number of reasons, Flash was the only player in the RIA arena for a long time. The situation changed when Microsoft released the first version of Silverlight in the summer of 2007. Silverlight 1.0 wasn't all that powerful in terms of programming, but it carried a key message: "Microsoft is back in the RIA arena."

I like to think of Silverlight 2.0 as the old idea of ActiveX revamped, adapted to current times and, last but not certainly least, done properly in terms of both security and interoperability. Equipped with a Microsoft .NET Framework client framework, Silverlight makes it possible for you to write .NET applications that run within the browser, sandboxed and not limited to Windows.

> **Note** Microsoft has made Silverlight available for a number of Windows and Mac platforms. For the Linux platform, you don't have any runtime directly available from Microsoft, however. Microsoft is working with the Mono group at Novell to produce a run-time environment for Linux. At this time, though, there's no released Linux product that matches the capabilities of Silverlight 2.0 for Windows and Mac. In summary, Silverlight addresses the theme of full interoperability in a much better way than in the past, but Flash's market penetration is still deeper.

Browser Plug-ins

The Web went through several phases of standardization. Many vendors over the years proposed their own solutions to the problems and limitations perceived as hurdles on the way to making the Web a success. One problem for which vendors attempted to devise a common solution was the ideal way of running native code from within a Web browser.

A Brief History of Plug-ins

The aforementioned ActiveX technology is just Microsoft's attempt to make binary code run within a Web browser, thus giving developers the opportunity to embed non-HTML objects in pages.

Before ActiveX, Netscape developed the concept of a browser plug-in in conjunction with Adobe. A browser plug-in is a program that simply adds new capabilities to the browser, possibly in a cross-platform manner. After it's registered with the browser, the plug-in can display content that the browser doesn't know how to handle.

The first example of a plug-in was an embeddable component capable of displaying a PDF file directly inside the browser. Other popular plug-ins that followed were the QuickTime and RealPlayer plug-ins used to play videos from within Web pages.

A plug-in relies on the browser's user interface and underlying infrastructure. For security reasons, the range of a plug-in is limited to a possible set of actions.

Netscape was the first vendor to develop and implement plug-ins. Netscape developed the Netscape Plug-in Application Programming Interface (NPAPI) technology and implemented it for the first time in Netscape Navigator 2.0. Subsequently, nearly all other browsers have supported NPAPI, including Firefox, Safari, Opera, and Konqueror. Recently, Google Chrome also included support for NPAPI plug-ins. Internet Explorer supported NPAPI for a few versions but stopped supporting it with version 5.5.

The NPAPI architecture evolved in *npruntime*, an NPAPI extension that enables scripting. Thanks to *npruntime*, a plug-in can both access any script objects in the browser and be scriptable itself. For more information on NPAPI and *npruntime*, have a look at *https://developer.mozilla.org/en/Plugins*.

Security Concerns

Overall, ActiveX didn't capture the heart of developers for a variety of reasons, and security concerns (along with interoperability limitations) were at the top of the list. However, note that technologically speaking NPAPI and ActiveX are not too different as far as security is concerned.

Once they're hosted in a browser, an NPAPI plug-in and an ActiveX component execute binary code and enjoy the same privileges as the browser process. Therefore, an NPAPI plug-in and an ActiveX component can be equally harmful.

The popular idea of NPAPI being somewhat more secure than ActiveX is justified by a couple of other points. First, it's the download model supported by the browser. With the best intention of making the user's life easier, Internet Explorer automatically downloads any missing ActiveX controls that the page references. This type of security can be fully configured by users and administrators, but it's inherently more prone to having users install undesired code.

The other option initially pursued by Netscape and Firefox consisted of either blocking any automatic download or accepting downloads only from trusted locations.

A second reason NPAPI is considered more secure than ActiveX is that a deep sense of insecurity has arisen with regard to ActiveX. Born as an adaptation of Component Object Model (COM) and OLE2 technologies, ActiveX was not specifically targeted to the Web. This means that a wide choice of components was available for developers to include in Web pages. And these components were created to provide a given functionality, regardless of the platform and location. The likelihood of hosting potentially dangerous components was inherently higher than with Web-specific NPAPI plug-ins.

The *<object>* Tag

ActiveX lost its appeal quite soon, and in the late 1990s it was already clear that ActiveX would never come anywhere near to being a de facto standard. The plug-in technology evolved and consolidated, but it did so mostly as a way to host unsupported file types within the browser.

In HTML, the *<object>* tag is the standard way to include objects such as images, videos, and special files (such as PDF files) inside a browser. The *<object>* tag provides the *type* and *data* attributes through which you indicate the type of content you are embedding and the content. Here's an example:

```
<object data="TheContentToShow.pdf"
        type="application/pdf">
    <a href="TheContentToShow.pdf">
        Click here to save a local copy
    </a>
</object>
```

If the content referenced by the *<object>* tag can't be displayed, the content of the tag is processed and displayed alternatively. For the browser to display the specified content, a plug-in is required. But what's a plug-in exactly?

Characteristics of a Browser Plug-in

A plug-in is a platform-specific binary library that gets hosted within the browser. The plug-in knows how to deal with a given content type and how to create a graphical representation for it.

A browser that encounters an *<object>* tag first reads the *type* attribute and figures out what plug-in to load. The browser reserves a portion of the page user interface for the plug-in and loads it. Finally, the browser streams the content of the referenced file to the plug-in.

By design, a plug-in must implement a given set of interfaces to write to the browser's client area, initialize and position itself, and support scripting and streaming. Among other things, a plug-in receives pointers to the browser networking infrastructure for any outside connection it might need. Installing a plug-in is usually a smooth experience, but it typically requires local administrative privileges.

Plug-ins for Hosting Applications

A plug-in doesn't necessarily have to be a viewer of some special graphic or a multimedia player. It can be a sort of virtual machine instead and host and run external code. In this case, the *data* attribute of the *<object>* tag describes the program to run and the *type* attribute indicates the type of the executable being passed to the plug-in.

Adobe Flash and, more recently, Microsoft Silverlight are two excellent examples of browser plug-ins that operate as a sort of virtual machine running external code.

On one hand, people want the ability to run rich applications over the Internet. On the other hand, though, people want to do it in a fully secure way. Is the browser's sandbox enough?

The *browser sandbox* is a run-time environment used to host executable Web content in a way that doesn't cause damage to the local machine. The sandbox is a restricted environment that doesn't allow hosted content to access protected resources, such as hardware and the local file system.

A sandbox, though, relies entirely on the security model and tools of the host operating system. If there's a way to work around the operating system security mechanism, the sandbox can't stop malicious users from running arbitrary code.

For a rich Internet application, therefore, the browser's sandbox is necessary but not sufficient. Each RIA virtual machine must provide its own made-to-measure security model to prevent arbitrary and potentially harmful code from being run.

Adobe Flash provided a solution to the issue by essentially developing a custom language and its run-time interpreter. The interpreter acts as the virtual machine and permits only operations considered legal.

In Microsoft Silverlight, an existing and familiar programming model is used—the .NET Framework and related languages. Because the .NET platform was not originally designed to be used within a Web browser, an ad hoc virtual machine is required with a brand new, tailor-made security model. The virtual machine is known as the CoreCLR (or sometimes the "mini-CLR"), and it implements its code access security layer on top of the concept of transparent code. I'll return to this topic later in the chapter.

In a nutshell, browser plug-ins are the means through which the old dream of running binary code over the Web is currently realized. The plug-in operates as a virtual machine, and its content is the source code of the external application to be run.

Let's discover more about the latest plug-in for building RIAs—Microsoft Silverlight.

Microsoft Silverlight at a Glance

The quest for an RIA environment is the result of the inherent limitations of the AJAX approach. AJAX solves many issues and can definitely make for smoother and better received Web applications. AJAX, however, is based on HTML and JavaScript. The difference between a classic Web (plus AJAX) application and an RIA is found in the quality and capabilities of the user interface and the programming power.

An RIA offers a new delivery format (for Silverlight, it's the Windows Presentation Foundation markup language) and compiled programming languages for expressing any related logic.

Microsoft Silverlight offers a .NET-based programming model, rich programming languages, code libraries, and controls for quick UI prototyping. All that you need to run .NET RIAs is incorporated in a small, 4-megabyte (MB) executable. (See Figure 8-1.)

FIGURE 8-1 Downloading the Silverlight 2.0 plug-in

Architecturally speaking, Silverlight is based on a core version of the full .NET Framework common language runtime (CLR) and doesn't require the .NET Framework to be installed on the local machine.

Elements of the Silverlight Architecture

The Silverlight platform is a Web platform that runs partially trusted applications. However, from a graphical standpoint it sits somewhere between a classic browser-based Web user interface and a smart client.

Silverlight vs. AJAX

Silverlight provides obvious benefits beyond what is offered by AJAX solutions. It offers compiled code written in high-level languages such as C# instead of interpreted JavaScript code. It offers the rendering power of Windows Presentation Foundation (WPF) instead of plain HTML. Beyond the mere syntax, the key point here is the design of the markup languages. The WPF markup—the XAML language—is in effect an application delivery format; the HTML language, conversely, is a plain document format. HTML lacks a powerful layout manager, rich graphics and multimedia, and expressivity.

Silverlight vs. Smart Clients

As mentioned, a Silverlight application is a Web solution, although it might look like a smart client solution. A Web solution is characterized by easy deployment and wide reach. To deploy or update an application, you need to touch only one server. At the same time, clients can connect from whatever platform understands HTML and HTTP.

A smart client solution is a desktop solution and has an inherently strong link to the client operating system. By using a technology such as ClickOnce, you can ease deployment and update your applications quite simply. A smart client solution, though, still requires Windows and a version of the .NET Framework on the client.

Recently, the WPF platform on .NET 3.x started supporting a new type of application known as XAML Browser Application (XBAP). What's the difference between this and Silverlight?

An XBAP is a full WPF application packaged and is deployed over the Web in a way that mimics a typical browser's behavior. Internally, the application is deployed via a ClickOnce manifest file. The manifest file causes the WPF application to be loaded into Internet Explorer.

The XBAP application runs in partial trust and is subject to all the typical limitations of partial trust applications, such as no free local file access and no URLs accessible outside the same origin domain.

Both Silverlight and XBAP applications are partially trusted. XBAP applications support the full range of elements of the XAML syntax, including the 3D application programming interface (API). In addition, XBAP applications require the .NET Framework on the client. Functionally speaking, XBAP and Silverlight are not all that different. With the release of the recently announced Silverlight 3.0, the two technologies could likely be nearly the same.

Today, a Silverlight application is a full Web application; an XBAP application is a smart client application running within the browser in partial trust mode. That's the key difference.

Running Silverlight Applications

A Silverlight application is a piece of binary code hosted in a classic Web page, no matter how you write that. It can be an ASP.NET (AJAX) page as well as an HTML page written using PHP Hypertext Preprocessor (PHP) or perhaps Active Server Pages (ASP) or Java Server Pages. To run the Silverlight application, a user must have the Silverlight plug-in installed on the local machine. In addition, the visited page must reference content of the Silverlight type, as shown here:

```
<object
data="data:application/x-silverlight-2,"
type="application/x-silverlight-2" >
    <param name="source" value="ClientBin/HelloSilver.xap" />
    <param name="onerror" value="onSilverlightError" />
    <param name="background" value="blue" />
```

```
    <a href="http://go.microsoft.com/fwlink/?LinkID=108182" style="text-decoration: none;">
      <img src="http://go.microsoft.com/fwlink/?LinkId=108181"
           alt="Get Microsoft Silverlight"
           style="border-style: none" />
    </a>
</object>
```

You can use either the *data* attribute on the *<object>* tag or the *source* parameter to make the browser point to the URL of the Silverlight application. The application is represented as a XAP (pronounced "zap") package and contains XAML markup plus compiled managed code. (XAP files contain the compressed assemblies and resources necessary to run a given Silverlight 2.0 application, as you'll see later in the chapter.)

The browser streams the XAP package to the installed Silverlight plug-in and has the plug-in execute it within the embedded core CLR.

If you write the host page using ASP.NET, you can resort to an ad hoc server control to emit any required HTML markup:

```
<asp:Silverlight ID="Xaml1" runat="server"
    Source="~/ClientBin/Helloworld.xap"
    Version="2.0"
    Width="100%"
    Height="500px" />
```

The main benefit of using the Silverlight server control is that it can automatically handle for you any trouble related to a missing plug-in.

Silverlight is a cross-platform product that Microsoft releases for a number of Windows and Mac platforms. The Moonlight group associated with the Mono project is porting Silverlight to Linux. A version of Silverlight for Linux is expected sometime around the fall of 2009. Check out the following URL for the latest news and an updated roadmap: *http://www.mono-project.com/MoonlightRoadmap*.

Graphics and Multimedia

Because it was created to deliver a pleasant experience to Web users, Silverlight naturally features strong capabilities in graphics and multimedia. In the current version, graphics are limited to 2D, but 3D capabilities are expected to be included in the next version. Graphics support is provided by the WPF engine, which is a much better tool to use to design a graphically interactive user interface than HTML.

Silverlight also has excellent capabilities when it comes to playing videos, especially high-quality videos.

Media Pack

Media support in Silverlight is provided by the *MediaElement* control, which delivers high-quality media without any additional components, such as Windows Media Player or other vendors' players.

Silverlight supports a number of formats, including a variety of Windows Media Video (WMV) formats such as WMV7, WMV8, and WMV9, plus WMV advanced profile VC1 and non-VC1. Audio formats include Windows Media Audio (WMA) and MP3 with various bit rates.

Finally, Silverlight supports ASX playlists over a number of protocols, including HTTP, HTTPS, Microsoft Metadirectory Services (MMS), and Real-Time Streaming Protocol (RTSP).

The *MediaElement* component also supports streaming from an enabled server. Depending on the protocol available, streaming can be live or occur through buffering and progressive download. It's also worth mentioning a feature named *Smooth Streaming* that Silverlight supports in combination with a media extension for Microsoft Internet Information Services (IIS) 7.0 on Windows Server 2008. It's a sort of adaptive streaming of media to Silverlight clients over HTTP.

Basically Smooth Streaming detects the media capabilities of the local PC and bandwidth, and it determines the ideal video quality of a media file. In cases where there is a large bandwidth, users can experience true high definition; otherwise, the quality is adequate to the situation and still no buffering occurs.

Animation

Again, because it was created to deliver a better user experience, Silverlight supports animation. Coded via the markup syntax of the user interface, animation is achieved by varying individual properties of visual objects over a period of time and within a range of values.

Based on the data type of the property being animated, a few different types of animation classes have been defined. You have *DoubleAnimation* for double types, *ColorAnimation* for colors, and *PointAnimation* for varying the value of a *Point* property between two target values using linear interpolation.

In addition, to animate properties of other types you can switch to a form of discrete interpolation, which consists of jumping from one value to another in a predefined sequence. This form of animation is represented by the *ObjectAnimationUsingKeyFrames* object in Silverlight.

Deep Zoom

A unique capability of Silverlight is a technology called *Deep Zoom*, which allows users to zoom to an almost arbitrary depth in properly configured images. Once you define the size of the image to appear in the screen, you define the only parameter that actually affects performance—the number of pixels to be displayed. By clicking or using the mouse wheel, you can zoom in on and out from the image without actually downloading more data than you can fit in the area.

The Silverlight engine loads progressively higher resolution images and applies smooth fading and panning to them to provide a better experience to users. Over the Web, you are often torn between providing high-quality images full of details that are clear and crisp or opting for blurry, low-level images that are far quicker to download.

Deep Zoom offers a good way out by letting you initially link a low-resolution image and then have users interact with that to see more details quickly and efficiently. More importantly, you have available a powerful API to write the zoom code yourself, the way you want it to be.

Deep Zoom requires images to be expressed in a richer format that doesn't simply include the pixels for a given resolution. The trick consists of representing the image through an "image pyramid," which is essentially a collection of copies of the image for each zoom step you want to support. All the information is wrapped up in an XML file that the Deep Zoom engine in the Silverlight plug-in processes.

As it turns out, you can't simply reference a native JPG or PNG image through Deep Zoom. Microsoft provides an ad hoc tool to create Deep Zoom–compatible images starting from the original one you would like to display. The tool is Deep Zoom Composer. You can download it from *http://go.microsoft.com/fwlink/?LinkId=116569*.

Building Applications

When it comes to building a Silverlight application, Visual Studio 2008 provides you with two project templates: the Silverlight application and Silverlight class library. That a Silverlight application is something special is fairly obvious. It's a bit less obvious that you also need a Silverlight-specific class library.

A Silverlight binary is different from other .NET binaries. The .NET CLR is slightly different from the Silverlight CoreCLR, and the two CLRs support different formats. This is one of the reasons why you can't just reuse any existing .NET class library in Silverlight. Another reason is that the Silverlight and .NET environment are backed by different versions of the .NET Framework with a different set of classes. In summary, code compatibility between .NET and Silverlight might exist at the source level; it doesn't exist at the binary level.

Note that this aspect is expected to change with the release of Silverlight 3.0 and .NET Framework 4.0. It's reasonable to expect by then that the .NET CLR will be split into a core CLR plus some extensions. And, at that point, the Silverlight CLR will match the .NET core CLR exactly.

Code and Markup

The overall structure of a Silverlight application is not that different from a Windows or ASP.NET application: it's always made of markup and a code-behind class. The markup describes the user interface and is expressed using the XAML language. The code-behind class contains any code and event handlers that relate to user interface elements. The code-behind class can address any class in the referenced assemblies. The code-behind class is ultimately compiled to an assembly.

The following markup shows the header of a typical Silverlight application. The root tag *UserControl* groups the entire user interface:

```
<UserControl x:Class="HelloSilver.Page"
    xmlns="http://schemas.microsoft.com/client/2007"
    xmlns:x="http://schemas.microsoft.com/winfx/2006/xaml"
    Width="500"
    Height="500"
    Loaded="UserControl_Loaded">
  <Canvas x:Name="LayoutRoot" Background="Cyan">
     ⋮
  </Canvas>
</UserControl>
```

The *x:Class* attribute specifies the name of the code-behind class. The *Loaded* attribute refers to the handler of the load event of the page. The handler is defined in the code-behind class, as shown here:

```
void UserControl_Loaded(object sender, RoutedEventArgs e)
{
   ⋮
}
```

As in ASP.NET Web Forms, you can programmatically refer to user interface elements by name. In particular, the name is given by the content of the *x:Name* attribute of the markup tag.

Programming Languages

The code-behind class can be written in C#, Microsoft Visual Basic .NET, plus a few dynamic languages such as IronPython and IronRuby. The CoreCLR provides the capabilities to process code compiled to the CLR's intermediate language.

In a Silverlight project, you can refer to an external library written in a different (but supported) .NET language.

No JavaScript is required within the Silverlight page. However, you can still have JavaScript in the Web page that hosts the Silverlight plug-in. The script in the page can access the Silverlight plug-in and script its content. At the same time, managed code within the Silverlight application can access and invoke JavaScript functions and any objects published to the browser's scripting engine.

In one word, the browser-to-Silverlight communication is bidirectional.

XAP Packages

A Silverlight application is deployed as a XAP package file. The package contains an assembly that results from the compilation of the code-behind class, plus any referenced assemblies and a manifest file. The markup is appended as a resource to the primary assembly.

As Figure 8-2 clearly shows, the XAP package is actually a ZIP archive just renamed to a different extension.

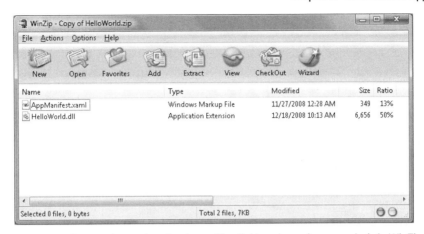

FIGURE 8-2 Renamed to a *.zip* extension, a Silverlight package shows up nicely in WinZip.

The XAP package must be deployed to the host Web application, preferably to the ClientBin Web server folder. Note, though, that using the ClientBin server folder is merely a convention. You can actually reference the XAP package from everywhere in the Web server.

What about the size of the XAP package? A package that contains only code is hardly larger than a few kilobytes (KBs). In .NET and Silverlight, the base size of any assembly is 4 KB. In 10 KB of Silverlight code, you can normally pack quite a bit of logic. The size of the package might grow significantly if you reference several external assemblies (not already part of the Silverlight platform) or include as resources graphic files or multimedia content. For really large packages, streaming and on-demand download are options to consider carefully.

Like any other resource downloaded through the browser, XAP packages end up going to the Temporary Internet Files folder. This means that clearing your browser's cache removes the Silverlight application from the local machine. At the same time, if an unexpired copy of the package is already available in the cache, the browser receives an HTTP 304 not-modified status code and no copy is downloaded.

CLR Instancing

You'll have a single copy of the CLR per browser process. Next, for each browser process there will be an AppDomain for each Silverlight plug-in. This means that if the same page contains multiple Silverlight plug-ins, each plug-in will live in its own space within a distinct AppDomain.

Nothing will be shared between plug-ins at the system level. Two plug-ins that want to communicate must do that through code. The simplest way, though, is by using the HTML Document Object Model (DOM) of the surrounding page. For example, the code in one plug-in might write data to, say, a hidden field in the page DOM. A second plug-in might access the same hidden field by name and read any content written by another Silverlight application.

The Programming Model of Microsoft Silverlight

Programming Silverlight is not much different from programming any other .NET application, whether it is an ASP.NET, Windows Forms, or WPF application. In all cases, the application is made of a collection of source code file pairs—a markup file plus a code-behind class file. Differences in the code-behind class are only the result of the different set of classes supported by the Silverlight CoreCLR. The Silverlight markup has little in common with ASP.NET or Windows Forms markup, but it's a compatible subset of the WPF 3.5 markup language.

Because it's a compatible subset of WPF, you're not going to have the same set of syntax elements, but the provided set makes it possible for you to build similar solutions. For example, you might not be able to use the same WPF syntax to add, say, a ToolTip to a Silverlight control; however, you'll definitely have a way to add ToolTips to a Silverlight user interface.

WPF-Based User Interface

The subset of WPF made available to Silverlight applications should be intended as a way to enable Web developers to create rich user interfaces rather than as an attempt to port desktop WPF applications to the Web.

Space constraints make it hard to stuff the whole WPF machinery into less than 5 MB. As a result, some features have been dropped (for example, 3D) while others have been trimmed down (for example, triggers and data templates). The Silverlight WPF-based user interface, though, is powerful enough to let you port a moderately complex WPF application to the Web without much pain.

In addition, some new controls and features have been added to Silverlight that weren't part of WPF 3.5. This includes ad hoc controls such as the *DataGrid* and *DatePicker* controls. These controls have been added to WPF recently with the WPF Toolkit. (See *http://wpf.codeplex.com* for more information.)

A few components characterize the user interface of a Silverlight application. In the first place, you find the layout manager to determine the shape of the visual tree of UI elements. In addition, controls, the data binding manager, and the style (or layout) manager are other aspects of the Silverlight UI that deserve a closer look.

Layout Manager

A typical Silverlight application is built from a tree of objects where *UserControl* is the root of the tree. In turn, the *UserControl* element contains a number of child elements laid out or stacked in a variety of ways. Elements refer to basic shapes, layout managers, storyboards, and controls, including custom third-party and user controls.

There are four main ways to lay out visual elements in a Silverlight user interface that correspond to the same number of layout managers—*Grid*, *StackPanel*, *Canvas*, and *ScrollViewer*.

The *Grid* element divides the entire user interface into a matrix of rows and columns in a way that is similar to the HTML *table* element. Each subtree contained within the *Grid* is then mapped to a grid cell for display. Following is a brief example of a grid with one column and three rows. In practical terms, it means that the overall UI will display in three horizontal panes, two of which have a fixed height (a sort of header and footer).

```
<Grid x:Name="LayoutRoot">
  <Grid.RowDefinitions>
      <RowDefinition Height="30" />
      <RowDefinition />
      <RowDefinition Height="40" />
  </Grid.RowDefinitions>
  <Grid.ColumnDefinitions>
      <ColumnDefinition />
  </Grid.ColumnDefinitions>

  <StackPanel Grid.Row="1" Grid.Column="0">
    ⋮
  </StackPanel>
  ⋮
</Grid>
```

The *StackPanel* element lays out elements side by side either horizontally or vertically. As a developer, you have no way to control the exact *x,y* position of each element; you can control only its relative location with respect to the previous one. With a *StackPanel*, the order in which elements are declared in the source code does matter.

The *Canvas* element is the one to choose if you need to control the exact coordinates of where each visual element should display. You use the *Top* and *Left* properties and assign them values related to the top-left corner of the canvas:

```
<Canvas x:Name="LayoutRoot" Background="White">
    <Button Canvas.Left="10" Canvas.Top="10" ... />
    ⋮
</Canvas>
```

Finally, the *ScrollViewer* element is useful when you need to display more content in a smaller space with horizontal scrollbars, vertical scrollbars, or both.

Common Controls

Silverlight provides many of the base controls of WPF, including *TextBox*, *Button*, *RadioButton*, *CheckBox*, *ListBox*, and *Slider*. In addition, it offers a set of controls not natively available in WPF 3.5, such as *DataGrid*, *HyperlinkButton*, *WatermarkTextBox*, and *DatePicker*. It doesn't yet support some advanced controls you have in WPF such as the *RichTextBox* control.

The framework for visual controls is totally extensible and allows you to easily create your own controls. It should be noted, though, that in WPF (and subsequently in Silverlight) you don't need to plan a custom control with the same frequency you do from Windows Forms or Web Forms.

WPF and Silverlight controls provide excellent support for styles and templates. If all that you need from a control is simply a different set of visual styles or alternate content, you can resort to a different style. For example, to add an icon to the caption of a button you don't need a specialized control; it will suffice to use a plain *Button* control with an ad hoc style that overwrites the *Content* property.

Likewise, if you want to give a control a different shape (say, create a rounded button), you simply opt for a custom control template and store it in an ad hoc style. The following code shows how to arrange a button with a circular shape and a background with grades of a certain color:

```
<Button x:Name="Button1" Click="Button1_Click" Content="Hi" >
    <Button.Template>
        <ControlTemplate>
            <Canvas>
                <Ellipse Width="50" Height="50">
                    <Ellipse.Fill>
                        <RadialGradientBrush GradientOrigin=".3,.2">
                            <GradientStop Offset=".2" Color="White"></GradientStop>
                            <GradientStop Offset="1" Color="Blue"></GradientStop>
                        </RadialGradientBrush>
                    </Ellipse.Fill>
                </Ellipse>
                <ContentPresenter Canvas.Left="15" Canvas.Top="15" />
            </Canvas>
        </ControlTemplate>
    </Button.Template>
</Button>
```

In the end, when do you really need to create a custom control? In two cases: when you need a control that provides functionality that doesn't exist and when you want to give a control a behavior that doesn't exist. But for purely visual changes—no matter how complex and sophisticated—you can do it with styles and templates.

The Data Binding Manager

Data binding is one of the most powerful features of the WPF platform. In particular, data binding in WPF can also be bidirectional, and it can both update the UI when the data store changes and update the data store when the content displayed in the UI changes. The overall functionality is preserved in Silverlight, but some syntax differences apply. Let's dig into the details.

In Silverlight, there are two ways to do data binding—via code and declaratively. To bind via code, you create an instance of the *Binding* class and set its *Source* property to the object that provides data. The constructor of the *Binding* class also takes the name of the property on the source that contains the value to bind.

```
Binding binding = new Binding("DisplayName");
binding.Source = new MySourceObject(...);
Label1.SetBinding(TextBlock.TextProperty, binding);
```

In the preceding code snippet, the value of the property *DisplayName* on the specified instance of the *MySourceObject* class is used to populate the target of the binding operation—the *Text* property of the *Label1* control. In the example, *Label1* is assumed to be an instance of the WPF's *TextBlock* element.

Alternatively, you can accomplish this declaratively, as shown here:

```
<TextBlock x:Name="Label1"
           Text ="{Binding DisplayName}" />
```

In the markup, the *TextBlock* element has its *Text* property set to an expression. The keyword *Binding* indicates a data binding operation and specifies the content. The declarative syntax, though, lacks a fundamental piece of information—where's the source object?

For the sake of simplicity, in Silverlight the data source of declarative forms of data binding is assumed to be the nearest data context object. In WPF, the property *DataContext* indicates an implicit data source shared by multiple elements. Once set, the *DataContext* property represents a valid data source for all data-bound elements in its scope. If there's data binding in action and the source object is not explicitly indicated, it defaults to the currently set *DataContext*. The reason for such an implementation is to avoid multiple source objects in the markup code.

```
Label1.DataContext = new MyDataSource(...);
```

In Silverlight, you set the *DataContext* property programmatically for the element you're interested in binding or for one of its parents. In the latter case, all child elements of the parent will share the same data context.

Finally, to bind a collection of objects to a rich control such as the *DataGrid*, you use the *ItemsSource* property and bind it to a .NET collection of objects with public properties:

```
DataGrid1.ItemsSource = collection;
```

If you want the data binding to be two-way, make sure the bound collection is of type *ObservableCollection*.

Compatibility Between Silverlight and WPF Code

Simplifying the porting of existing WPF code to the Web certainly is not the primary goal of Silverlight. This said, to some extent porting is possible, but it depends on how the WPF API is used in the original desktop application.

To start, in Silverlight you have no triggers or, more precisely, you don't have triggers in all places. For example, there is a *Triggers* collection on UI elements—descendants of *FrameworkElement*—but not in styles, data, and control templates.

Likewise, data binding is supported in Silverlight but not in the same manner as in WPF. For example, you have the *Binding* element and you have data context, data templates, and observable collections. However, you have no triggers and you don't have the same set of markup elements. Also, the internal implementation is quite different. The *Binding* object in Silverlight has far fewer properties than in WPF.

Globalization is another area that might be a source of headaches for you. For performance reasons, the Silverlight CLR doesn't include its own globalization data for all supported cultures. Instead, the *CultureInfo* class in Silverlight relies on the globalization functionality provided by the underlying operating system. This means that there's no way for you to give applications the same globalization settings across different operating systems.

Finally, WPF has a richer set of controls that are not available in Silverlight. A good example is the *RichTextBox* control.

In summary, porting a Silverlight application to WPF is relatively trivial, although as a developer you should be concerned about possible performance "gotchas" that could be caused by the richer object model. Porting in the opposite direction is not realistic, unless we are talking about a moderately complex WPF application that doesn't extensively use cool and effective WPF features such as triggers and data binding.

The .NET Base Class Library

The .NET Base Class Library available to you in Silverlight isn't the same one you have available in any other .NET application. There are various reasons for this, including space constraints and security.

In Silverlight, you find threads, timers, LINQ, XML, isolated storage, and networking, as well as cryptography, sockets, and proxies for remote services. You won't find ADO.NET or anything that looks like a client-side database. Likewise, you won't find full file system access. In general, though, you have quite a powerful programming model that is incomparably richer and faster than with JavaScript.

Support for LINQ

In the .NET Framework, most of the time you enjoy LINQ capabilities through the keywords added to the C# and Visual Basic .NET languages. Keywords such as *from* and *select*, though, are just syntactic sugar and simply build on top of some classes defined in the .NET Framework. The same set of classes is supported in Silverlight.

In particular, in Silverlight you have LINQ-to-Objects, LINQ-to-XML, and also LINQ-to-JSON. LINQ-to-Objects allows you to query over collections and arrays of in-memory data. LINQ-to-XML allows you to query over the content of XML documents. Finally, LINQ-to-JSON (at this time, a Silverlight-only feature) lets you query over a stream of JSON objects. Here's a brief code snippet that shows LINQ-to-XML:

```
String xml = ...;
XDocument doc = XDocument.Parse(xml);
```

```
List<MyButton> buttons = (from b in doc.Descendants("Button")
                          select new MyButton
                          {
                              Enabled = Boolean.Parse(b.Attribute("Enabled").Value),
                              Text = b.Attribute("Text").Value
                          }).ToList();
```

The XML content is first loaded into an *XDocument* object and then used as the input for a LINQ query. The query selects elements from the root of the XML documents that match a given set of criteria and projects the output to a collection of data transfer objects.

In a similar manner, you can proceed with JSON data that you might have received from a RESTful (Representational State Transfer) service:

```
JsonArray data = (JsonArray) JsonArray.Load(stream);
var members = from member in data
              where member["Age"] > 20
              select member;
foreach (JsonObject member in members)
{
    string name = member["Name"];
    int age = member["Age"];

    // Proceed ...
       ⋮
}
```

To use LINQ-to-JSON, you need to import the *System.Json* assembly and add the *System.Json* namespace to your source code.

Support for Threads

In Silverlight, you can create threads in two ways. You can use the *Thread* class directly, or you can rely on the system-provided *ThreadPool* class that manages a pool of threads for you. Here's how to create a thread explicitly. As you can see, the code is not really different from the code you would use from a classic .NET application:

```
ThreadStart code = new ThreadStart(DoSomething);
Thread t = new Thread(code);
t.Start();
```

The body of the thread is given by the *DoSomething* function with the following prototype:

```
private void DoSomething()
{
    // Do the work
       ⋮

    // Update the UI
    this.Dispatcher.BeginInvoke( delegate {
        lblThreadOutput.Text = "Updated from a background, non-UI thread.";
    });
}
```

The *Dispatcher* object allows you to access the UI thread from the outside so that you can include UI code right in the external thread. (Achieving this same effect in Windows Forms would require more effort on your part.) The *BeginInvoke* method just takes a delegate (including anonymous delegates) and runs it on the correct UI thread from where updating UI controls is safe.

Just as in full .NET, in Silverlight you can rely on the advanced services of the *BackgroundWorker* class. The class encapsulates a background task and fires common events such as start, completed, progress made, and canceled. More importantly, the class completely shields you from the details of marshaling UI tasks over to the correct thread. You just provide event handlers and the class does the work of running them appropriately:

```
bkgndWorker = new BackgroundWorker();
bkgndWorker.DoWork += new DoWorkEventHandler(_bkgndWorker_DoWork);

// Register additional event handlers for "completed" and "progress" events
bkgndWorker.RunWorkerCompleted +=
    new RunWorkerCompletedEventHandler(_bkgndWorker_RunWorkerCompleted);
bkgndWorker.ProgressChanged +=
    new ProgressChangedEventHandler(_bkgndWorker_ProgressChanged);

// Enables additional features (report progress, and cancel)
bkgndWorker.WorkerReportsProgress = true;
bkgndWorker.WorkerSupportsCancellation = true;

// Start (passing some input values)
object data = ...;
bkgndWorker.RunWorkerAsync(data);
```

The background task represented by the *DoWork* event runs on a distinct thread. Every time the task invokes the *ReportProgress* method, the *ProgressChanged* callback is invoked on the UI thread to update the user interface.

```
private void _bkgndWorker_DoWork(object sender, DoWorkEventArgs e)
{
    // Do some work
    for (int i=0; i< (int) e.Argument; i++)
    {
        // Update UI to reflect what you're doing
        bkgndWorker.ReportProgress(i / 100);

        // Check whether cancellation was requested
        if (bkgndWorker.CancellationPending)
        {
            e.Cancel = true;
            return;
        }
    }
}
```

The background worker class also provides a mechanism to intercept requests for canceling the pending task and then proceed.

The *BackgroundWorker* class should be your primary choice for threading needs in Silverlight, notably because of its automatic context switching to the UI thread.

Support for Timers

One of the most common scenarios for using Silverlight is for making asynchronous requests to some remote HTTP façade. Most of the time, though, these requests must go out periodically; a timer, therefore, is a much needed utility. The following code shows how to initialize a timer object in Silverlight:

```
Timer timer = new Timer(new TimerCallback(DoWork),
                data,                 /* some input value: indicates the user context */
                Timeout.Infinite,     /* wait this time before starting */
                Timeout.Infinite);    /* period */
```

The timer constructor takes the callback that will be repeated periodically plus one object that represents input data. Finally, you can specify in milliseconds the time to wait before starting the timer and the period. The timer callback takes the following form:

```
void DoItPeriodically(object userContext)
{
    // Do some work
    ⋮

    // Update the UI if needed
    Label1.Dispatcher.BeginInvoke(delegate {
            Label1.Text = DateTime.Now.ToString();
      });
}
```

As you can see, the timer callback runs on a different, non-UI thread, meaning that you need a dispatcher to update any visual control.

If you need to start or stop the timer programmatically, you can do that using the *Change* method, as shown here:

```
// Start the timer in 1 second and set the period to 2 seconds
timer.Change(1000, 2000);
```

To stop the timer, you set the period to *Infinite*.

Isolated Storage

Nearly all applications greatly benefit from local data storage. By *local storage*, I mean the application's ability to save some data on the client machine. This has never been an issue for desktop applications, which have full access to the local disk and file system.

For Web applications, though, it has always been a mission-impossible task. For security reasons, any code hosted by Web pages—typically, JavaScript code—can't just access the file system of the local machine. For years, Web page developers resorted to cookies, or server-side storage, to save some user-specific information.

As far as local storage is concerned, Silverlight is a platform sitting somewhere in between the Web and desktop. A Silverlight application can't freely perform I/O operations on the user's hard disk because those are considered critical from a security perspective. However, a Silverlight application takes advantage of a special and constrained programming interface that permits disk access only under certain conditions. This .NET Framework API is known as *isolated storage*, and Silverlight fully supports it.

Why Is Local Storage Important?

What kind of content should an application store on the user's local disk? Although it mostly depends on the particular application, a couple of categories of data can be easily identified. First, applications might need to save application settings and everything that can be filed under that tag. Application settings include user preferences, configuration, extra features installed, and also user-specific data that is helpful and useful to the application.

Second, applications might need to temporarily save any data that the user is still working on and that has not been committed yet. For example, you could save in the local storage the draft of a form so that users can come back later and fill out the rest of the form without losing any information. The user will eventually submit this work to the server, but until then data has to be maintained on the client and updated as needed.

These two broad categories of data going into the local storage of a Silverlight application have significant differences as far as their size is concerned. Application settings are usually short pieces of data limited to just a few KBs. Working data, on the other hand, is usually a much larger chunk of data, even in the order of MBs, that contains text or binary data representing a piece of work. The storage system of Silverlight lends itself very well to accommodating user preferences, but it might not be as effective for larger blocks of data.

In the .NET Framework, isolated storage is a storage mechanism that enables partially trusted applications to save data on the local machine without violating any security policies set on the computer. Isolated storage has been around since the first version of the .NET Framework and is especially useful for downloaded, partially trusted components that are not usually given access to the standard I/O mechanisms. Through isolated storage, applications coming from potentially untrusted sources can still do some disk I/O, albeit in a controlled and safe way.

Note Silverlight has its own implementation of the isolated storage feature and doesn't directly rely on the bits provided with the .NET Framework. This is not surprising because Silverlight is not a desktop platform and doesn't rely on a full edition of the .NET Framework installed on the client machine.

The Storage System

The entry point in the Silverlight isolated storage subsystem is the *IsolatedStorageFile* class and in particular one of its static methods: *GetUserStoreForApplication* or *GetUserStoreForSite*. Both methods get you a logical token that can be used to perform any supported operation on the virtual file system. Here's how to get a token:

```
using (IsolatedStorageFile iso =
      IsolatedStorageFile.GetUserStoreForApplication())
{
   :
   :
}
```

When you call one of the initialization methods, the system creates a subdirectory specific to the application or the site (if it doesn't exist already). The token that is returned to you tracks which part of the physical file system your application is enabled to work on.

The root of the isolated storage file system is located in a hidden folder within the subtree reserved for the current user. If you're using Windows Vista, the hidden isolated storage folder lives under the *Users* directory. If you're using Windows 2003 Server, it is located under the *Documents and Settings* folder for the current user.

In summary, each Silverlight application has its own virtual file system that is completely separated from the file system that's visible to other full-trust applications. A Silverlight application can't just navigate out of its personal file system. File names are always intended to be relative, meaning that you can't use absolute paths that include drive information. At the same time, any relative path that includes ellipses (\.\.\) is not allowed.

Working with Files and Directories

The *IsolatedStorageFile* class features a number of methods to perform Create, Read, Update, Delete (CRUD) operations and lookup operations on files and directories. Here's a quick example that shows how to create a new directory:

```
using (var iso = IsolatedStorageFile.GetUserStoreForApplication())
{
   iso.CreateDirectory("MyData");
}
```

What if you need to create a child subdirectory? All that you have to do is create a directory name that includes both the parent directory and the new directory. If you can't provide the full name of the directory as a hard-coded string, you can use the *Path* class to build the name programmatically. Here's how to do it:

```
string dir = Path.Combine("MyData", "Pictures");
iso.CreateDirectory(dir);
```

To enumerate the content of a directory, you use ad hoc methods such as *GetFileNames* and *GetDirectoryNames*. Both methods return an array of strings with all the names that match the specified search criteria:

```
string[] filelist = iso.GetFileNames("*.dat");
```

In Silverlight, you can't make any use of the *DirectoryInfo* and *FileInfo* classes that in the full .NET Framework are so helpful when it comes to doing any special work on files and directories.

The classes exist, but your application code is just not allowed to use it. The following code compiles successfully, but it throws an exception once it is executed:

```
DirectoryInfo dir = new DirectoryInfo(@"c:\");
```

The problem with the previous code is just security; I'll return to the topic of security later in the chapter.

Working with File Streams

The content of a file is available as a stream for reading and writing purposes. The *CreateFile* and *OpenFile* methods on the *IsolatedStorageFile* class just return the stream to the application code.

Silverlight supports one particular type of stream, represented by the *IsolatedStorageFileStream* class. Therefore, an alternative way of getting a file stream in Silverlight is to explicitly create a new instance of the file stream class. Here's how you can proceed:

```
using (IsolatedStorageFile iso =
        IsolatedStorageFile.GetUserStoreForApplication())
{
    IsolatedStorageFileStream stream;
    stream = new IsolatedStorageFileStream(TESTFILE, FileMode.OpenOrCreate, iso);
        ⋮
}
```

The constructor of the *IsolatedStorageFileStream* class accepts the name of the file to access and a *FileMode* value (*OpenOrCreate*, *Append*, *Create*, *Open*, and so on) that sheds some light on your intentions regarding the file. Finally, the third parameter is the reference to the root of the virtual file system.

Once you have a stream to operate on the content of a file—for reading or writing— you have two options to proceed. The first option entails that you use the synchronous or asynchronous API for I/O defined for stream classes. The stream class features pairs of methods such as *Read/Write* and *BeginRead/BeginWrite* in addition to classic stream methods such as *Flush*, *Close*, *SetLength*, and *Seek*. Finally, a stream lists a number of properties, including *CanRead*, *CanWrite*, *Length*, and *Position*.

The second option is based on the fact that you leverage a helper reader or writer class to work with the stream content. As in the full .NET Framework, these classes are named *StreamReader* and *StreamWriter* and have nearly the same programming model. The following code snippet shows how to create a file and write some content to it using a stream writer helper class:

```
using (IsolatedStorageFile iso =
        IsolatedStorageFile.GetUserStoreForApplication())
{
    IsolatedStorageFileStream stream;
    stream = new IsolatedStorageFileStream(TESTFILE, FileMode.OpenOrCreate, iso);
    StreamWriter writer = new StreamWriter(stream);
```

```
    writer.Write(DateTime.Now.ToString());
    writer.Close();
    stream.Close();
}
```

Largely similar is the code that reads content from a stream. Here's the part that relates to the *StreamReader* class:

```
StreamReader reader = new StreamReader(stream);
content = reader.ReadToEnd();
reader.Close();
```

The *Write* method of the *StreamWriter* class has a number of overloads to let you write the content of a bunch of types—bytes, arrays, characters, Booleans, and objects. The *StreamReader* class, on the other hand, is mostly a text reader class and offers facilities to read text files.

What if you need to deal with binary content? Silverlight also has in store for you a tailor-made version of the *BinaryReader* and *BinaryWriter* pair of .NET Framework classes.

Storage Management

When the *GetUserStoreForApplication* method is invoked, it first checks whether the proper subtree exists and, if not, it will create it. As an application developer, you have to worry only about your own files and directories. The system guarantees that the isolated storage infrastructure is always up and running for you. But does it really?

To sum it up, there's a possibility that the end user, deliberately or not, could clear stored data or disable the isolated storage feature altogether. By right-clicking on a Silverlight window in any browser, you get the dialog box shown in Figure 8-3.

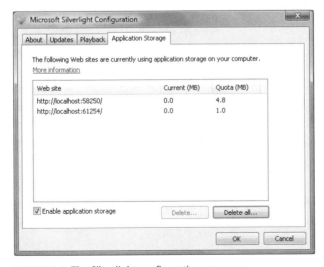

FIGURE 8-3 The Silverlight configuration manager

The check box at the bottom of the Application Storage tab says it all. If the user deselects that button, isolated storage stops working and any call made to any API results in an exception. In light of this, it is recommended that you create your own helper at least for the initialization methods, such as *GetUserStoreForApplication*, that do include some exception handling.

In Figure 8-3, the two delete buttons also enable end users to erase any content in the selected isolated storage. This means that as an application developer you must be ready to handle the possibility that all of your previously stored data is gone. The suggestion is to store in the Silverlight storage only data that you know how to re-obtain or data that you can do without. No data that is critical for the application should be stored in the Silverlight storage. The risk is only that the user might delete it.

> **Note** Is Silverlight good for building occasionally connected applications? There's no technological reason for not doing that. However, such applications need to work offline and save data locally. This can raise two issues in a Silverlight environment.
>
> First, what if the user deletes data or disables storage? Second, what if the disk quota for the application (or site) is exceeded?
>
> The answer to the first question is that there's no answer. However, an occasionally connected application sounds like an application for a small and smart category of users who can be instructed and informed about the configuration dialog. The risk, however, is that by misusing the Silverlight environment they end up losing their own work. For the second question, the size of the disk quota (as we'll see in a moment) can be adapted to any need.

Disk Quotas

To avoid having downloaded applications flood the local hard disk with their settings and user-specific data, a threshold has been set that indicates the maximum capacity of the user store for a given application.

By using the *Quota* property on the *IsolatedStorageFile* class, you can learn about the current quota of disk space that the current application is assigned. The *AvailableFreeSpace* property, on the other hand, informs you about any remaining space. By default, each Silverlight application is given 1 MB of disk space on the local user's machine to save its own data. The quota is per application and per site, meaning that if you download multiple Silverlight applications from the same site, the current quota is the maximum amount of disk space that Silverlight applications can consume in total.

There might be situations, though, where the limit of the disk quota is too low. In these cases, the Silverlight base class library makes available a method on the *IsolatedStorageFile* class through which the application can ask the local user to increase the quota to a given value. The method is *IncreaseQuotaTo*.

```
using (IsolatedStorageFile iso =
      IsolatedStorageFile.GetUserStoreForApplication())
{
    bool ok = iso.IncreaseQuotaTo(5000000);
    MessageBox.Show(ok ? "Accepted" : "Denied");
}
```

The method accepts a long value that indicates the larger size you request and returns a Boolean value that indicates, instead, the user response to the request. Any attempt to increase the application's quota, therefore, must be explicitly approved by the user. Applications are not allowed to silently and arbitrarily increase the quota. Any call to the *IncreaseQuotaTo* method results in a dialog box being displayed to the user, as shown in Figure 8-4.

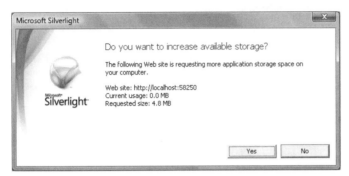

FIGURE 8-4 The dialog box displayed when the application attempts to increase the disk quota

Note that the *IncreaseQuotaTo* method throws an exception if the new quota is not larger than the old quota. To reset the quota and clear any stored data, you resort to the dialog box that was shown in Figure 8-3, select the site of choice, and delete the data store. The next time the storage is initialized, a new subtree of directories will be re-created.

Networking

For an RIA, communication is a fundamental asset. Through communication, the application calls for data to process and passes the results back to the server. The big difference between an RIA and a JavaScript application is found in what each can do on the client; both types of applications are dependent on the server for input and output.

Network communication in Silverlight is singularly based on an asynchronous API. The application code invokes a component and asks it to download a resource; the component starts working and fires an event when it has finished retrieving the resource. The provided callback does the rest, which consists of updating the user interface with the results calculated on the server.

Invoking services—whether WS-* Web services, WCF services, or perhaps ADO.NET Data Services—is also asynchronous. In Silverlight, synchronous calls are not supported.

Note By playing a trick, you can invoke a URL in a synchronous manner. The trick, however, is just a trick. Although it doesn't rely on hacks and undocumented features, still it might be the source of performance issues. Use this trick if you need it, but be careful.

So what's the trick? It basically consists of using the Silverlight-to-DOM API and invoking the browser's *XMLHttpRequest* object. Here's an example:

```
ScriptObject xhr = HtmlPage.Window.CreateInstance("XmlHttpRequest");
xhr.Invoke("open", "POST", url, false);
    :
xhr.Invoke("send", body);
string response = (string) xhr.GetProperty("responseText");
```

A synchronous call blocks the application until a response is received from the remote server. For this reason, you should use this approach very carefully.

Downloading Data

The communication API in Silverlight comes in three flavors. You have a simple API to download resources from the Web. You have a bit more sophisticated API to issue HTTP requests, including POST requests. Finally, you have an ad hoc API for invoking services over HTTP. Let's attack with the API to get some text or binary content downloaded to the client. The API is centered around the *WebClient* class.

The *WebClient* class is an extremely simple class that basically operates as a downloader. The class offers two pairs of methods to download text and binary content in an asynchronous manner. Here's some code that gets a string from a URL:

```
WebClient client = new WebClient();
Uri endpoint = new Uri("http://YourServer/Samples_Web/test.ashx");
client.DownloadStringCompleted +=
    new DownloadStringCompletedEventHandler(OnDownloadStringCompleted);
client.DownloadStringAsync(endpoint);
```

The *DownloadStringAsync* method connects to the specified URL and retrieves data. After data has been fully downloaded on the client, the *DownloadStringCompleted* event is fired so that the client can handle any response.

```
void OnDownloadStringCompleted(object sender, DownloadStringCompletedEventArgs e)
{
    string response = e.Result;
    :
}
```

The *WebClient* class performs an HTTP GET and returns the raw response as returned by the endpoint. If you use *WebClient* to connect to an AJAX-enabled WCF service, you'll get back a JSON string and you're entirely on your own when parsing that to a JavaScript (or other) object.

To download binary content (for example, an image or an on-demand XAP package), you follow the same pattern, except that you need to call into another method—*OpenReadAsync*. The syntax is exactly the same as before:

```
WebClient client = new WebClient();
Uri endpoint = new Uri("http://YourServer/Samples_Web/extra.xap");
client.OpenReadCompleted +=
    new OpenReadCompletedEventHandler(OnReadCompleted);
client.OpenReadAsync(endpoint);
```

The response from the invoked URL is exposed to the callback via a *Stream* object. The following code snippet shows how to process a dynamically downloaded XAP package and transform its content into a user control object that can be plugged into an existing Silverlight object model:

```
private void OnReadCompleted(object sender, OpenReadCompletedEventArgs e)
{
    if (e.Error != null)
        return;

    // Load a particular assembly from XAP
    Assembly a = GetAssemblyFromPackage(assemblyName, e.Result);

    // Get an instance of the XAML object
    object page = a.CreateInstance(className);

    // Get the user control object that represents the visual tree in the package
    UserControl uc = page as UserControl
    :
    :
}

private Assembly GetAssemblyFromPackage(string assemblyName, Stream xapStream)
{
    // Local variables
    Uri assemblyPath = null;
    StreamResourceInfo packageBits = null;
    StreamResourceInfo assemblyBits = null;
    AssemblyPart part = null;

    // Initialize
    assemblyPath = new Uri(assemblyName, UriKind.Relative);
    packageBits = new StreamResourceInfo(xapStream, null);
    assemblyBits = Application.GetResourceStream(packageBits, assemblyPath);

    // Extract an assembly
    part = new AssemblyPart();
    Assembly a = part.Load(assemblyBits.Stream);
    return a;
}
```

In the example, the stream you download represents the content of the XAP package. Some work is required to unzip the package and extract the bits of the entry point assembly—that is, the assembly that contains the code-behind for the new Silverlight application.

After the bits for the assembly have been found, you create an *Assembly* object out of it using the Silverlight-specific *AssemblyPart* class. From the *Assembly* object, with a bit of reflection you can dynamically create an instance of the code-behind class and cast that to the *UserControl* type.

Managing Web Requests

The *WebRequest* class offers a richer interface for when you need to arrange HTTP calls using POST or other verbs. Generally, the *WebRequest* class helps you whenever you need to perform more than just a GET from a plain URL. The programming interface is also more sophisticated. Let's see how to post some data to a URL:

```
Uri endpoint = new Uri(...);
WebRequest request = WebRequest.Create(endpoint);
request.Method = "POST";
request.ContentType = "application/x-www-form-urlencoded";
```

At this point, you need to prepare the body of the request. The *WebRequest* class makes available a request stream, but it forces you to fill the stream asynchronously. (Not exactly a delicate touch!) The preceding code snippet continues with the following lines:

```
// Data to pass down to the request body builder
MyRequestState state = new MyRequestState();
state.Request = request;
state.Symbols = symbol;
request.BeginGetRequestStream(new AsyncCallback(InitializeRequest), state);
```

Any data to write into the body are grouped into a custom data object (for example, *MyRequestState*) that also references the current request object. The data object is then passed as context to the *BeginGetRequestStream* method along with the callback that will physically write to the stream:

```
private void InitializeRequest(IAsyncResult asyncResult)
{
    MyRequestState state = asyncResult.AsyncState as MyRequestState;
    WebRequest request = state.Request;

    Stream requestStream = request.EndGetRequestStream(asyncResult);
    StreamWriter writer = new StreamWriter(requestStream);
    writer.Write("Symbols=");
    writer.Write(state.Symbols);
    writer.Flush();
    requestStream.Close();

    request.BeginGetResponse(new AsyncCallback(HandleResponse), request);
}
```

Finally, the *BeginGetResponse* method kicks off the call, and *HandleResponse* will be invoked when results are received:

```
private void HandleResponse(IAsyncResult asyncResult)
{
    WebRequest request = asyncResult.AsyncState as WebRequest;
    using (WebResponse response = request.EndGetResponse(asyncResult))
    {
        using (Stream responseStream = response.GetResponseStream())
        {
            // Read and process
            :
        }
    }
}
```

The response is made available through a *Stream* object.

Consuming Services

Consuming services from Silverlight couldn't be easier. All that you have to do is link the Web or WCF service to the project through the canonical *Add Service Reference* dialog box, as shown in Figure 8-5.

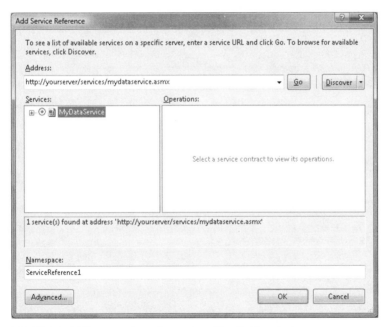

FIGURE 8-5 Adding a service reference to a Silverlight project

When you're done with the configuration, you can start writing code against the proxy class that Visual Studio 2008 automatically generates for you. Here's an example:

```
StockServiceClient client = new StockServiceClient();
client.GetQuotesCompleted += new
        EventHandler<GetQuotesCompletedEventArgs>(OnGetQuotesCompleted);
client.GetQuotesAsync(symbols);
```

The entire process is in no way different from what you would do in a Windows Forms or ASP.NET project.

When you add a WCF reference, Visual Studio 2008 also generates a client configuration file where it specifies the binding mode, address, and contract name. In Silverlight, WCF services can be called only by using the *basicHttpBinding* mode.

Silverlight also fully supports ADO.NET Data Services. After you've linked in this way as a service to a Silverlight application, you can proceed with the following code:

```
private void UserControl_Loaded(object sender, RoutedEventArgs e)
{
    Uri svc = new Uri("SimpleNorthwind.svc", UriKind.Relative);
    ctx = new NorthwindEntities(svc);
    coll = new ObservableCollection<Customer>();
}
```

An ADO.NET Data Service is a service wrapper around an object model created with Entity Framework. When you instantiate the *xxxEntities* class, you also indicate the URI of the service that exposes it. The instance of the "entities" class is referred to as the data context.

Next, you use the data context to fire a query against the service using the rich syntax supported by ADO.NET Data Services:

```
private void Button1_Click(object sender, RoutedEventArgs e)
{
    Uri query = new Uri("CustomerSet?$orderby=Country", UriKind.Relative);
    ctx.BeginExecute<Customer>(query, OnExecuted, ctx);
}

void OnExecuted(IAsyncResult result)
{
    try
    {
        NorthwindEntities ctx = (NorthwindEntities) result.AsyncState;
        IEnumerable<Customer> results = ctx.EndExecute<Customer>(result);
        foreach (var item in results)
            coll.Add(item);

        // Update the UI
        Dispatcher.BeginInvoke(() =>
        {
            grid.ItemsSource = coll;
        });
    }
    catch (DataServiceRequestException ex)
    {
        MessageBox.Show(ex.Response.ToString());
    }
}
```

Cross-Domain Requests

By default, from Silverlight you can place calls only to URLs located in the same server domain that has served the calling page. If needed, the local service then places a server-to-server call to the desired server on any domain you want. This restriction, known as the Same Origin Policy (SOP), is applied by browsers for security reasons.

In AJAX sites, SOP is often overcome by using a trick in which the remote Web service returns executable script rather than plain data. You reference the service through the *<script>* tag, and it downloads executable script that builds data. In this way, you get data from an external site in full respect of SOP. The *<script>* tag (as well as the *<img>* tag) is not subject to SOP. The trick requires the collaboration of the remote Web service, which must be designed to return script code.

Flash introduced a more formal (and also secure) mechanism. According to this model, a Web site can declare that it is happy to receive calls from JavaScript code hosted in external domains. It does that by putting a file named *CrossDomain.xml* in its root directory. Here's possible content for such a file:

```
<?xml version="1.0" encoding="UTF-8"?>
<cross-domain-policy xmlns:xsi= http://www.w3.org/2001/XMLSchema-instance
 xsi:noNamespaceSchemaLocation="http://www.adobe.com/xml/schemas/PolicyFile.xsd">
  <allow-access-from domain="*" />
</cross-domain-policy>
```

The value of the *domain* attribute indicates which sites are enabled to call in resources in the site. By using *, the site declares itself open toward external Flash applications that are calling.

The format of the *CrossDomain.xml* file allows for filtering of which caller is accepted and which is not, but once a caller has been accepted it gains full access to the site. In other words, there's no way to limit, say Site, to access only a given subtree of the site. To make up for this, Silverlight also supports another configuration file—the *ClientAccessPolicy.xml* file. Here's an excerpt:

```
<access-policy>
   <cross-domain-access>
      <policy>
         <allow-from>
            <domain uri="*" />
         </allow-from>
         <grant-to>
            <resource path="/PubServices/" include-subpaths="true" />
         </grant-to>
      </policy>
   </cross-domain-access>
</access-policy>
```

The *uri* attribute of the *<domain>* element indicates a site that is welcome, while * just opens the server to accept any incoming call from Silverlight clients. However, the *<grant-to>* node lets you restrict the areas of the site an external caller can programmatically access.

Note Unfortunately, no configuration file is supported for JavaScript callers. Today, no browser script engine supports this mechanism or anything similar. This situation penalizes the *XMLHttpRequest* object and makes it impossible for the component to place cross-domain calls. Internet Explorer 8, in fact, provides an ad hoc component for cross-domain script calls—the *XDomainRequest* object. We'll see what other browsers will do in the upcoming months. Some good news is also expected from the W3C, which is working on standardizing a mechanism for enabling *XMLHttpRequest* to make calls to external domains that in some way have opted in.

Microsoft Silverlight and Code Security

Users and administrators are always concerned when it comes to downloading executable code that comes from the Internet. In which way is Silverlight better than ActiveX and at least as secure as Flash? How can Silverlight's runtime prevent risky code from executing? How can it recognize that now it is enabled to execute a large share of the .NET Framework classes? Let's explore the security model of Silverlight.

The Security Model

Silverlight's CLR uses an innovative security model that is a sort of simplified version of the security model employed for the .NET Framework. Silverlight doesn't use the Code Access Security (CAS) model of .NET; instead, it opts for an adapted version of the concept of *code transparency*. Code transparency is an attribute-based security model that was introduced in .NET to distinguish critical and noncritical code. With some simplification and adaptation, the model has been ported to Silverlight, which makes it a really safe and secure platform.

Code Access Security

In the .NET Framework, in the process of loading an assembly, the CLR gets some evidence about it. Based on the evidence, the CLR figures out the *code group* of the assembly.

A code group defines the list of privileged actions that participating assemblies are allowed to perform. Whenever some code is about to execute a privileged action, the CLR verifies its permissions through the code group and throws an exception if it finds out that anything is wrong. Permissions for code groups are determined by the machine administrator.

The role played by the administrator in a CAS scenario is just what makes the CAS model critical if you consider its porting to Silverlight. What if the administrator (that is, in many cases the end user) doesn't do much to protect the system? Or he isn't very restrictive?

Code Transparency

The CAS model therefore is not supported in Silverlight. Instead, code access security in Silverlight is guaranteed by a brand new security model.

Silverlight's CoreCLR reverses the basic principle of CAS completely. Any code that goes through the CoreCLR is not trusted; no evidence is ever checked, and no code group is ever created. Any code that goes through the CoreCLR is simply not allowed to call into other methods that require higher privileges.

This model is also referred to as *code transparency*, meaning that any code is transparent unless it's marked at the assembly level with a different security attribute. Can you see the difference between this and CAS?

Like CAS, code transparency lets you distinguish in some way between *safe* and *unsafe* code; however, in Silverlight the security level is an attribute of the code and does not depend on the settings and choices of some administrator. Additionally, security attributes are fixed forever and cannot be changed by an administrator at some time.

This is an important point, and not one most new Silverlight developers are aware of. So let's delve deeper into the security attributes of Silverlight code.

Security Attributes

Any code that runs within the Silverlight run-time environment belongs to one of the following categories: transparent code, critical code, or safe-critical code. The level of security hazard associated with any method on any class is identified with an attribute: *SecurityTransparentAttribute*, *SecurityCriticalAttribute*, or *SecuritySafeCriticalAttribute*.

Transparent Code

The concept of code transparency is nothing new in the .NET Framework. It refers to code that is marked as unable to call into full-trust code. Transparent code is not allowed to perform any actions that would possibly elevate the permissions of the call stack. Transparent code is determined differently in the .NET fully fledged CLR and in the Silverlight CoreCLR.

In the .NET CLR, only the code in methods or assemblies explicitly decorated with the *SecurityTransparent* attribute is transparent. In other words, all code is fully trusted unless it is downgraded via the *SecurityTransparent* attribute.

In the CoreCLR, conversely, all code is transparent unless a different security attribute is used. In particular, this means that by default all the code in a Silverlight application cannot directly execute any critical operations such as invoking unsafe or unverifiable code or attempting system-wide changes through the P/Invoke subsystem. Any application code in the Silverlight virtual machine runs as partially trusted and can invoke only other transparent code or, at most, code marked with the *SecuritySafeCritical* attribute. In no way can any transparent code call directly a piece of code marked as *SecurityCritical*.

In case you're still a little uncertain about it, let me rephrase the explanation. In Silverlight, all application code—that is any code written by developers within a project—can only be transparent. As such, it's not allowed to call into any method of any class that is declared as *SecurityCritical*. At most, transparent code can call into methods declared as *SecuritySafeCritical*. These rules are strictly enforced by the CoreCLR, and they do not depend on any external configuration or settings being managed by an administrator.

Critical Code

In Silverlight, critical code runs in full-trust mode with none of the limitations that affect transparent code. Critical code has unlimited access to all machine resources, including installed hardware and the file system.

Although uncontrolled execution of critical code downloaded from a Web site can put any local computer at risk, still it is viable for applications to access resources such as the file system. Critical code is not absolutely evil. More simply, the attribute refers to code that can manage valuable resources of a computer. Thus, if executed in an uncontrolled way it can create a security hazard.

Executing critical code safely in the context of a Silverlight application still makes a lot of sense and, additionally, it's sometimes unavoidable, legitimate, and desired. The whole point is about how to execute it in a safe way. Enter *safe-critical* code.

Safe-Critical Code

The CoreCLR invariably throws a method-access exception every time that the application code attempts to execute any critical code. For example, most of the methods in the *System.IO.DirectoryInfo* class are marked as critical, as you can see in Figure 8-6.

```
Disassembler

[ComVisible(true)]
public sealed class DirectoryInfo : FileSystemInfo
{
    // Methods
    [SecurityCritical]
    public DirectoryInfo(string path);
    [SecurityCritical]
    public void Create();
    [SecurityCritical]
    public DirectoryInfo CreateSubdirectory(string path);
    [SecurityCritical]
    public override void Delete();
    [SecurityCritical]
    public void Delete(bool recursive);
    [SecurityCritical]
    public DirectoryInfo[] GetDirectories();
    [SecurityCritical]
    public DirectoryInfo[] GetDirectories(string searchPattern);
    [SecurityCritical]
    public FileInfo[] GetFiles();
    [SecurityCritical]
    public FileInfo[] GetFiles(string searchPattern);
    [SecurityCritical]
    public FileSystemInfo[] GetFileSystemInfos();
    [SecurityCritical]
    public FileSystemInfo[] GetFileSystemInfos(string searchPattern);
    [SecurityCritical]
    public void MoveTo(string destDirName);
    public override string ToString();

    // Properties
    public override bool Exists { [SecuritySafeCritical] get; }
    public override string Name { [SecuritySafeCritical] get; }
    public DirectoryInfo Parent { [SecurityCritical] get; }
    public DirectoryInfo Root { [SecurityCritical] get; }
}
```

FIGURE 8-6 A class with security-critical members

This means, for example, that because the class constructor is critical, the simple instantiation of the *DirectoryInfo* class will throw an exception in Silverlight:

```
// Throws a security exception (an absolute file path is required to instantiate the class)
DirectoryInfo dir = new DirectoryInfo("c:\new folder");
```

However, some directory operations might still be useful and required in a Silverlight application. In this case, a different attribute is used to indicate a member that works with critical resources, but which does it in a controlled and therefore safe way.

In Figure 8-6, you see that the *get* accessor of the *Exists* property is declared as *SecuritySafeCritical*. This means that security-wise, it is acceptable that some application code gets to know whether a given directory exists. It is not acceptable, though, that the code can freely navigate within the file system to find it.

In summary, safe-critical code is full-trust code and acts as a smart proxy toward critical code. A safe-critical method does a number of checks before passing control to a critical method. Security checks can include parameter validation and any sort of API-specific checks aimed at ensuring that the application state is acceptable for the call to continue. Safe-critical methods are a delicate element because they represent the gateway for downloaded application code to access a critical method.

Application code is allowed to call into safe-critical code, as Figure 8-7 shows.

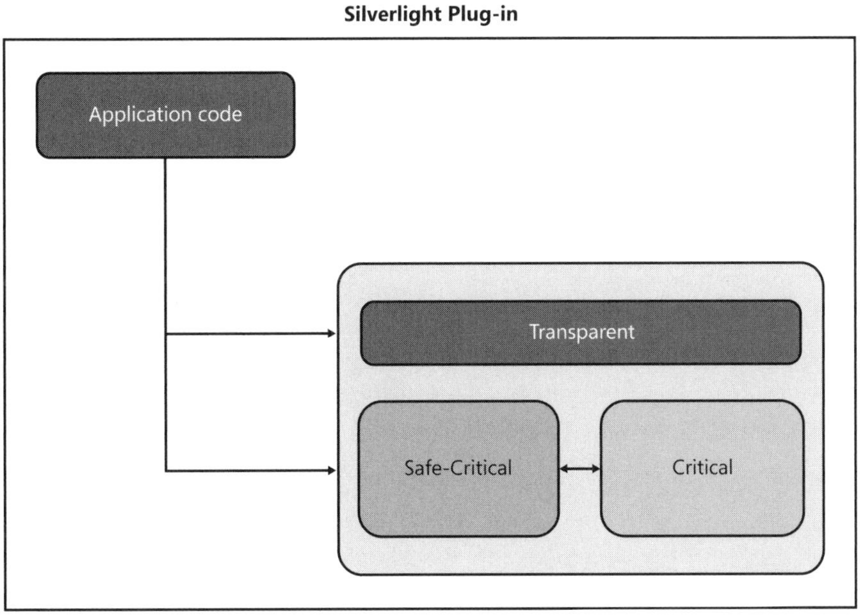

FIGURE 8-7 Types of Silverlight code and security attributes

The perfect example of safe-critical code is the isolated storage API. It wraps access to the local file system, but it exposes a safe API that enables application code to see and work only with a secure subtree of the disks.

> **Important** The *SecuritySafeCritical* attribute is new to Silverlight. The whole concept of code transparency, though, is nothing new in the .NET Framework. Attributes such as *SecurityCritical* and *SecurityTransparent* have existed for a long time in the .NET Framework.
>
> Another long-standing security attribute defined in the .NET Framework is the *SecurityTreatAsSafe* attribute. Why has *SecurityTreatAsSafe* not been ported to Silverlight, and why has it been replaced by *SecuritySafeCritical* instead?
>
> In the desktop CLR transparency model, all public critical methods are automatically marked as *SecurityTreatAsSafe*. In the context of Silverlight, a similar setting would enable transparent code to call into any public critical methods, thus severely invalidating the whole security model. In addition, a distinct *treat-as-safe* attribute applicable to transparent code make little sense because transparent code is safe by nature. So the *treat-as-safe* attribute makes sense especially if combined with critical code. The *SecuritySafeCritical* attribute is just the combination of *SecurityCritical* and *SecurityTreatAsSafe*.

Secure by Design

Safe-critical code is the layer shielding application code from critical local resources. But who provides safe-critical methods? Or, put another way, is it possible for a developer to inject her own set of safe-critical methods in a Silverlight application? As you can understand, the ability to create safe-critical code is essential to assessing whether Silverlight is safe or not.

Application Code vs. Platform Code

Regardless of the security attributes, any piece of Silverlight code falls into one of two families: application code and platform code. Application code is any custom code that developers write for an application and that users download to their machines. Platform code is all the system code that makes Silverlight run.

Application code can only be transparent; any attempt to directly invoke a critical method results in a method access security exception. Platform code can be of any type: transparent, critical, or safe-critical. How do you distinguish between application and platform code?

For the CoreCLR, safe-critical code can be defined only in an assembly recognized as platform code. This fact eliminates at the root the possibility that malicious application developers write their own safe-critical methods that are, in the end, a vehicle for attacks.

Platform code is not written by Silverlight application developers.

The CoreCLR recognizes as platform code only code defined in assemblies loaded from the local Silverlight installation directory and digitally signed by Microsoft. Only such assemblies are allowed to contain safe-critical or critical code.

In no way can the CoreCLR be fooled to consider safe-critical code a piece of application code. To state it clearly, no code downloaded from the Internet by a Silverlight application can be treated as safe-critical, and only Microsoft can create safe gateways to access critical APIs within the .NET Framework.

Inheritance Rules

The Silverlight security model doesn't prevent inheritance, but it limits the way in which you derive new classes from existing ones. Security attributes apply to methods, so in principle you can derive your classes from any existing class. The overriding of methods, though, is strictly governed. In particular, you can override transparent methods as well as safe-critical methods. You can't override, though, any virtual method that is marked as critical.

Is it safe to override a safe-critical method from a Silverlight application? Doesn't this represent a possible breach in the overall security model?

When you override a method, which actions can you reasonably take? For example, you can invoke the base method implementation and code some extra tasks. Alternatively, you can completely change the implementation of the method by having the code do radically different things.

In both cases, you are still limited to calling into transparent or safe-critical code. Unless the base class contains security holes (for example, it doesn't mark as critical an internal virtual method that manipulates critical resources), overriding safe-critical methods isn't riskier than any other application code. The following code shows a typical (and allowed) way to derive a new class while overriding a safe-critical method:

```
public class StreamReader : System.IO.StreamReader
{
    static StreamReader()
    {
    }
    public StreamReader(Stream s) : base(s)
    {
    }

    // This method was originally a safe-critical method. It is now
    // a transparent method.
    public override string ReadToEnd()
    {
        string text = base.ReadToEnd();

        // Does some extra work; for example, turn to JSON
        return ToJson(text);
    }
}
```

The same restrictions apply to interfaces. An application class can implement only security-transparent interfaces that don't contain critical methods.

Summary

Microsoft's answer to users' demands for ad hoc tools for building rich Internet applications is Silverlight. Silverlight places itself in the same product area as Adobe Flash, but it is not a standalone product. It comes with strong connections to ASP.NET AJAX, WPF, the .NET Framework 3.x, and the Expression suite of products.

Silverlight represents Microsoft's way of building a compelling user interface for Web applications in a cross-browser and cross-platform scenario. A browser plug-in, Silverlight focuses on .NET Web applications that need media support, sophisticated forms of interactivity, and client processing power.

In a way, Silverlight can be seen as a .NET-in-the-sandbox solution because it brings most of the programming power of the full .NET Framework to the client browser and—here's the most important point—without the need to have the .NET Framework installed on the local PC.

Silverlight and AJAX are two faces of the same coin, as both aim at improving the overall user experience over the Web. Silverlight requires a browser plug-in to be installed, and a browser plug-in requires administrative privileges. AJAX is entirely based on HTML and JavaScript and, as such, guarantees an unparalleled reach.

In the end, you choose between Silverlight and AJAX based on application-specific tradeoffs. I like to summarize this as the *rich versus reach* dilemma. If you value the richness of the user interface and application more than reach, the natural choice is Silverlight. Instead, if reach counts more, you should go into the AJAX arena.

Index

Symbols and Numbers

About the Author

Dino Esposito

 Dino Esposito is an IDesign (*http://www.idesign.net*) architect and a trainer based in Rome, Italy. Dino specializes in Microsoft Web technologies, including ASP.NET AJAX and Silverlight, and spends most of his time teaching and consulting across Europe, Australia, and the United States.

Over the years, Dino has developed hands-on experience and skills in architecting and building distributed systems for banking and insurance companies and, in general, in industry contexts where the demand for security, optimization, performance, scalability, and interoperability is dramatically high. Every month, a variety of magazines and Web sites throughout the world publish Dino's articles on topics ranging from Web development to data access and from software best practices to Web services. A prolific author, Dino writes the monthly "Cutting Edge" column for *MSDN Magazine* and the "ASP.NET-2-The-Max" newsletter for *Dr. Dobb's Journal*. As a widely acknowledged expert in Web applications built with .NET technologies, Dino contributes to the Microsoft content platform for developers and IT consultants. Check out his articles on a variety of MSDN Developer Center topics, such as ASP.NET, security, and data access.

Dino has written an array of books, most of which are considered state of the art in their respective areas. His more recent books are *Microsoft .NET: Architecting Applications for the Enterprise* (co-authored by Andrea Saltarello) and *Programming Microsoft ASP.NET 3.5*, both from Microsoft Press (2008). Dino regularly speaks at industry conferences all over the world (including Microsoft TechEd, Microsoft DevDays, DevConnections, DevWeek, and Basta) and local technical conferences and meetings in Europe and the United States.

Dino lives near Rome and keeps in shape playing tennis at least twice a week at CT Monterotondo.

Best Practices for Software Engineering

Software Estimation: Demystifying the Black Art
Steve McConnell
ISBN 9780735605350

Amazon.com's pick for "Best Computer Book of 2006"! Generating accurate software estimates is fairly straight-forward—once you understand the art of creating them. Acclaimed author Steve McConnell demystifies the process—illuminating the practical procedures, formulas, and heuristics you can apply right away.

Code Complete, Second Edition
Steve McConnell
ISBN 9780735619678

Widely considered one of the best practical guides to programming—fully updated. Drawing from research, academia, and everyday commercial practice, McConnell synthesizes must-know principles and techniques into clear, pragmatic guidance. Rethink your approach—and deliver the highest quality code.

Agile Portfolio Management
Jochen Krebs
ISBN 9780735625679

Agile processes foster better collaboration, innovation, and results. So why limit their use to software projects—when you can transform your entire business? This book illuminates the opportunities—and rewards—of applying agile processes to your overall IT portfolio, with best practices for optimizing results.

Simple Architectures for Complex Enterprises
Roger Sessions
ISBN 9780735625785

Why do so many IT projects fail? Enterprise consultant Roger Sessions believes complex problems require simple solutions. And in this book, he shows how to make simplicity a core architectural requirement—as critical as performance, reliability, or security—to achieve better, more reliable results for your organization.

The Enterprise and Scrum
Ken Schwaber
ISBN 9780735623378

Extend Scrum's benefits—greater agility, higher-quality products, and lower costs—beyond individual teams to the entire enterprise. Scrum cofounder Ken Schwaber describes proven practices for adopting Scrum principles across your organization, including that all-critical component—managing change.

ALSO SEE

Software Requirements, Second Edition
Karl E. Wiegers
ISBN 9780735618794

More About Software Requirements: Thorny Issues and Practical Advice
Karl E. Wiegers
ISBN 9780735622678

Software Requirement Patterns
Stephen Withall
ISBN 9780735623989

Agile Project Management with Scrum
Ken Schwaber
ISBN 9780735619937

microsoft.com/mspress

Collaborative Technologies—
Resources for Developers

Inside Microsoft® Windows® SharePoint® Services 3.0
Ted Pattison, Daniel Larson
ISBN 9780735623200

Get the in-depth architectural insights, task-oriented guidance, and extensive code samples you need to build robust, enterprise content-management solutions.

Inside Microsoft Office SharePoint Server 2007
Patrick Tisseghem
ISBN 9780735623682

Led by an expert in collaboration technologies, you'll plumb the internals of SharePoint Server 2007—and master the intricacies of developing intranets, extranets, and Web-based applications.

Inside the Index and Search Engines: Microsoft Office SharePoint Server 2007
Patrick Tisseghem, Lars Fastrup
ISBN 9780735625358

Customize and extend the enterprise search capabilities in SharePoint Server 2007—and optimize the user experience—with guidance from two recognized SharePoint experts.

Working with Microsoft Dynamics® CRM 4.0, Second Edition
Mike Snyder, Jim Steger
ISBN 9780735623781

Whether you're an IT professional, a developer, or a power user, get real-world guidance on how to make Microsoft Dynamics CRM work the way you do—with or without programming.

Programming Microsoft Dynamics CRM 4.0
Jim Steger *et al.*
ISBN 9780735625945

Apply the design and coding practices that leading CRM consultants use to customize, integrate, and extend Microsoft Dynamics CRM 4.0 for specific business needs.

ALSO SEE

Inside Microsoft Dynamics AX 2009
ISBN 9780735626454

6 Microsoft Office Business Applications for Office SharePoint Server 2007
ISBN 9780735622760

Programming Microsoft Office Business Applications
ISBN 9780735625365

Inside Microsoft Exchange Server 2007 Web Services
ISBN 9780735623927

microsoft.com/mspress

For C# Developers

Microsoft® Visual C#® 2008 Express Edition: Build a Program Now!

Patrice Pelland

ISBN 9780735625426

Build your own Web browser or other cool application—no programming experience required! Featuring learn-by-doing projects and plenty of examples, this full-color guide is your quick start to creating your first applications for Windows®. DVD includes Express Edition software plus code samples.

Microsoft Visual C# 2008 Step by Step

John Sharp

ISBN 9780735624306

Teach yourself Visual C# 2008—one step at a time. Ideal for developers with fundamental programming skills, this practical tutorial delivers hands-on guidance for creating C# components and Windows–based applications. CD features practice exercises, code samples, and a fully searchable eBook.

Learn Programming Now! Microsoft XNA® Game Studio 2.0

Rob Miles

ISBN 9780735625228

Now you can create your own games for Xbox 360® and Windows—as you learn the underlying skills and concepts for computer programming. Dive right into your first project, adding new tools and tricks to your arsenal as you go. Master the fundamentals of XNA Game Studio and Visual C#—no experience required!

Programming Microsoft Visual C# 2008: The Language

Donis Marshall

ISBN 9780735625402

Get the in-depth reference, best practices, and code you need to master the core language capabilities in Visual C# 2008. Fully updated for Microsoft .NET Framework 3.5, including a detailed exploration of LINQ, this book examines language features in detail—and across the product life cycle.

Windows via C/C++, Fifth Edition

Jeffrey Richter, Christophe Nasarre

ISBN 9780735624245

Jeffrey Richter's classic guide to C++ programming—now fully revised for Windows XP, Windows Vista®, and Windows Server® 2008. Learn to develop more-robust applications with unmanaged C++ code—and apply advanced techniques—with comprehensive guidance and code samples from the experts.

CLR via C#, Second Edition

Jeffrey Richter

ISBN 9780735621633

Dig deep and master the intricacies of the common language runtime (CLR) and the .NET Framework. Written by programming expert Jeffrey Richter, this guide is ideal for developers building any kind of application—ASP.NET, Windows Forms, Microsoft SQL Server®, Web services, console apps—and features extensive C# code samples.

ALSO SEE

Microsoft Visual C# 2005 Step by Step
ISBN 9780735621299

Programming Microsoft Visual C# 2005: The Language
ISBN 9780735621817

Debugging Microsoft .NET 2.0 Applications
ISBN 9780735622029

For Web Developers

**Microsoft® ASP.NET 3.5
Step by Step**
George Shepherd
ISBN 9780735624269

Teach yourself ASP.NET 3.5—one step at a time. Ideal for developers with fundamental programming skills but new to ASP.NET, this practical tutorial delivers hands-on guidance for developing Web applications in the Microsoft Visual Studio® 2008 environment.

**Microsoft Visual Web
Developer 2008
Express Edition
Step by Step**
Eric Griffin
ISBN 9780735626065

Your hands guide to learning fundamental Web-development skills. This tutorial steps you through an end-to-end example, helping build essential skills logically and sequentially. By the end of the book, you'll have a working Web site, plus the fundamental skills needed for the next level—ASP.NET.

**Introducing Microsoft
Silverlight™ 2,**
Second Edition
Laurence Moroney
ISBN 9780735625280

Get a head start with Silverlight 2—the cross-platform, cross-browser plug-in for rich interactive applications and the next-generation user experience. Featuring advance insights from inside the Silverlight team, this book delivers the practical, approachable guidance and code to inspire your next solutions.

**Programming Microsoft
ASP.NET 3.5**
Dino Esposito
ISBN 9780735625273

The definitive guide to ASP.NET 3.5. Led by well-known ASP.NET expert Dino Esposito, you'll delve into the core topics for creating innovative Web applications, including Dynamic Data; LINQ; state, application, and session management; Web forms and requests; security strategies; AJAX; Silverlight; and more.

**JavaScript
Step by Step**
Steve Suehring
ISBN 9780735624498

Build on your fundamental programming skills, and get hands-on guidance for creating Web applications with JavaScript. Learn to work with the six JavaScript data types, the Document Object Model, Web forms, CSS styles, AJAX, and other essentials—one step at a time.

Programming Microsoft LINQ
Paolo Pialorsi and Marco Russo
ISBN 9780735624009

With LINQ, you can query data—no matter what the source—directly from Microsoft Visual Basic® or C#. Guided by two data-access experts who've worked with LINQ in depth, you'll learn how Microsoft .NET Framework 3.5 implements LINQ, and how to exploit it. Study and adapt the book's examples for faster, leaner code.

ALSO SEE

**Developing Service-Oriented AJAX
Applications on the Microsoft Platform**
ISBN 9780735625914

Microsoft ASP.NET 2.0 Step by Step
ISBN 9780735622012

Programming Microsoft ASP.NET 2.0
ISBN 9780735625273

**Programming Microsoft ASP.NET 2.0
Applications: Advanced Topics**
ISBN 9780735621770

What do you think of this book?

We want to hear from you!

To participate in a brief online survey, please visit:

microsoft.com/learning/booksurvey

...and enter this book's ISBN number (appears above barcode on back cover).

Tell us how well this book meets your needs—what works effectively, and what we can do better. Your feedback will help us continually improve our books and learning resources for you.

Thank you in advance for your input!

Where to find the ISBN on back cover

ISBN: 000-0-0000-0000-0

9 0 0 0 0

0 000000 000000

Example only. Each book has unique ISBN.

Stay in touch!

To subscribe to the *Microsoft Press* *Book Connection Newsletter*—for news on upcoming books, events, and special offers—please visit:

microsoft.com/learning/books/newsletter